Arbeitskommando

Elvet Williams

827-8883

Vince

CORONET BOOKS
Hodder and Stoughton

Copyright © Elvet Williams 1975

First published in Great Britain 1975
by Victor Gollancz Ltd

Coronet edition 1978

This book is sold subject to the condition that
it shall not, by way of trade or otherwise, be
lent, re-sold, hired out or otherwise circulated
without the publisher's prior consent in any
form of binding or cover other than that in
which this is published and without a similar
condition including this condition being
imposed on the subsequent purchaser.

Printed and bound in Great Britain for
Hodder and Stoughton Paperbacks, a
division of Hodder and Stoughton Ltd.,
Mill Road, Dunton Green, Sevenoaks,
Kent (Editorial Office: 47 Bedford
Square, London, WC1 3DP) by
Hunt Barnard Printing Ltd.,
Aylesbury, Bucks.

ISBN 0 340 22010 4

CONTENTS

PREFACE

It is strange that I should now feel a compulsion to record my memories of captivity, thirty full years after my escape from Germany.

My compulsion derives from viewing, and enjoying, the many films recently satisfying an apparent demand for P.O.W. escape stories. As escape films they are admirable – fitting memorials to men who shrugged off bitter disappointments and occasionally chalked up spectacular successes. Yet I, an ex-prisoner, am increasingly left with a feeling of having heard only half a tale.

As backcloth to thrilling escapes we have repeatedly been shown a captivity bearing little resemblance to that endured by most men in German hands, and escape stories which all too often ended where they should have begun, just outside the wires. The former point of criticism is perhaps unavoidable, the object of the films being to portray the spectacular escapes; the latter is more difficult to understand.

To reveal that the conditions which made the 'spectaculars' possible, even inevitable, applied to relatively few prisoners is not to belittle the deeds we have witnessed, but to view them against a truer background. The normal conditions of captivity were not those of the Oflag, Luftlag or Stalag with which we have all been made familiar, but of the Arbeitskommando, of which there has been no sight. As regards escape, the greatest problem, and the real object, was not to get out of a camp but out of an enemy-occupied continent. The most brilliantly conceived and executed break-out was only the first, albeit vital, step in the long exhausting run for home, and the only one to be undertaken against known, calculable odds.

A mythology of captivity which ignores the Arbeit around which most lives inexorably revolved is at best incomplete; a mythology of escape which dismisses the efforts of hundreds who took the fateful plunge without benefit of Escape Commit-

7

tee, disguise, false papers or real money can only be a distortion. Recognition already freely accorded to backstage conspirators who produced tunnels between tea-breaks to work off boredom and frustration is a just due; reticence about men who, denied that therapeutic, intermediate aid to retention of sanity, cast themselves, in an instant, into the role of fugitives in a hostile land is an injustice. Mythology is in danger of fossilising into a shape too unmalleable to accord them their deserved niche.

Where enforced idleness dictated the pattern of life and escape for officers, forced labour imposed a different, more strenuous, routine on other ranks. At first, like their separated officers, concentrated in large camps, they soon found they were not to be allowed to choose their bunks, lie on them, and plot. Even while Stalag itself was still strange, inhospitable and bewildering, they were divided and despatched to Working Camps, often in very small groups; slave labourers hired out to civilian contractors. With hardly an unsupervised minute to call their own, they were left to sort things out for themselves, bereft of officers when they most needed them, and subject to both military guard and civilian bosses. Escape from such a life meant release from bondage rather than from captivity. They had their successes. Should they be denied them?

What follows in these pages is a tale of one man's progress through the Transit Camps and the Arbeitskommandos, a rounded story of a life of captivity about which little has been written and virtually nothing shown. In the narrower field of escape, the events I have recorded may be typical of many: if so, the case for a revision of the mythology is established. If they were exceptional, proving no rule, they should, for that very reason, assume their rightful place in the annals.

E.W.

BLACKWOOD
DECEMBER, 1974

8

Chapter 1

TRANSIT

I was captured on Crete by a parachute patrol, late in the morning of Thursday, 29th May, 1941. Captured with me were a corporal and another private, both also of the Welch Regiment, though neither was of my company. The tide of battle had thrown us together two days before in an attempt to outflank the encircling Germans.

The patrol seemed glad of us. They could take us back and get out of the sun, for the day was already hot and they wore full drop kit. They set off in single file, waddling laboriously up the hill. We trudged dejectedly in the middle of the line. After about twenty minutes we all stopped and sat down so that the Germans could rest and mop their brows. We were lighter clad, in drill shirts and shorts, pullovers and hose-tops. Our captors spoke no English and we had no German. They pulled out captured Craven A and Woodbines and asked us to join them in a smoke. Each side took stock of the other. Their conversation was obviously about us, while we watched them in silence till presently Corporal Jones spoke:

'These chaps could never beat our boys.'

Against all evidence I felt he was right. These were crack troops of the German Airborne Division, the pride of their army and the envy of our own. Yet they did not impress me. Their equipment did. I felt better for knowing that Corporal Jones with the professional eye of a regular soldier had dismissed them so lightly. By the time we were motioned to our feet to walk to whatever awaited us things seemed just that little bit better.

Our journey continued uphill through craggy gullies until, at the top of a rise, we came to a village. Germans swarmed everywhere, some in full fighting kit, others in only British shorts and British pith helmets. Red swastika flags draped balconies and adorned rooftops. One graced the bonnet of a British three-ton lorry parked in the square. The startlingly

9

colourful flags were not just ornament; they were there for the benefit of German pilots. Our escort turned along an alleyway ending at a church gate, before which stood a sentry. Across the churchyard women in black peered out of the church door.

We passed through a gate set in the stone walling flanking the lane to our right and into an enclosure surrounded by the same stone walling. Prisoners, stretched out around the perimeter or propped up against the wall, followed us with their eyes as we were led halfway along the compound and through another gate into a garden. The patrol commander left us in the charge of the sentry at the gate while he himself marched up to a group of scantily-dressed Germans bathing and drinking in the shade of a building. A stark-naked man, certainly an officer, came back with him. Looking at our brass shoulder-badges, he said:

'Ach so. I see you are three Welshmen.'

He was concerned to know whether we had fought at Galatos, where, he alleged, some of his men had been found pinned to doors. He was of the opinion that the New Zealanders were most probably the guilty ones, not the British. I ventured to assure him that New Zealanders were also British. He changed the subject, much to my relief: we would be sent to Germany where we would be well treated; anyway, the war couldn't last much longer . . . A wave of his British army issue towel implied that till we got to the haven of Germany we shouldn't expect too much. The sentry directed us back into the enclosure.

Most perimeter space had already been taken, but we found room for three to lie against the wall in full glare of the midday sun. What little narrow shade was thrown by the low walls was fully occupied, yet no one seemed to be completely shaded. Nowhere could we see any familiar face, no one else wearing Welch flashes, nor any trace of an officer. A disconcerting feature was the number of men who, in spite of uniform, had lost all semblance of being soldiers. Some prisoners were in plimsolls, a couple were without boots or any kind of footwear, and one showed up vividly in kitchen whites. Everyone looked wilted. The sun roasted us. We three new arrivals gradually fell silent.

The unthought-of had happened. I had often visualised getting killed or being wounded, but never being captured. I had dealt with Italian prisoners in Egypt, and with German prisoners, only a week before, on Crete, but they too had only just been taken. What lay ahead was a closed book I had never thought of reading. Sailing from Liverpool round the Cape in 1940 I had been fully reconciled to exile until the end of the war. Even so, there had always been the hope of an earlier return. Now all chance had gone. Having savaged Europe, swiftly and brutally, the Germans were in process of spilling into the Middle East and Africa. Thoughts, of home, of the battle, of captivity, just churned about in my mind.

My musings were interrupted when a soldier entered the compound carrying British respirators, without their satchels, under one arm, face-masks dangling in front, canisters behind. He motioned men opposite us to rise. Half a dozen or so rose slowly and doubtfully to their feet. No interpreter was needed to explain what was afoot, and no one would envy the men their task: to collect and bury the blackened and bloated bodies which had lain for days strewn in the hills, each with its stench and its own black, buzzing colony of flies. The working party disappeared.

Loosening my shorts I examined the wound in my left thigh. Using my sweaty hand I rubbed away at the blood caked on the outside of my leg, from wound to hose-top. Corporal Jones suggested I got it dressed. Concluding it was worth a try I strolled over to the sentry at the garden gate. I showed the wound and tried to indicate a dressing. Another soldier came down, took a look at my thigh and departed towards the building. Soon he was back with some wide plaster which he carefully stuck over the small, round hole. Sensing rather than understanding that both Germans were showing concern I endeavoured to convey that I was all right. Pointing to the thigh I gave a shrug; then, patting my stomach, I made a kind of grimace, indicating as best I could that my empty stomach concerned me more than my wounded leg. The message penetrated, with a most unexpected result. The soldier who had dressed the wound went back into the house, while the sentry barred the way back into the enclosure. His comrade returned with a tin of British sausages, opened but untouched.

As I walked back to my place at the wall, astonished faces regarded me and my prize as if I were a magician, for no one had eaten all day. We three Welshmen shared half the contents of the tin, deciding to leave the rest till later. Then we washed our mouths with swigs from our water-bottles, refilled only a quarter of an hour before capture. A feeling almost of guilt had lain on us while we'd been eating; but it was worse while we drank. Few men appeared to have water-bottles, and those who had had long since emptied them.

We lay back and attempted to sleep, but it was too hot for comfort. I dozed and turned, dozed and turned, vainly trying to avoid the sun. Each return to awareness brought me alive with an awful feeling of something very wrong. Then I would jerk myself awake to begin again all the futile ponderings, snap out of it, and doze again. Every time I awoke it was to find that nothing had really changed, except that I was even more drenched in sweat. Towards evening a little shade began to creep out from the wall to make sleep possible. I must have slept for some time when I awoke to find prisoners getting to their feet. Guards rounded us up into one sorry-looking group, counting and recounting us.

The knowledge that we were moving brought a feeling of inexpressible relief: it was not the release from the sun, for the heat was already subsiding; nor the ending of boredom, for an eternity of meaningless days lay ahead; nor the anticipation of a chance to escape, for we Welshmen had made our bid the night before; nor was it the prospect of movement itself, for I had lost a lot of blood and had already walked till my boots felt over-full of feet. Rather was it a hope of getting out of limbo, of nearing some unimagined permanence, some new base. On Crete our last chance had gone. Even had we had the luck to remain free until darkness the odds against us slipping through the Suda-Canea neck and over the horny hump of the island before all evacuation from the south coast ceased would have been enormous, even if, somewhere, the British still held a front. The Germans marched us westwards, towards Canea. On the last, long slope down to the town landmarks became familiar. There, on the right, the M.O. had roused me from an off-duty siesta under a fig-tree; apologetically, he had asked me to move, the Greeks having assured him that the blobs of white sap poised on the branches could be fatal; he hadn't believed it either, but he couldn't allow me to take the risk. To the left I picked out the dark scar of the ditch where we had kept our German prisoners until, like us, they had been marched away at dusk. Somewhere, close by, would be the shredded remains of the kit I had slashed with my razor, to leave nothing of use to the Germans.

12

As the Germans escorted us into the first suburbs of the town, past those few buildings still rising scarred amid the rubble, an incredible sight affronted us, rubbing salt into wounds of defeat and capture. Lights blazed from open, unshuttered windows. The contempt they expressed was tangible, as violent as any blow: the new champ was sticking his chin out, confident no one could hit it. The all-conquering enemy felt utterly secure in shattered Canea, taken only two days earlier. One building, conspicuously illuminated, already displayed a large banner with huge letters proclaiming KOMMANDANTUR. The greater part of the town, including all the ruined centre, was different, darker than it had been on the Monday night when I had last trodden its streets. Then its ruins had been still lit by the glow of gutted buildings; now the last embers had died.

The column had perforce to struggle as it picked its way past the obstructions. Leaving the town I saw the bullet-spattered front of the small house against which I had leaned on Tuesday morning, only to be pulled violently away: a sniper had put those marks on the wall, and I had obligingly put myself in his sights. Inside the house we had laid C.S.M. Ashman down on his stretcher, while Harbinson, the dispatch rider, had got me to examine his back. Shrapnel had travelled down through his right elbow, but it was the pain in his back he couldn't stand.

West of the town we crossed the river bridge. To the left lay the clearing where P.S.M.* Simms had been murdered on the day the battalion had left Monastery Camp. Only a little farther on I had received my wounds. We had cursed the gas-capes rolled behind our backs, as well as the respirators on our chests which had propped us up as if on stilts in face of machine-gun fire. But I had reason to bless my gas-cape. It had spent the force of the first mortar-bomb splinter which had travelled through its folds before lodging in my right shoulder. The second bomb, with the splinter which had really drawn blood, had struck immediately afterwards. Some miles farther on the column turned right through a fence into a field. I knew where we were: Lower Galatos, where we had had a hospital, white marquees between road and sea. Rumour had had it that

* At the time of the events described the rank of P.S.M. – Platoon Sergeant-Major – had disappeared (most probably in 1940) except in respect of men already bearing the rank.

Max Schmelling had dropped, and been wounded, there. In the field the shapes of sleeping men became gradually discernible. One or two sat up and spoke. Answering with brief references to our identity and counter-questions to establish whom we were joining, we took our places among them. The most shattering day of my life had ended.

Next morning we were left to face the day as best we could. The marquee still served as a hospital, packed with the wounded of both sides. The space between it and the road was a prison compound, a staging post for those still sound in wind and limb and a dressing station for the lightly wounded. A search revealed none of my friends, no one from my section and hardly any acquaintance. The Germans showed little intention of feeding their prisoners, who for the most part appeared to be still too dazed to be very concerned. We finished the sausages, again conscious that we were the only ones eating.

An N.C.O. ordered me to report at a table set up in the sun. I joined a queue. Behind the table sat a British M.O.,* while orderlies, moving along the line, exposed each wound in turn. The M.O. glanced at my thigh, expressed himself satisfied, and referred me to an orderly who cleaned the wound and replaced the old strapping. Early in the afternoon all walking wounded were warned to be ready to move out.

An hour later I was once again on the road westwards, this time in a slow-moving procession of walking-wounded, headed for Maleme, which, since its beach had been our airfield, had taken the brunt of the air bombardments and witnessed much of the heaviest fighting. All British planes had been ordered off Crete one day before the assault began. Even so, as we got nearer to Maleme evidence increased that the Germans must have found it a touch-and-go battle. Scores of planes and gliders, crashed, riddled, crumpled and charred, lay scattered in and out of the water or perched crazily on rocks and trees. The ceaseless air traffic between Greece and Crete must have been considerably thinner on the northbound lanes.

Our destination at Maleme proved to be a two-storeyed stone structure at the far end of the air strip. A bare room taking up most of the first floor was already almost full of other walking wounded, mainly Australians and New Zealanders.

* The reader may find difficulty with the word 'British'. Sometimes it will be used to denote British as distinct from Australians or New Zealanders, or others, and more generally, as here, to include Anzacs.

More serious cases, on stretchers or simply lying on the floor, occupied the ground floor. Among the stretcher cases I found one man of the Welch. Lying on his stomach, he looked up over his shoulder and recognised me. While we talked I tried hard to work out how he could have received his wound; there was no need to wonder why he didn't roll over to face me. His bottom was exposed, the one cheek flat to the size of a breakfast plate, raw flesh heaving with flies. I could visualise no weapon capable of so neatly carving that round, flat area of flesh.

That night our rest was not to be undisturbed. A tall Australian, wrapped in a blanket from shoulder to ankle and with a tall hat on his head which made him appear even taller when viewed from our positions on the floor, kept everyone awake long after dark and alerted us at intervals throughout the night. His illusion, as he paced the centre of the room, was that he had a parachute. He would break off his restless pacing in order to get to one of the unglazed windows to make his drop. His mates would intercept and restrain him, then resettle him in the middle of the floor before resuming their own places so as to bar all access to the windows. Towards morning the Aussie must have exhausted himself. Daylight found him peacefully asleep, still wrapped in his blanket and still retaining his hat.

Everyone, though very hungry, was reconciled to remaining empty-stomached until reaching Greece. It could only be conjectured whether it was the policy of our captors to weaken us, or whether they had no spare food or organisation to cater for the needs of prisoners. We hoped that the Germans wished to get us off the backs of their fighting troops as quickly as they could. Some of the stretcher cases had already disappeared from below; the rest hoped to be air-lifted out shortly. We, the luckier ones, would have to tighten our belts at the end of the queue. It needed only one visit to the butcher's shop of a ground floor to see the justice of our being held back.

In the heat of the afternoon, about twenty of us were led down to the airfield. Seated on grassy hummocks in the sand, we watched at leisure the relentless operation of the mighty Luftwaffe which had so remorselessly crushed us. It was with very mixed feelings that we regarded the scene. In a queer way it did us good to see, from another angle, further indisputable proof of why, after initial, heartening success, defeat had been inevitable, unprotected as we had been against that overwhelming air power. It did us even more good to survey the damage we had inflicted, the havoc on the ground and the lines of enemy wounded. The battle hadn't been so one-sided as the result seemed to indicate. I was not alone in feeling a little more kindly disposed towards the R.A.F. It would have been needless suicide to have retained our few planes for launching against the Luftwaffe. Had they been able to get into the air in time to have a field-day among the cumbersome Junker 52s (the troop-carriers), once they'd relanded – and reland they would have had to – the enemy swarms would have instantly blasted them off the beach.

More depressing was the evidence of how much leeway would have to be made up in order to get on near level terms 'with the enemy in material, or, as one Aussie acidly observed, in numbers of P.O.W.s. On that long, hot, dusty afternoon on the busy beach at Maleme, to contemplate a captivity of ten or so years seemed not unreasonable, to think hopefully in terms of much less required a faith in miracles stronger than mine. While no one even hinted that his belief in final victory had been shattered, all agreed it was time we stopped 'farting about' and took the enemy on on equal terms somewhere, or by the time we had the stuff to do the job we'd have no men left to use it.

Twice we were called out on to the runway. The first time it was a German N.C.O. in search of a working party. Wounded or not, there was no option but to obey. Before we reached the taskmaster another German intercepted us, waving us back. Across the sand I heard the word 'Verwundet'. It sounded so like English that there was no mistaking the gist of the conversation. The first man sought his labourers elsewhere. When next we got on to the runway we were actually lined up to board a Junker 52. Then came a late switch of plan. A file of German wounded shuffled towards us, and boarded instead of us. As the plane headed out to sea it took with it our last hopes of food for that day.

We settled down that night anxious to sleep and so forget our stomachs. The tall, wandering Digger having departed, it promised to be more peaceful than the night before. It must have been about midnight when the totally unexpected droning brought everyone awake. We'd had our fill of planes, but this had to be different. The Luftwaffe hadn't flown at night. What we were hearing was a sound for which we had waited and prayed in vain ever since the invasion had started. It had to be the R.A.F. For more than a week we had prayed for them to come to our aid; now they had to arrive when we least needed them. For over a week we had been bombed and strafed by the Luftwaffe; just when they had left off the R.A.F. had to take over.

The droning passed and repassed overhead. Guns cracked. A couple of heavy thuds rattled and shook the building. Several times the planes returned while we listened intently in the darkness. Relief each time a thud announced a bomb had missed us mingled with hopes that the boys had scored a hit. After all was quiet again we found ourselves excited and encouraged, and very relieved. If the planes had left their mark it would be hard to detect among the litter on the beach.

Sunday, 1st June, opened with more promise. A British 15 cwt. pick-up ferried the badly wounded down to the airfield. A few hours later, after another hot, hungry wait on the beach, I found myself aboard a Junker 52. British and German wounded sat in two rows, intermingled, facing each other across the body of the fuselage. The last sight of Crete as the plane flew low over the calmest of blue seas was of a mountain with its snow-capped peak silhouetted brilliantly against a sky as dazzlingly blue as the sea beneath. When the plane began to circle over an airfield crammed with enemy aircraft there was no mistaking where we were. A large city lay spread below us, with Minerva's temple, the Parthenon, clearly visible on its hill. As the wheels touched the ground, the row of men opposite, German and British, rose as one man to their feet, hung peculiarly bent and poised on tip-toe, and then plunged in a heap on top of us. After the confusion of arms and legs had been disentangled, we found that everyone was unharmed, but the plane had acquired an unusual list. Standing under the one wing to get some shade, we could see that tyre had burst and that the tip of the other wing had carved a semi-circle in the dust.

Our new home in Piraeus, the port of Athens, was a fairly large compound containing a number of low, wooden huts and several smaller ones in an area of brown earth enclosed by a high, barbed-wire fence. For the first time since capture we were required to give some particulars. Everyone was well aware that he should confine himself to giving name, rank and number, but since we had all been committed to battle complete with badges and flashes, not to mention, as in my own case, with regimental garters, that part of our orders seemed not a little ridiculous. It was hardly surprising that we were asked nothing about our units, but we were asked for our addresses. There seemed little point in refusing: knowing our addresses could hardly have helped the enemy, but might do some of us a lot of good, particularly since we were assured that a short selection of names would be broadcast to England, to the comfort of our families.*

Each long hut could hold over two hundred men lying side by side on long, wooden platforms running the full length of the side walls and in double rows down the centre. The side platforms sloped gently up to the walls, the centre ones backed on to each other to look like long cricket covers. It soon transpired that the camp was an annexe to a hospital situated about a mile away. Its function combined that of convalescent camp and out-patients' department. Most prisoners, taken in the battles of Greece in April, had been there some weeks, and their wounds were already on the mend. The casualties who really caught the eye were the dozens of dysentery sufferers, many severe, continually slouching between the huts and the latrines, or, often, strategically squatting within striking distance of the latter, which, providentially, were sited reasonably distant from the sleeping quarters. The most repeated sentence in Piraeus referred to the ability to shoot through the eye of a needle at fifty paces.

Our first taste of food was an evil-smelling, repulsive bowl of sauerkraut which, nevertheless, everyone ate gladly. The food was to remain bad, alternating between thin soup or sauerkraut once every midday, with a ration of coarse, brown bread which most men endeavoured, not always successfully, to keep until evening. A hot drink, neither tea nor ersatz coffee nor the mint tea we were to know so well later on nor, indeed, anything identifiable, was ladled out each morning, and sipped enjoyably because it was hot.

My trifling shoulder wound had never troubled me, but I had got into the habit of picking at the scar until, eventually, the jagged splinter of shrapnel worked loose and came away in my fingers to reveal a small, round hole which had healed perfectly. As for my thigh, a New Zealand doctor gave a look at it every

* In my case the Germans were as good as their word. News of my capture first reached my family via a friend who had heard it from Lord Haw-Haw, broadcasting from Hamburg and Bremen.

few days. On one visit, after remarking on how quickly and well that second injury was healing under conditions conducive to making most minor cuts troublesome, he noticed my psoriasis spots and made an observation which my subsequent history tends to confirm: 'That's your safety-valve. You'll never have trouble with healing.' It was at that same sick-parade that I re-found Harbinson, whom I'd last seen groaning in Canea.

Harbinson's was the only familiar face from pre-capture days. Otherwise I had to fit in among the hundreds of strangers, no difficult task where so many had so little to anchor to. Some men stood out immediately: the half-dozen or so Maoris; the L.A.C. in his conspicuous, solitary, blue uniform; the pipe-major, complete with tartan trews and bagpipes. The Maoris entertained us one evening with cheerful harmonies, evoking pictures of peaceful beaches lapped by warm seas, while most evenings the pipe-major played the sun down with laments to pull at the heart-strings. The lone R.A.F. boy had to stand the frequent but good-natured references to the conspicuously absent 'glamour boys' who had left him behind.

Days, hardly distinguishable one from another, soon merged into a shapeless monotony of idleness.

The shortage, often complete lack, of the small comforts of normal life hit more and more men with every passing day. In spite of all attempts to conserve them, soap cakes became smaller, razor-blades blunter, and toothpaste tubes emptier. Without hot water or soap, washing sweaty clothes was not easy. The most desperate shortage of all was that of paper of any kind. How the dysentery cases managed only they themselves knew as degradation was added to sickness which tore at their bowels. For myself, I counted myself more than fortunate. 'The runs' never touched me, and, on my second day, during my only visit to the hospital, I acquired, by sticking it under my pull-over, the greater part of an American glossy magazine. It made depressing reading, composed as it was of adverts either for luxuries I'd never been able to afford or for toilet articles I'd have given anything to possess at that moment, and of an article which took pages to prove painstakingly that Britain would probably end up by being able to boast 'sure, we lost the war, but our equipment was better'. It could very well have been produced by Dr Goebbels for special distribution in P.O.W. compounds. But the stiff, shiny pages went a long way towards solving my own personal hygiene problem.

The most exciting and heartening event to occur whilst at Piraeus was the bursting of the news that Russia was in the war. At first received incredulously, the rumours persisted until when, after a day or two, they were backed by astronomical figures of miles advanced, tanks destroyed, prisoners taken and towns overrun, the most sceptical and least optimistic were convinced. The boost to morale was enormous, raising some of the gloomiest spirits to unreasonable heights of optimism, only to plunge them back to a depth almost as low as before when no perceptible change occurred either in the conditions of captivity or in the attitude of the guards. But for most men the war had taken a vast turn for the better. At worst Britain was no longer alone and could, at least for another year, forget the threat of invasion. Some of us had read enough Tolstoy and history to doubt the ability of even the blitzkrieging Germans to swallow and digest Russia in a campaign started halfway through the summer.

At the end of June or the beginning of July, a party of us were marched down to the docks where we boarded a small coastal coaler, Climbing on board I saw, for the first time, Piwi Pirini, the Maori. One could hardly have missed him. He was sitting on a hatch-cover, with his broad, flat face creased in a cheerful smile, as if he were the official 'welcome-on-board' receptionist, and with the merriest pair of eyes I have ever seen. The startling, unmilitary cut of his huge, Oxford-bags drill trousers would alone have made him the most conspicuous man on board. The boat carried thousands of life-jackets in her hold, no doubt left over from the abortive sea invasion attempt on Crete. We were put on top of the life-jackets but were allowed the freedom of the well-deck during most of the day; a freedom of which we were not slow to take advantage, preferring the heat of the sun and the feel of the warm breeze to the stinking stuffiness down below.

For three days, and escorted on the port side by a rolling porpoise for most of the way, we sailed slowly up the beautiful, placid waters of the Aegean Sea, along rugged coasts, through clusters of islands looking strangely remote from the turmoil of war.

It was early evening when we landed in Salonika, As we filed up the steps to the promenade dozens of cameras clicked at us. Every off-duty soldier, like a uniformed tourist, seemed to have one. It was amazing, for I could not, and still cannot, recall ever seeing a Tommy with a camera. Equally puzzling was that most of the cameras seemed to be directed at me. Only later did it dawn on me that, among the leading file, I had been the only prisoner in tropical shorts. That was the most photographed moment of my life. Later, I visualised my photo in homes throughout Hitler's Reich and, I could not refrain from hoping, on corpses sprinkled all over Russia. One other thing surprised us as we were paraded along the sea-front: convoy after convoy of German horse-drawn transport vehicles, all solidly purpose-built and brand new. The sight was hard to reconcile with Blitzkrieg and Fallschirmjäger.

Greater, less palatable surprises lay in store. After entering the camp through two sets of wires and two double gates, we were drawn up in threes at the bottom of a central parade ground, where a sergeant-major, wearing the black beret of the tanks, together with a supporting entourage of Germans, took up position facing us. The sergeant-major called out: 'Any Irishmen here?' At first no one moved. The purpose of the question had everyone baffled. Then, just as it seemed there were no Irishmen prepared to admit the fact at such abrupt notice, Harbinson, standing next to me, stepped forward, calling out 'the one and only'. Taken aback, I watched him being led away on his own. Until that moment, in spite of Sir Roger Casement, it had never occurred to me that, in German eyes, there was any difference between a Paddy and a Taffy.

Tanky addressed us: there wasn't to be any nonsense; the Germans were in charge and we were to carry out their orders. Immediate, instinctive protest rose from the ranks. Unmoved, Tanky cut it all short with the never-to-be-forgotten words: 'That will be enough of that. You'll have to listen to the Germans after the war, so you'd better start getting used to it now.' It was said with unmistakable conviction. The captive audience let Tanky get on with it. Hating and contemptuous, they heard out the rest of the welcoming speech in silence, and refrained from further interruption even when the speaker assured them that Germany had already won the war and that Russia was already beaten.

Next, we found ourselves in an empty barn of a room at the top of the compound, segregated from the other inmates. After the door was locked, leaving us to pass the night on the floor-boards, the smouldering wrath kindled by Tanky's address burst into flame: who the —— did the —— think he was? he was only a prisoner like the rest of us; if he did think the Jerries would win the war he didn't have to help them to do it; he hadn't spoken for the Jerries but for himself; he was a Quisling, who, having gone over to the other side, was using his rank to carry the rest of us over too; he should help us, his own men, not the enemy.

The conversation gradually changed, lingering on the idea of escape. This might be our last, our only, chance for a long time. Turkey couldn't be too far away, and we would never be nearer any neutral country, if, as we all assumed, Germany was to be our ultimate destination. How far were we from Turkey? There I was able to help; map-making had been part of my business in the Intelligence Section. Turkey would be about two hundred miles away, due east. Could anyone reach Turkey, if he got out? The Greeks might, almost certainly would, help, with clothes, food, shelter and guides.

It was well into the following morning before the door was unlocked to admit a bevy of Germans, self-importance writ large on every face, gesture and stride. They lined us up around the walls and searched us, pitiful belongings and persons, all the while recording particulars. Then we were led back down the compound, to the hut nearest the gates, where again we were shown into a large, bare, but not quite empty room. There were two occupants. Almost in the centre of the floor, where no one could overlook him, sat a naked man, elbows resting on raised knees while he picked through his scanty rags. He was unbelievably thin. It took a while for most of us to grasp what he was doing; searching out lice and killing them, click, click, click, click, between his thumbnails, a natural technique we were all soon to master. Meanwhile, the other occupant, an enormous, grey rat, had scurried away.

The P.O.W. camp at Salonika had unquestionably been a Greek barracks. The main prison compound contained all the central parade-ground of brown earth, with the barrackrooms for other ranks, including Yugoslavs, running at right-angles up the right side and along the top. The buildings to the left of the parade-ground were separated off by a barbed-wire fence, and housed captured officers, the first I had seen if one excepted the doctors and a Catholic padre at Piraeus. At the bottom of the compound, either side the gates, lay the German blocks, contained within the strong outside wires but divided from the main compound by another fence and gate. Each barrack hut, raised up on brick foundations, consisted of a long room and, at the end farthest from the parade-ground, primitive latrines. From the long room two doors led outside, one at the end facing the parade-ground, the other in the middle facing the next hut. A third door gave access to the latrines.

As at Piraeus, the Germans provided nothing apart from a minimum of food, while the latrines and an unreliable water supply were the only toilet provisions. Medical facilities, of which there was great need, were nowhere in evidence. Not even the crudest of 'eating irons' were issued. Numerous men had to improvise or borrow just to ensure being able to eat at all: empty tins, scrounged during prior weeks of captivity, were cleaned up and their serrated edges filed smooth. The tins, many with ingenious, bound-on handles, dangled from almost every other waist, their owners determined never to let go of them. It was the same with boots: men who were barefooted remained barefooted, those who had boots hardly let them off their feet, and when they did so they kept them in sight or under the protecting eye of a friend.

The prisoners had to share their accommodation with the rats, their clothes with the lice. By day the rats roamed boldly about the latrines and under the huts: at night their forages penetrated to the barrackrooms. After only a night among the huddles of men on the floor, new arrivals developed the automatic reflex action which sent leg kicking and arm flailing to speed the loathsome prowlers through the dark, a habit adding greatly to the burden of the dysentery sufferers picking their unlighted ways to and from the latrines. A more constant, personal and degrading discomfort was the lice. From firm strongholds in seams of vests, pants and shirts, especially ensconced under armpits, the pale, swollen parasites gave their hosts no respite, by day or night. Each fresh, still hopeful, victim, defying all retailed experience, endeavoured to halt the invaders at the first onslaught. A vain folly! All that remained was to follow the time-hallowed prescription: strip, and slaughter each fresh brood, seam by noxious seam, at least twice a day, thereby ensuring that the next day would not be much more uncomfortable than the present.

Two other dark clouds loomed constantly over the camp. One was the blight cast over spirits by the hated presence of the Senior N.C.O. Many could have understood, and, on available evidence, even forgiven his expressed belief that Germany was bound to win the war. What was unforgiveable was that he should exert the authority of his rank and role to impose the enemy's will, with his blessing, on his own men. Prisoners who had already reconciled themselves to having been sacrificed on the altars of war strategy and high diplomacy found it harder to swallow that they were now not only being abandoned but also handed over naked to their enemies. The other cloud, more immediate and darker for those who had fallen under it, was the daily threat of work in the Timber Yard.

Salonika held many times more captives, Yugoslavs, Palestinians, Anzacs and British, than had Piraeus, so it was not surprising that on the first morning I found several men of the Welch, only two of whom I remembered by name, Privates Ash and Ashford. Ash and Ashford had seen one or two officers of the battalion in the adjacent compound, and had spoken to one of them through the wires. To my genuine sorrow they reported that our C.O., 'Daddy Ford', was there: he was too old for the game. Later in the morning I bumped into Harbinson and went with him to his quarters, a hut not far from mine, but furnished with widely spaced iron bedsteads and blankets. Further evidence of preferential treatment for the Paddies came a few days later when, having missed him for a day or so, I went on the search for Harbinson. He, and most of his room-mates, had been moved on.

The rats, the lice, and the stumbling dysentery victims were not alone in disturbing our nights. Odd rifle shots often brought one awake, although most men took little notice and simply waited for more shots to follow before falling back into their own private cocoons. Next day rumour would be rife: one, two, even three bodies had been seen lying where they had been hit, at the foot of the wires, as warning to the rest of the internees. Only once did I actually see a body, still half-draped on the wires in mid-afternoon, but there was no reason to doubt the veracity of the rumour-spreaders.

About a week after my arrival the disturbance from outside was much more alarming and too close for comfort. It all began in the small hours with a loud shouting of 'Kamerad! Kamerad!' The highly excited voice of someone urgently in need of assistance sounded near, the words clear and distinct. More voices joined in, with sounds of running feet, The firing increased, automatic bursts and single shots, punctuated by the cracks of stick-bombs. Lights, voices, feet, obviously inside the compound as well as alongside the hut, over the dividing wire. Something big was happening. Sitting up, we listened, shushing eager, whispered questions. What was it all about? Who were the targets? Gradually the noise subsided, leaving only the intermittent passing of less urgent feet and less excited voices, until at last all was silence again apart from our own continued whispering as we speculated on what daylight would reveal.

The morning looked in no way different from those that had gone before, but the air was full of an extra crop of rumours somewhere concealing the true facts. Slowly some part of the likely picture began to emerge: a drain had been discovered leading out of the compound; a long line of prisoners had crawled through; twenty (some said more) men had got out to freedom by the time the alarm had been raised; most men still in the tunnel had managed to crawl back, but some, dead or alive, might still be trapped; others had been caught emerging. It was certain that a number were missing: how many it was difficult to tell. There had been no beds left unoccupied, no kits strewn about without owners, no one had neighbours, and some missing men might have been 'loners' with no friend to note their absence.

One of the Welch told me he had seen Ash and Ashford among the leading men going into the drain. That I could well believe: they had been on the prowl for a means of escape, and South Walians would be more used than most to squeezing through dark, confined spaces. Throughout the day I kept my eyes open for the two men, who, I suddenly realised, had become a vital part of my tenuous link with the past. They were of my unit and country, and who was there to look out for them? Were they alive or dead? In the drain or out of it? Had they got free and into hiding? Three-and-a-half years later I was to learn the answers.

A true gauge of the measure of confidence in which the Senior British N.C.O. was held is the fact that it never occurred to me to turn to him for information in such a life and death matter. It would have been more natural to ask the Kommandant to return a brick one had just hurled through his window. For a while I did indeed contemplate lobbing a stone, not through the Kommandant's window, but over the wires into the adjacent officers' compound, together with a note for the Senior British Officer. The idea was dismissed: the officers must have heard the alarm and would, no doubt, have made what enquiries they could. I was left to reflect on how quickly the Welch, who had not been numerous to start with, had thinned on the ground. Harbinson, Ash and Ashford, the only fellow captives I had known by name in the days of freedom, had all gone. How different had been their departures!

The morning Appell was always a tiring, protracted affair, as we endured count after count. While, after each apparent miscount, the Germans got into a huddle trying to get their sums right, the khaki lines would shuffle, fidget and droop as the sun's angle grew warmer. When at last the count was agreed, every eye watched the next move. Where would the guards pounce? A number of prisoners, usually selected from one end of the front ranks, would be separated off. That was the moment when relief became audible, when tensions relaxed and men dropped their guards; for that day the Timber Yard would not have them. The two or three smaller parties still to be counted off were of no importance. It was the Timber Yard which caused men to dread each morning's inevitable parade and to jockey for position, safe and inconspicuous, in the middle of the rear lines.

Only once was I unwary enough to be caught. Standing up, crowded on to the backs of two open Greek lorries, we were driven through the crowded main streets to the western out-skirts of the town. The Yard consisted of an extensive area covered by high stacks of cut timber of all sizes. In addition to the escorting sentries there appeared to be a permanent staff of German soldiers in control, the worst sort of occupation troops, lords of all they surveyed. Contrary to anticipation, much of the work was not really heavy, and the midday break lasted two full hours, but when the work was heavy, it was very, very heavy, while the generous break turned out to be a form of deliberate torture. For prisoners who had existed for weeks on a diet of bread and thin, questionable soup, and many of whom still suffered from severe dysentery, the combined effects of the hard driving by the resident taskmasters, the lifting and carrying, the bending and shuffling to and fro with heavy loads under a baking, July, Mediterranean sun were crippling.

Ill-luck or design so arranged things that when dealing with light planks there was no walking or carrying involved, just the sliding of planks from one stack to another, either adjacent or near by; but, when we had to move long, weighty beams, they required to be lifted on to shoulders and carried a good hundred yards. Three men were assigned to each beam. On that uneven ground, deeply rutted where previous stacks had stood, the man in the centre had the worst of it. Over each rise he took the full weight, and the sharp edges cut into his shoulder. Putting the shortest man in the middle didn't help, neither did lining the team up from shortest to tallest, since in both cases the same victim suffered in the centre. Most took it in turns to carry front, middle and back, an arrangement which still meant that on every third trip the tallest, least-suited man bore the brunt of the weight, buckling over on every rise while his mates tried, with extended arms, to ease the burden off him.

For the protracted lunch-break we were shepherded into a paddock in whose centre a cluster of bushy trees cast an inviting shade which was immediately monopolised by the Germans. The prisoners spread themselves out in the sun, the sentries taking it in turns to patrol the outside of the circle. The meal was soon over. The Latins take their siesta in the shade behind closed shutters. We took ours that day in the heat of the blazing sun, sweating and turning in discomfort while the overseers and guards not on duty slept in the tantalising shade. Before going back to work, I removed my sweat-soaked under-pants and folded them into a soft, damp pad for my sore shoulder.

The longest days end. So did that one in the notorious Timber Yard. One day's experience had confirmed all the evil reports associated with it. We were reloaded on to our lorries, dirty, exhausted and reeking with sweat, silent and sullen in relief and resentment. In the main street we passed a youth carrying a basket of appetising bread-rings hooked over his arm. The lorry had to slow. As it began to speed away from him again the youth sent a bread-ring looping into our midst. The guards suddenly came to life. Thumping with their rifle-butts on the back of the cab, they reinforced their frenzied yells. The lorry flung everyone into a heap as the driver braked. Guards jumped out, pounding back down the road, brushing aside pedestrians overflowing from the pavement. They hauled the youth along and flung him roughly in amongst us. Never have I felt so little, mean and helpless as on the rest of that journey, standing powerless within feet of a boy about to face the un-predictable consequences of his good-natured but futile gesture. At the entrance to the camp the unfortunate baker-boy was bundled with small ceremony into the yawning doors of the Kommandantur.

My only other Salonika experience of a working party was an unexpectedly different affair. Instead of being driven to the distant western outskirts we were marched a short distance to the eastern edge, where a white-coated cavalry officer awaited us. He took the lead into a cool barn where he made signs to us to lay down our inseparable messtins and sidepacks. After seeing that every man was issued with a long-handled, crutchless shovel or a pick, he made his way in front of us into another field. There we were paired off, shovel with pick, our task being to dig holes for fence-posts. In astonishing contrast to the Timber Yard, the Germans let us get on with the work at our own pace, the only overseer being the white-coated officer who contented himself with occasionally inspecting the line of holes to judge the depth. As for the sentries, they took their stance a fair distance away.

Throughout the morning we couldn't fail to observe Greek women, usually in small groups, leisurely passing along a well-worn path running diagonally across the field just beyond the beat of the sentries. Frequently, after a group had sauntered by, a little brown or white packet would be noticeable on the track, left by the women to be picked up by the nearest German, brought towards us and inside the circle of patrol, and then laid on the grass. Everyone could see what was happening, spot the offenders, guess the intentions of the women as well as the purpose of the packages. Still the package-dropping continued, with the heap on the grass growing bigger. Only when a solitary woman sent her young mite stumbling towards us clutching a present did the guards intervene. A sentry headed the boy off, while his mother called out to him to drop his load and run. He did as instructed. The sentry contented himself with urging the woman along by a couple of two-handed shoves in the back. Returning to his station, he picked up the child's packet and added it to the others.

We returned to the barn, our chore finished, followed by a sentry with both arms full of packets. They were deposited in a corner where they remained only long enough for the officer to make us understand that the contents, bread, tomatoes, oranges and olives, were ours, but that they would have to be eaten there and then, in the barn, away from all inquisitive eyes, with not a crumb or sliver smuggled into the compound.

As I stood eating my small share of the unexpected titbits I had time to reflect that Ash, Ashford and any others who might have been at large, would not have lacked assistance and sustenance, if the women and the baker-boy were a fair sample of the Greeks, and on how unfortunate that youth had been compared with the women.

The unscheduled snack was a sharp contrast to meal times in the compound where the starvation diet stayed depressingly foreseeable, but for dozens of prisoners unobtainable without a physically-tiring, mentally-torturing wait full of suspense. Day after day the same soup slopped into the motley of messtins held out by an endless queue whose appetites grew daily even after ample confirmation that the only meat unloaded at the cookhouse was horses' heads. Sidling alongside the queue, or, having learned from empty-bellied experience, hovering in the middle of the compound to waylay luckier fellows with tins already full, those lacking containers suffered agonies of hunger, sharpened by the sight of others eating, and of doubt, intensified by fear of the food running out before they could get their hands on a tin. I had adopted the habit of taking both halves of my messtin with me and handing the spare half to one of the unfortunates on my way to the queue, a practice which soon marked me off as one of the many willing and able to help. The tin, never on permanent loan, always returned without prompting.

The sheer resilience of human nature ensured that even at Salonika all was not gloom. Men could still laugh whilst de-lousing, could still joke over the backs of the rats dodging between their feet. They even played. Most evenings a football was kicked around the parade ground; sometimes a challenge match was held between the Yugoslavs and the British. Most remarkable of all, perhaps, was the complete lack of impression Tanky's defeatist lead had on the attitudes of Aussies, Kiwis and Pommies alike. While making himself hated, and adding another needless cross to be borne, his words and officious actions had had no appreciable effect on morale, had converted no one, except possibly the insignificant handful of his im-mediate associates. The Anzacs, only in the mess because they had volunteered to fight our war, dismissed him more easily than we did, and didn't hold him against us.

On Tuesday, 29th July, with hardly an hour's warning, my

stay in Salonika came to an end. To the very last, our hosts ran true to form. As some hundreds of us were lined up in the German enclosure to receive rations of biscuits and tinned paste for the journey, my end of the line were amused by the playful antics of a spirited young tabby cat on the branches of a tree above us. With one well-aimed shot from his Luger an officer put a swift and bloody end to both play and entertainment, whilst, predictably, producing instant mirth among his cronies.

No regret at leaving the place was noticeable as we marched out through the gate.

As a change from plane and ship transport, I left Salonika by train, by cattle-truck. Whether the wagons standing in the dusty siding bore the legend '*Chevaux* 8, *Hommes* 40' I don't know, but, after we had pushed and pulled each other aboard, the *hommes* in my wagon totalled sixty-nine. The truck had four grills, two either side, high enough up to require one to stand on tip-toe to peep through the heavy criss-cross of barbed-wire nailed on the outside. I was lucky enough to obtain a spot to sit, under a rear grill opposite the door. By the time the sliding door was clanged-to and locked, the prisoners had already divided themselves into first-class passengers, sitting propped up by the walls, and second-class, standing in the middle and wondering how they would ever be able to sort themselves into some semblance of order. If it was a wagon for forty *hommes*, it was for *hommes debouts* or *assis,* certainly not *couchants.*

In addition to the overcrowding, discomfort was with us from the start. The sun had converted the train into a string of over-heated ovens. Once shut in, dependent on what little air could penetrate through the grills and the huddles of heads blocking each one, we began to pour sweat. It seemed as if the train, not sharing our eagerness to be quit of Salonika, would never pull away. Eventually it did move, bringing a breeze of warm air to the faces at the grills but not to those in the body of the stifling truck. As evening approached to make the temperature more tolerable a kind of squatting order gradually emerged, the majority ranged round the sides, the less fortunate making do with the limited space among the outstretched feet.

Sooner than expected or desired a new problem arose. The neighbours to my right were a group of Aussies, one of whom had lingering dysentery and had to do something about it. One small hole in the floor would have provided an acceptable solution. There wasn't one. A messtin was called into service, so producing a further problem: how to get rid of the foul mess and clean the tin. The only outlet was through a grill, and paper and water were at a premium. The barbed-wire above my head was prised to enable the tin to be held out. A couple of swills with urine and a polish with two or three pages of a Pay Book did the rest. The group in the corner took stock of their resources and determined which pockets, sleeves or other refinements of clothing were dispensable in the interests of comfort and hygiene. That is how I lost one breast pocket off my cellular shirt.

How we slept that and subsequent nights will forever be a mystery. Everyone was overlapped by feet and legs, and incessantly prodded by restless knees and elbows. But at least the nights were cooler than the days.

By the return of daylight things were desperate. The toleration and assistance shown the dysentery sufferer could not be extended to all and sundry, no matter how acute the need. The uncertainty as to whether the train would stop, and if so for what purposes, created a terrible predicament. Those who had water were afraid to drink, both from fear of overloading already swollen bladders and from fear of being unable to replenish supplies. Some time in the morning, after hope had been abandoned, the train halted in the countryside, the doors were slid open, and we were ordered out on to the track. The long row of squatting prisoners performed their functions, so intent on making the most of the opportunity that few took in the full ludicrous scene, the obscene vista. Water was available. I managed to refill my bottle.

After the welcome break, the wagon held fewer fears. While discomfort did not diminish with time and familiarity, the dread of being left to accumulate our own filth had been lifted. No one could guess when the next halt would be made. There was still need to conserve the water which few possessed, still doubt about many things, especially the duration of our journey, but the morning had lightened mental and physical loads. And resignation to our lot was made easier by reports that other trucks held eighty or more prisoners. Outrage at our treatment was softened by the thought that greater outrage was being perpetrated on others.

31

In the afternoon, as the sun played on the wagon during a protracted halt, a discordant note was struck when a man opposite began to beg for, then demand, water. The longer his pleadings were ignored the more abusive and demanding he became. I was particularly conscious of the voice, for it was Welsh, and I had water. Water was scarce and under the desperate conditions it could no longer be regarded as the private preserve of the men who owned the bottles. I couldn't drink and ignore the thirsty men around me, the neighbours whose cramped discomfort was personalised by my wriggling legs and by my hot, sticky, smelly body. My compatriot, thirsty as he no doubt was, looked in better shape than many, and in less need of the water which he would have to do without, at least until such time as everyone decided it was time to drink.

Towards daylight on Thursday the temperature dropped. The train must have travelled well inland and also climbed. It was cool enough to make me conscious of my bare knees for the first time since capture. We actually looked forward to the sun making an impact. Around midday the train pulled up in a large siding among hundreds of similar wagons, most of which also had human occupants, not prisoners peeping out on the world through wired grills, but civilian families visible through open doors, together with the sticks of furniture they had been able to salvage. Men with briefcases and girls with shopping-bags kept disappearing along the tracks. It must have been Belgrade, which had suffered severely in the German advance.

It was my twenty-third birthday. Incredibly, I was not denied my birthday party, the most unexpected and welcome, if far from the most lavish, I'd ever had. Our door slid open to reveal, in addition to the expected guards, the wonderful sight of Yugoslav Red Cross ladies encircling a trolley. Biscuits, more acceptable than the hard-tack ration, a few sweets and three or four cigarettes per man were handed up, while tins were passed down to be filled with a kind of fruit drink, very pleasant and refreshing to our taste. Pitifully little as it may now sound, it was a god-send, manna from above. The group in my corner drank my health, considerately refraining from wishing me many happy returns of that day.

The event of the Friday morning was the presence of a German troop-train carrying armoured units drawn up along-side us during a long wait. Judging that the guards would not dare to intervene between the fighting troops and prisoners we felt free to try scrounging matches through the grills from the Jerries perched on the hot armour of their tanks. Our scroungings succeeded.

On Saturday the doors opened once again for an unknown purpose. This time nothing was handed in. We were in a town. British medical orderlies with stretchers, sent to remove the sick off the train, stood along the track. We called out, eager to know where we were. The town was Marburg, on the Austria-Yugoslav border. No one was taken from our truck, but every stretcher was put to use, several of the cases passing beneath us looking lifeless. Perhaps there had been eighty or more in some wagons!

The nightmarish journey ended, not a minute too soon, on August Sunday* morning. The train halted as if for the morning toilet, but this time we were not to get back on board, nor soil the countryside.

* The first Sunday in August.

Chapter 2

STAMMLAGER XVIIIA

For the dishevelled prisoners entering Stalag XVIIIA, Wolfsberg, Austria, on August Sunday, 1941, the immediate burning question was whether, and in what ways, their new home would be better or worse than preceding camps. They assumed that, for good or evil, the gates receiving them would not open to release them until the issue of the conflict in Europe had been settled. The weary weeks of transit from distant battlefields had left marks which time still to be spent behind wires would only very slowly erase. No appreciation of the mental approach to subsequent confinement is possible without an understanding of the conditioning effects of protracted degradation, deprivation and uncertainty, however philosophically endured, during those first formative months. The prisoners themselves would only begin to realise the extent to which they had been pulled down as each small token and symbol of civilised living returned.

Greater in area than previous camps, Stalag's defences were also much more imposing, with layers of fences, watch towers and sub-divided compounds. The hope that the end of the weary trail had been reached was very soon blunted. After lengthy delay and repeated checking inside the narrow administrative area, our immediate destination proved to be a no-man's-land in the centre of the camp, between the French area, through which we had passed, and the British sector, which we were not yet deemed fit to enter. For days our accommodation was a large, white marquee on the grass, which made softer bedding than any encountered so far, our water supply a low, wooden trough fed by an exposed pipe, and our latrine a long, heavily limed trench surmounted by a wooden bar on which we could roost and simultaneously survey the greater part of the new prison. We had closer contact with the French than with our own countrymen, for everyone had to be processed, and most of that took place in, or adjacent to, the French enclosure.

34

The presence of so many Frenchmen was a matter of great surprise, and some interest. More than a year had elapsed since their country had capitulated, yet there they were, as securely 'in the bag' as the tattered rest of us. The sight both intrigued and depressed. On the brighter side – and it was already revealed as a soul-saving characteristic of prisoners that they usually found a brighter side – the reflection that the French, in spite of longer and more humiliating captivity, at least looked in better shape than most of us did strengthened the hope that the worst was behind us.

Part of the processing resulted in the loss of the few valuables we had managed to retain. The confiscated articles were entered in a register against each prisoner's name and number, and a solemn, straight-faced assurance was given that the surrendered property would be returned to the owners after the war. I met no one who gave the assurance much credence. The haul obtained from me consisted of a wrist-watch and several pounds in Egyptian piastres and Greek drachmas, the sum total of my visible and tradeable assets.

Another part of the processing gave us new identities, new numbers and oblong, metal tags, perforated across the middle, each half proclaiming that the wearer was No. such-and-such from Stalag XVIIIA. I became No. 5841, from which I concluded that 5,840 prisoners of all nationalities had previously been registered as domiciled in Stalag XVIIIA. The French wore identical-looking discs, and on mine there was no marking to denote I was British. I added my tag to the two British fibre discs already dangling from my neck. Next day I had to take it off again when everyone was innoculated against something or other and proof of the fact was punched on the back of the metal oblong.

By far the most welcome part of the processing came when we were fed into the de-lousing shed. Nobody grumbled as we tied our clothes by sleeves and trouser-legs into individual bundles and waited around in the nude for them to finish cooking. On the contrary, everyone prayed that German efficiency would live up to its much-vaunted reputation. No clothes have ever been so closely examined by bargain hunters as were those hot, steaming bundles by their scraggy, hopefully-anticipating owners. Fingers poked into seams trying to stir up dreaded displays of life. The vermin appeared to be well and truly deceased; it could only be taken on trust that the same effect had been produced on the nits.

One further, important operation remained before the gates of the British compound could open to receive the new arrivals, an operation as welcome to some men as the universally acclaimed de-lousing. There had been nothing approaching equality of suffering. Except for being in tropical kit, I, like most infantrymen, had been far better equipped for withstanding the deprivations than had the majority. I'd had good boots, spare socks, razor, shaving-brush, toothbrush with paste, comb, handerchief, messtin, water-bottle, knife, fork and spoon, and of basic essentials had lacked only towel and soap. Support and supply troops, men not normally expected to carry their all on their backs, had been taken less well prepared and lacked most, if not all, the small but so important items I had clung to. It was long overdue for someone to consider their needs. Stalag made a beginning.

An assortment of second-hand war-booty clothing was issued to those most in need, with many comical results, since the items originated from French, Belgian and Dutch depots. Men in tropical kit were also included in the issue, so, in preparation for the winter, I emerged most elegantly rigged out in French cavalry breeches reaching only to my calves, a green Belgian jacket with chrome buttons and deficient in length of sleeves, a long French overcoat, and a French sidecap to replace the steel topee in which I had met my fate.

Men without boots received Dutch clogs, great barges of rigidity, with thick soles and uppers; those without socks were handed, to their utter astonishment, Fusslappen or footrags. The Fusslappen were simply squares of limp cloth, like large, unhemmed handkerchiefs: one placed the foot on one diagonally, turned the side-corners up over the instep and the front corner up over the lot, then slid the foot into the boot, leaving the spare material from the corners to dangle outside. Maximum discomfort and inelegance were achieved by combining clogs with footrags. It was probably at the same distribution that we each became the possessor of an off-white handtowel, barely larger than a footrag, and hardly any thicker.

The British compound was surprisingly small. Three or four wooden buildings, side by side, with spaces between, each of which could have taken a hut of similar size, the whole wired-off sector considerably smaller than either previous camp, was the total extent of the accommodation reserved exclusively for the British. The formidable wires at the back formed part of the perimeter fence, the less imposing ones on the other three sides divided the British from their neighbours, the French, and from an empty compound which contained an extension of the British row of huts.

Our barracks, as well as the rest of the row continuing into the empty compound, differed from every other structure in sight. Whereas the size, shape and position of doors and windows in the others were such as to pass unnoticed, our centrally placed doors, one on either side of each hut, were big enough for a barn and, when both open, gave the impression of a squat archway, while the narrow windows snuggled, lengthwise, high up under the eaves. Those particular features, combined with the fact that, inside, shallow channels ran the length of the concrete floors, convinced us that the buildings had once been stables on a grand scale, a conviction soon strengthened by the discovery that the space between the first and second huts was partly taken up by a couple of large squares surrounded by low, concrete walls. At the time filled with rubbish, some of which excited us, revealing as it did a glimpse of empty tins, from their labels definitely of British origin, the squares could have been previously used to hold the droppings swept up from the stables.

The greatest, single improvement at Stalag was that each man, at long last, got a bunk, a place he could call his modest own. This advance meant much more than an end to sleeping on hard, dirty floors in crumpled, sweaty clothes. The bunks, rising in three tiers, with very little space between each group, offered added identity as well as a refuge formerly lacking. The initial reaction was one of pure joy at the sight of the bunks, each with its loosely filled palliasse and its couple of blankets. For most, at that moment, the bunks signalled the end of the road; they had reached their resting-place.

I had stumbled along harbouring an assumption that all roads in captivity converged on, and ended in, Stalag; that, like the local agricultural show of happier days, it would be the place where new and old friends would meet, to patiently sit out the war. Nowhere in the crowded huts was there a sign of anyone I'd known, other than those already met in Greece, the one or two men of the Welch being as much strangers as any Aussie or Kiwi. There was substantial news that others of the battalion had passed that way, but nothing more.

Disappointed as I was, the prospect of being a 'loner' did not unduly depress me. By nature somewhat independent, I had already discovered that I was, fortunately, endowed with a considerable part of the make-up needed to overcome what could have been a fearful handicap. Being a loner was hard, and it had daily become clear that some few men who had trailed through the transit camps had neither the physical nor mental resources to face it. For such men the possession of a bunk made life more bearable; for it provided them with a retreat and, more important still, it gave them regular, recognisable and recognising neighbours. They were much less likely to be allowed to spend their brooding hours on a bunk without well-meant interference than on any odd bit of unclaimed floor space.

For my own part, two gratuitous attributes helped enormously: I was Welsh, and also an infantryman. Because my shoulder badges, unlike the majority which on Pommie uniforms generally indicated R.A.S.C., R.E. or R.A., proclaimed my origin, I had instant address as 'Taffy' at the briefest encounter. Those same badges also marked me down as a footslogger, and British footsloggers were a rarity in the compound. In the bantering bouts on the theme of 'how many Pommies does it take to keep one Anzac in the line?' I found myself referred to, and drawn in, impartially, by both sides, the British using the Black Watch and the Welch as well as the Yorks and Lancs to illustrate their infantry commitment, Aussies and Kiwis doing likewise to prove that once the British had stubbornly fought on to the last man from 'down under', they would naturally continue to fight to the last Jock and Taff. The hard-hitting Aussies and Kiwis, volunteers almost to a man, being more British than the British themselves, did not hesitate to call a spade a 'bloody shovel' or a Tommy a 'Pommie Bastard', an epithet which, according to stress and intonation, could convey anything from the most intense loathing to the tenderest endearment, while the man they took to their hearts was the one who could retaliate with an equally heartfelt 'Ball-and-Chain Bastard'.

Almost from the first day life settled down into the same dull routine which had bored us stiff in Greece. But Stalag, although conveying a sense of anti-climax by virtue of being so poorly endowed with the wherewithal for lasting out a lengthy war,

38

was a great improvement on anything which had gone before, not merely because we had lost our lice and gained our bunks, but even more on account of the lighter, more united spirit prevailing throughout the compound.

The Senior British N.C.O. and others of the 'Inner Circle' carried out their not-too-pleasant duties as prisoners like the rest of us, inspired, or instinctively impelled, by the same common aim as ourselves: to put up with what couldn't be avoided, and to avoid whenever possible what didn't have to be put up with, either way making things satisfying for the prisoners in proportion as they were irritating for the Germans.

Food routines differed little from past experience: the same non-breakfast, the same one-course midday meal of soup or potatoes, or of potatoes and sauerkraut, the same daily bread ration and the same weak mint tea, the same lack of eating irons and the same improvised bowls, with the same hope of a 'back-up', the coveted extra which could sometimes come one's way by rejoining the queue after everyone had been served. The front of the queue seemed always to be monopolised by the same people, for two quite different reasons; most, the 'backers-up' having taken their positions early in order to stake an equally good claim to any leavings; the others, so that they could finish early and hand their tins to empty-handed mates hopefully waiting at the back of the line. It was not always greed which prompted the rush for a back-up. Some tins were so pathetically inadequate that without a second fill-up the owner would have been existing on barely half the absurdly small rations.

In Stalag, my spare half messtin obtained me many a share in a back-up without my having to depart from my practice of never racing back into line. A 'swedebasher' from East Anglia, one of the men who had shared my water-bottle on the train, possessed only a miserable little tin. He joined me on the grass as I sat down to spoon my soup on my first day in the camp. I gave him my spare container. As long as I stayed in Stalag he used my tin and repaid me by queuing early and trying for a back-up. When his luck was in, he shared with me.

The coarse bread was issued by the loaf, a basic fact of life which brought men nearer to blows than any other regular event. The loaves came in all shapes, weights and sizes, large and round, long and flat, thin and tapering, squat and bulbous, never small enough to be simply divided in two, never regular enough to be cut into evenly-shaped portions. As the loaf varied, so did the number of men to share it, the Germans counting off sometimes more than ten men to accompany the holder. Few were prepared to tolerate a sliver too thin, fewer still were ready to chance their arm at slicing. Dividing a loaf, either round or tapering, into an uneven number of nine or eleven pieces with eight or ten hungry, critical men directing each cut demanded the nerves and skill of a surgeon. No cut was ever dared until each line of incision had been marked and approved.

The sole addition to the diet at Stalag was the distribution of margarine or jam, but since that tasty extra, in the case of margarine, was also issued at the bread queue on the same basis of one pack among so many men, and the number per loaf never coincided with the number per slab of fat, it became one more source of anxiety and friction, half the men having to keep an eye on the division of their bread while not losing sight of the people walking off with their margarine. As a final refinement in complications, most food was issued away down past no-man's-land, so that, as often as not, one trekked back behind one's loaf group with half one's attention glued to a quite separate margarine group which sometimes headed for a different hut.

Parades and queues took up only a small part of each day. Killing time, other than by talking, dozing or brooding proved little easier than before. Washing had been reduced to a quick, soapless sluice, shaving from a daily lathering to the once-or-twice-weekly, self-inflicted torture of a damp scrape, or, as in my own case, when my one-and-only blade split right across the middle, abandoned altogether. There was nothing to read if one excepted the couple of identical, prominently-displayed posters warning all P.O.W.s to lay off German women on pain of the most dire consequences, notably DEATH – given a line of large, red print all to itself – for anyone committing the 'ultimate offence'; and there was a limit to the amount of time even the most imaginative prisoner could devote to the intriguing speculation as to what diabolical deed constituted the said 'ultimate offence'.

Several huddles of men were able to entertain themselves, and their over-critical spectators, by playing bridge or whist with treasured, dog-eared cards which had begun active life back in the desert. At least one prisoner was the lucky owner of a pocket chess set, but only two could play; even counting the initiated, the eager to learn, and the curious, chess was hardly the greatest spectator sport. The football had travelled from Salonika to find no worthy pitch, but was still the main source of recreation. We made do with the parade area between the huts, re-learning the schoolyard skills of beating opponents by the nice rebound off walls which a far-sighted architect had kept uncluttered by windows for at least nine feet from the ground.

The Australian 'Two-Up' addicts found no apparent difficulty in occupying their days. At a quick, first glance the narrow strip separating the first hut from the neighbouring empty compound could have been mistaken for a dirt-street set in a Wild West film. Tall, bronzed men in wide-brimmed hats jostled, shouted and gesticulated incessantly. After one's curiosity had driven one to elbow a way through to the centre of the circle one saw the handsome hero, not with guns a-smoking, but with nothing more lethal than a bit of stick and twopence. The pennies were laid flat on one end of the stick so that a practised flick of the wrist sent them twirling high in the air before landing on the ground. The noisy excitement arose from the complicated system of side-bets bawled across the circle. What was used as stake money remains a mystery to this day. The 'Two-Up' school was as mystifying as it was interesting to ignorant Pommies, and it remained one of the few spots in which to find men totally dedicated to oblivion of their surroundings.

On a bunk opposite mine a pale Aussie spent odd moments blowing into a mouth-organ without producing audible sound. In other barracks could occasionally be heard the strumming of a banjo or the blare of a wind instrument. There must have been a wealth of talent awaiting an outlet, and part of it was revealed one evening at an outdoor concert. More than one singer had a trained voice; several more had strong, beautiful voices which had never been encouraged except amid the fug of a bar or barrackroom. Among them was a dark-haired Welshman of medium build. He sang with his thumbs stuck in the leather belt curving under his stomach. The stance of the man and his rich tenor voice conjured up vividly pictures of home. Had my eyes turned to alight on a group of figures resting in a 'collier's crouch', backsides on heels, it would at that moment have been no matter for surprise.

41

Two much-longed-for interruptions to monotony and boredom brought everyone alive in common interest and activity. The first was the issue of one lettercard and one postcard per man, giving us, at long last, a chance to write home. Until that moment it had merely been assumed that some hidden machinery of which we knew nothing might have been set in motion to get news of capture to parents, wives and sweethearts puzzled by the long silence. Many prisoners had neither received nor sent any letter for months, and those then received had been weeks in transit, conveying news of events long past, something which was the cause of great concern to men whose homes lay in cities known to have been heavily blitzed in the weeks prior to capture. In many cases the main anxiety was not whether families knew prisoners were alive, but whether mother, wife or child were themselves dead, injured or bombed-out.

I sent the postcard to my father, the longer lettercard to my fiancée. Both were lined, limiting the amount which could be written, but by the time I had crammed as many close, upright words as possible into the restricted space, I felt I had fallen back into an old habit. At the same time the realisation struck home that the greatest deprivation had been the inability to scribble even a line of reassurance to the people who meant most to me. Once all cards had been written the general relief pervading the camp was infectious: a milestone had been passed, and there was another one, more significant and exciting, to look forward to within a roughly predictable period of time. I swear I had never heard one of my neighbours speak a word of his own volition until that evening, when he asked if he could borrow my pencil. Afterwards, he must have told me every word he had written to the wife he had married on his short embarkation leave.

The second morale-booster, an evening or two later, involved everyone even more effectively than the first. We were on the receiving end of a substantial link with home to more immediate, material advantage. The first batch of Red Cross food parcels was issued. Only one who has shared the experience could remotely gauge the impact of that first issue of one parcel for every two men. While we queued feelings of anticipation and curiosity predominated, with few daring to pitch their hopes too high. We were still at the stage when we would have willingly lined up all night, and felt well rewarded, to get our hands on nothing more exciting that a packet of hard-tack biscuits. The nearer one filed to the distribution point the higher expectations rose, as the more obvious it became, from the reactions of those already scurrying away with their substantial-looking boxes, that hopes had more likely been exceeded rather than merely fulfilled.

Memories of that joyous evening are confused, some details standing out clearly while others of no less importance are irretrievably buried in the mists of time. I remember how I shared my parcel, but have no recollection of whom I shared it with. The large, corded box, with a slip-over lid as deep as the box itself, weighed about ten pounds and held an unexpected amount of varied food with a surprisingly civilian look about it. The tins could have been gathered from any grocer's shelves as part of the weekly shopping. Occasionally, a flat pack of toilet-paper, as useful and welcome as the food itself, was snuggled amongst the paper-straw packing. No class of Mixed Infants can ever have shown the ecstasy and unashamed pleasure displayed throughout the compound during the next couple of hours as treasure after treasure was revealed, drooled over, fondled and sampled. It made no difference whether the recipient hailed from the Australian outback or was a product of more sophisticated city life; the cooing noises sounded identical.

My partner, whoever he was, and I, split the chocolate and dates; he got the corned-beef; I, the pilchards; I took the tea while he clung to the condensed milk. The odd bits were divided in the same way. His hoard was carried off in the lid of the box, mine in the inner half, but not before we had partaken of a banquet of bread and corned-beef, followed by dates and chocolate. The fact that we ate perched on the concrete rim of the unappetising-looking rubbish dump, which conveniently enabled us to jettison our litter, in no way detracted from our pleasure. The dinner conversation was mainly confined to arranging our eating programmes for the next few days, beginning with a feast of pilchards fixed for the morrow, the division of the food being on the principle of both of us having an equal claim on the contents of every tin, regardless of who was its custodian. We could have scoffed the lot at one go, but the obvious best compact, with an inbuilt guarantee of restraint, was to spread the full variety between both of us and over as many days as possible. Other groups, of three, four, or more friends adopted the same plan, as so, although the word itself had yet to be coined, the 'combine' was born.

Absorption in eating did not diminish curiosity about the contents of other parcels exposed all around us: on the contrary, it added spice to the meal. We felt we had cause for self-congratulation that we had corned-beef and not meat-and-veg, which could hardly have been at its best spooned out cold and lumpy. At the same time there was cause for regret that our sponge pudding also needed heating to be properly appreciated, unlike the creamed rice slipping easily down the throats of a neighbouring party.

The practicability of heating food was the major topic already being discussed, more especially and urgently in order to make tea or coffee, drinks we had forgotten the taste of. The lack of a hot drink was accentuated by the possession of another delight which had come our way as a supplement to the food, a tin each of fifty English cigarettes. I was not, at that time, a regular smoker, but that evening I was as ready as the next man to lean back with a messtin of tea and a fag. The tea problem was solved, before the night was out, by queuing at a boiler stoked up in a little room at the end of one of the huts. The most heartening day of captivity to date ended in a blue haze of tobacco smoke and a continued buzz of lighter-than-usual chatter carried on well after dark, and was followed by a night during which, as one lay back on one's bunk reflecting on the new turn of fortune, an unusual rustle of silver paper punctuated the stillness.

Every fresh twist of fortune only served to emphasise our ignorance of P.O.W. life. Hours of debate took place in an effort to resolve such elementary questions as whether army pay would continue to mount up in credit now we were no longer able to fight for our keep, a point to conjure up visions of Salonika Tanky being paid by both sides; whether being taken prisoner was a court-martial offence; whether all N.C.O.s, especially sergeant-majors, could be compelled to work within the terms of the Geneva Convention; and whether or not prisoners had to salute the Germans. No one had ever seen a copy of that much-quoted document, the Convention, and there was no authoritative opinion on which we could rely, so that all that could be done was to argue from every conceivable angle and pin one's hopes on what seemed the most common-sense solution. With regard to letters and parcels the same state of ignorance and doubt prevailed. The hope was that the rumour suggesting a normal weekly issue of both would prove correct, although quick mental calculation worked it out that a supply of one ten-pound parcel per week for each of perhaps as many as 60,000 prisoners would involve a fantastic distribution and transport problem which, it was dishearteningly felt, the Germans would be unlikely to undertake or permit, unless, as some sceptics hinted, rations were so poor precisely because the Boches were prepared to let anyone feed us so long as it saved them raiding their own larders for the purpose. The sceptics' theory seemed not entirely far-fetched. In that case there was all the more reason for pressurising the Germans to provide the means of brewing the tea and heating the food the British saved them the trouble and expense of providing.

Ever since the gates of the compound had closed behind us, the words 'working camp' had cropped up in all sorts of conversations: I had missed men of the Welch because they had been moved on to a working camp; the food would be better at a working camp; Stalag had to make do with Red Cross parcels left over after the needs of working camps had been met. Rumour even had it that wages were paid for the work extracted, with mention of actual rates of pay. Later on we were to realise that already in Stalag we had encountered that singular phenomenon of P.O.W. life, the receipt of true fact or news so wrapped in the false that it remained unrecognised or distrusted. On top of a natural revulsion against doing any sort of work for the enemy, most men had a cautious approach to the prospect of a war spent, as neither civilian nor soldier, labouring at whatever onerous tasks the Germans selected. Hard fact and experience on which to base a judgment was nowhere to be found. With no one to whom we could turn for guidance, we had to find everything out for ourselves the hard way, the only certainty being that each day would bring nearer the time when we would know, and become the only real authorities.

The life we could visualise ahead differed completely from anything any of us had imagined. There had been no need of a Convention to convince us that when the Germans said 'Arbeit' we would have to knuckle under and tackle whatever job was dictated; but to have thrust on us the knowledge that the whole Stalag system was based on Arbeitskommandos where prisoners became forced labourers or slaves was a horse of another, filthier colour. It was one thing to realise we had to work when ordered to, quite another to face up to what was virtually a sentence of hard-labour for the duration.

A substantial body of opinion, reconciled to the inevitability of work and impressed by the possible chance of an actual improvement in food and conditions, favoured an early departure from Stalag. I had strong reservations until converted by a parasite. The soldier shuffling along in front of me in the bread queue wore only shorts. In contrast to the short-back-and-sides styles still traceably visible as the starting point for most runaway locks in the queue, his recently tended blond hair fell in artificial curls down to his brown shoulders. I gathered from the talk behind me that he was a female part for a play about to be attempted. My admiring gaze dropped from his waves to his back. Squatting, fat and bloated, between the shoulder-blades, sat a louse, as shockingly healthy as any ever squelched at Salonika.

There had been no other evidence of reinfestation, but that one loathsome creature convinced me that within weeks the whole camp would be scratching, stripping and clicking. Any number of simple explanations sprang to mind to account for lice reaching the compound. Whatever the cause, my term in Stalag couldn't end a day too soon. I examined my clothes and kept my fingers crossed that when I did leave it would be with a small party of uninfected workers.

About three weeks after entering Stalag, forty-odd numbers were somehow selected and forty-odd men were rounded up with their slender bits and pieces ready to move out. There was no hint of destination or nature of employment. Accompanied by four or five guards we set off down the road towards the town of Wolfsberg. At the siding where we had left the cattle trucks from Salonika we boarded another, but this time it was better. The numbers were fewer, the door stayed open since the guards rode inside with their charges, there was no barbed-wire over the grills, and loose benches lined the walls. It was to be luxury travel.

How luxurious it was we were impressively reminded during one of the very first, brief halts. Only yards away, solitary and forbidding, a cattle truck stood on an angling line, its doors closed and its vents reinforced by networks of barbed-wire. From the gloom behind the grills tousled heads jockeyed for a view of us, and fingers like claws clutched the lower rims. They belonged to British prisoners arriving belatedly from Greece. We fully understood, from our own experiences, their plight, their curiosity and their misgivings. What they made of us, in our multi-national uniforms and clogs, was debatable, in spite of our assurances that their worst would soon be over.

The train took its time as with frequent pauses it travelled through the beautiful Austrian valleys bathed in dazzling, late-August sunshine. Our eyes had a chance to linger on sights straight from a Grimm's fairytale world of steep roofs, bell-towers, fancy aprons and decorated, narrow-brimmed hats. The small stations, with place-names still displayed to our great surprise, conveyed little to indicate our whereabouts, although one name stayed in the memory as being more than British – Rottenmann.

Night fell and further hours passed before the journey ended at a small, deserted station. After lengthy vacillation the guards shepherded their tired charges into a small room unlocked by a station official. They locked us in and left us. Our impression was that they were waiting for transport and had gone for a meal or a drink in the meanwhile. We settled ourselves as best we could on the cold floor. Gradually men began to doze off. I woke several times, each time feeling a little colder, until I finally came to in the light of the dawn. When the guards eventually let us out it was fully light.

My next clear recollection is of being marched across a wide, flat valley as the morning mists lifted in the sun. The man in front of me wore clogs, and I was fascinated by his laboured attempts to keep pace with the rest of the party striding out to restore warmth and circulation. Every few steps one thick, wooden upper clicked against the other as he failed to give clearance to the passing foot. Towards the foot of the mountains whose peaks had been visible through the mists, we passed along the fringe of a village or hamlet where someone named Lemmerer owned the Gasthaus. A Herr Lemmerer also sold Wintersport equipment. Further along a sawmill displayed the same name. Herr Lemmerer, as we were gradually to discover, owned much more than was then apparent to our eyes. That morning he became the proud possessor of us.

Just beyond the village we entered a narrow valley with its clear stream racing towards us on the left. A rough cart-track took us between the steep, wooded mountainside and the noisy, turbulent water, every twist of the road exposing a view more

47

breathtaking than the last, with no sign of life, habitation, or work. In places the track narrowed where its bank had collapsed into the river; at others its surface had been washed away or pitted by waterfalls from the hillside, causing us to bunch and then straggle. The more bends we rounded the less likely it seemed that any sort of camp would come into view. The little-used road was the only indication that there must have been life in the surrounding hills. The rocky, forested hill on the far side of the valley fell sharply to the water's edge as if never disturbed by man or beast.

Then suddenly, as if it had lain lurking in ambush and had jumped down from the thickets at sight and sound of us, there was the camp alongside us, lying flush with the road. Although it was the only building we had seen in the miles from the village, we would have passed by with nothing more than curious glances had not the Germans brought us to halt in front of it. It bore no resemblance to any camp we had passed through or visualised. An essential something was missing; there was no barbed-wire fence, not even a gate.

We almost felt we were being cheated.

Chapter 3

THE PINE CABIN IN THE HILLS

The guards drew us up in formation facing the building, a wooden construction which, both from its stained, dark-brown exterior and its sweet smell of pine, left no doubt it was brand-new. Lower and much smaller than the huts in Stalag, it had one similar feature, narrow windows running across under the eaves. Where the hut left off framing the road, a solid wooden fence, topped by a strand of barbed-wire, took over for a few yards before turning inwards towards the steep hillside.

The Gefreiter (N.C.O.) in charge of the escort came out of the building accompanied by a stocky Feldwebel (sergeant), whose short neck supported a round face and an equally round, smooth-shaven, blotchy head with a forage cap planted plumb centre on top of it. The Feldwebel received the report that all prisoners were present and correct with all the dignity owing to his rank, and slowly looked us over. What he saw appeared to impress him far less than his own rank and authority, both of which, I suspected, were not only as new as the building, but were also, like the building, entirely owed to the unprepossessing rabble awaiting his pleasure.

The door opened into an L-shaped passage whose longer arm led away to the left and the guards' quarters. We turned right, into a room occupying the greater part of the hut and its whole width. Just as the outside of the camp had taken us by surprise so did the inside. Most of us, long since conditioned to seeing to first things first, spent little time gathering more than a fleeting impression before making sure of securing as advantageous a position as possible by depositing our belongings on a bed. Only then could we take a long, hard look at what was to be, as far as we then knew, our home for the duration of the war.

The smell of newly planed wood pervaded the room and, as if that were not enough to convince us that we were to be its first occupants, two overalled civilians studied us from the farther, blank, end wall where they had been interrupted in their task of gathering up shavings.

Down the centre of the room ran a line of four strong, planed tables, each flanked by matching benches, the line broken in the middle by a tall, round, iron stove. We would be able to sit down and eat at a table!

It was the novelty of the sleeping arrangements which made the biggest impact. At Piraeus we had slept on bare, wooden platforms, at Salonika on bare, wooden floors, at Wolfsberg on three-tier bunks, but now we were literally being put on the shelf – or under it. A continuous, slightly-sloping shelf, projecting six feet into the room at a height of about five feet, stretched almost the entire length of each side wall. The outer edges of the shelves carried low footboards, at right-angles to which shallow, parallel dividers, running up to the walls, carved the shelves into bedspaces, rather like super stalls at a thriving fruiterer's. The same arrangement was repeated at floor level, to give a choice of top or bottom bunk, approached in either case by crawling or climbing over the footboard. I chose an upper berth in the middle of the side backing on to road and river. Above the sleeping shelf, a proper, shallow shelf provided space for storing our few worldly goods, and above that shelf ran the narrow windows. By the time we had settled in, about a quarter of the bedspaces remained unclaimed.

It seemed a remarkably good start, amply justifying the view expressed at Stalag, to the effect that things would be better at an Arbeitskommando. The gains indoors, however, were more than offset by the losses outside. There was virtually no outside. The stockade fence, crazily staggering an up-and-down course never more than ten yards from the hut, enclosed a wilderness of brushwood, hummocks, rocky slopes and boulders, with insufficient flat ground even to hold a Two-Up school. What little there might have been originally had been taken up by the latrine shed standing detached beyond the prisoners' end of the hut and by a see-through shed behind the Germans' section. About three yards from our back door a wooden trough caught the steady stream of crystal water fed into it by an iron pipe whose length could be traced back, diagonally and upwards, along supporting stilts of diminishing height until it disappeared into the bushes and the mountainside itself just below the foot of the fence, but at a level well above our heads. That was to be our compound: nowhere to sit, lounge or pace.

The water looked inviting. I scooped a drink in my hands and decided to get my towel for a refreshing swill to remove the sweaty grime of the journey and the uncomfortable bivouac of the night before. The atmosphere in the room was noticeably different from when I had left it. Instead of the usual backchat, there were earnest, resentful mutterings. Heaving myself up on to my bed, I reached for my towel.

'Don't put your head down, Taff. Baldy doesn't like it.'

'Anything up?'

I joined the men at the nearest table. They were worked up because, apparently, guards had ordered men sharply off their bunks. Until then we had at least been free to exercise about the only choice of activity left to us, whether to sit, stand, or lie down; and, since it was tiring to stand continually, idling, and we'd become accustomed to having nowhere to sit, flopping down on the floor or, since Stalag, on a bunk, had become a way of life. It was bad enough to have a useless compound pinning everyone indoors without being sentenced to sit on a bench. Close to the door, men were attempting to argue with two sentries, still shouldering their rifles and sporting their forage-caps. The chap next to me called out:

'Ask 'em to bring me a dunce's cap, and I'll stand in the corner.'

Someone suggested taking a bench outside. Those of us who had already surveyed the compound expressed doubts about whether any spot could be found suitable for taking a bench. The proposer decided to have a look for himself. He returned in full agreement with us: there was no spot, unless we cared to lean back against the latrine, a suggestion which found little favour.

'If I'd come for the music I'd have brought my piano.'

'No offence, Jock, but I never could stand bagpipes.'

I went for my swill. Glancing up beyond the fence I saw that part of the wood had been cleared and that a snow barrier had been erected to save the camp being engulfed by avalanches, a sight to make nonsense of the unlagged pipe bringing our only water supply out of the bowels of that same hillside; just double our period of captivity and we would be in the middle of an Alpine winter. The water, as it was, felt as if it had arrived direct from the last winter's snows.

Back in the room the mood had grown worse. No one had eaten for twenty-four hours, it was longer than that since any-

51

one had had a hot drink and, to cap it all, there had been little sleep. There were grumblings and rumblings that the Germans, instead of seeing that bunks remained unruffled, should be concerning themselves with providing hot water so that we could at least brew our own tea. Even stronger annoyance was seemingly caused by the continuous presence of guards in our only room, something we had not been used to and which threatened to take the gilt off all ideas about improved conditions at a working camp. Already they had become the butts of sarcastic sallies, received with grins, nods or blank confusion.

'If you're staying, come inside and get yourself a bunk.'

'You're a right grinning bastard, aren't you?'

The more cautious prisoners put a restraint on the baiting. At all other camps the guards, normally outside the wires, had been just faceless jailors, constantly changing and rarely distinguishable one from another. These would be living with us, under the same roof, for an indefinite period. The dullest of them would gradually pick up the odd word of English, and it required little imagination to visualise the sort of dog's life it might produce if one of them got his messer into a particular prisoner when, eventually, he discovered what insults he had unwittingly been subjected to, and there was no doubt which words would, by sheer repetition, first impress themselves on his mind.

Confinement in the Arbeitskommando brought the Germans unwelcomely close to all our movements, but there was a small consolation to be found in the thought that the out-of-door trek for food had gone with the privacy. A serving-hatch occupied a large part of the end wall containing the passage door and, towards midday, its shutters were opened and each man was issued with a white enamel plate and an enormous enamel mug, brown outside and mottled-grey inside. The issue did much to relieve the tension, as also did the fact that the articles were handed out from a kitchen where a male, civilian cook appeared to be making a show of producing a meal on reasonable-looking kitchen equipment. What the meal consisted of I have long since forgotten, but it was the first to be eaten off a plate whilst seated at a table, and also the first to be accompanied by a hot drink. The mugs were not filled to the top with mint tea. That was hardly surprising. Each held an incredible one-and-a-half litres, or over two-and-a-half pints.

It was obvious that our working camp – and we had no clue

52

as to whether it was typical – was to be a cheek-by-jowl-with-the-Germans captivity, totally different from Stalag where direct contact with our captors had been minimal. It is true that after that first meal the guards retired from our room and were subsequently to intrude only at irregular intervals, for checking, or when Baldy, the Kommandant, made an entrance accompanied by two civilians. They surveyed the quarters, pursuing a conversation of which we understood nothing, while we studied the civilians, bandied caustic, descriptive comments on what we saw, and wondered who they were – builders, employers, local bigwigs, or plain inquisitives. Later we were to hazard a guess that one of them was the Herr Lemmerer whose name had been so profusely displayed in the village.

The rest of the day passed idly. Penned indoors on our benches, away from the sacred beds, there was a good opportunity to get to know each other. The bag was a mixed one. Rank ranged down from the sergeant-major of the Northumberland Hussars and his quarter-master sergeant, through three or four sergeants and about the same number of corporals, to a medley of gunners, sappers and privates at the base of the pyramid. Although the most prominent accents were North Country, principally Lancashire, the forty-odd men formed a wide representation. Australia supplied three Diggers, including the youngest boy in the room; New Zealand contributed a sergeant and the Maori, Piwi Pirini of the twinkling eyes; India was represented by a dark-skinned man with the surprising name of John Cobb; while a fluent French speaker, with not too bad a grasp of English, claimed to be a Turk and something like a clerk or secretary to a French Cardinal. France could not quite be omitted, for, although, as his name suggested, he was English, Tom Bowman's home and business lay in Paris. He found it much easier to converse with Tony Vella, the Turk, in French than with the rest of us in English. Bowman was not alone in suffering the additional handicap of knowing his home was at the mercy of the enemy. There was also Moffatt, from the Channel Islands.

The United Kingdom's share included no one from Ireland, the Paddies having been extracted at Salonika. Scotland and Wales boasted equal representation in numbers, but the Jocks outranked the Taffs with a jolly, red-faced sergeant and a chubby corporal against a sapper and a private. But the sapper, Taffy Dennis, did Wales proud, for he was the man I had heard sing, thumbs in belt, at Stalag. The Lancashire men seemed to have belonged largely to the same Bofors crews or engineer detachments, with few, if any, loners amongst them.

Ill-assorted as the complement might at first sight have appeared, it gave every sign of knitting together, the numbers being small enough to make everyone noticeable. Conversation was actually helped along by the diversity of origins. Topics ranging from the mysteries of Australian Rules football or a Wakes Week in Blackpool to trotting in Auckland or life in the regular Army competed with analyses of our failures in Greece and Crete or assessments of Hitler's chances of getting to Moscow before the winter's snows. I got well and truly drawn into the discussions on making the interesting discovery that one of the Bofors crews had been my near neighbours for weeks prior to and during the battle on Crete.

With the fall of dusk half-a-dozen oil-lamps were brought in and hung about the rafters to give a dim, shadow-throwing light, which, since there was nothing to read, proved just about adequate. The idle storytelling continued in the gloom. Promptly at nine o'clock, guards entered with five or six zinc buckets which they proceeded to line up along the farther, blank wall, so conveying the unmistakable intention of locking us in for the night. That provoked another, unanticipated topic for discussion. We had not been locked in at other camps, where perimeter wires had always been lit by floodlights. Once more the all-embracing Convention was liberally cited by men who had neither seen nor read it.

The back door was locked and we were ordered to bed. Before anyone had time to peel off his clothes, another order transmitted via Edgar Parry, a prisoner who revealed an understanding of German, stopped us rigid, half-in and half-out of our clothes. Passed along from group to group, it sounded like a joke, but Parry's quiet, insistent voice dispelled any idea that he had got it all wrong: everyone had to put his boots and trousers into the passage. Few scenes from Dickens could have rivalled the ensuing sight: the bright light from the Kommandant's incandescent lamp thrusting through the passage into the comparative gloom of the big room, picking out the long-drawered, shirt-tail flapping procession emerging from our room with boots and trousers in hand, jostled by the emptyhanded queue trying to get back against the main tide, while Baldy and his henchmen solemnly supervised the hanging of trousers on wall hooks and saw to it that the right number of boots were arranged neatly around the floor. After that comedy had been played out amid mutterings and not a few giggles, there ensued another novelty, that of being counted in our beds. The lamps were turned out and carried away, except for one, which, turned down to a minimum glimmer, was destined to serve throughout the night to light prisoners to their slop-buckets and sentries on their periodic checks.

The morning started at six-thirty when guards ' 'raused' us from our beds. We elbowed and bummed each other in the narrow confines of the passage, tracking down trousers and pushing aside boots. For once, men with clogs had a quite definite advantage. I met no difficulty in finding my distinctive breeches, but I came across my boots nowhere near where they had been placed. More than one argument arose as some pairs turned out to be odd or to consist of two right or two left boots, while, much later, one man was still doing the rounds looking for someone with three to a pair, and to make it worse, as he repeatedly pointed out to anyone who stayed long enough to listen, the one boot he was holding was not only not his but was also much to small even to try on.

By the time the prisoners had come fully to life after a quick douse in the compound, they were able to appreciate the one unanticipated change in routine to be generally welcomed without reservation – the first breakfast for three months. It was fitting that on that day of all days we should qualify for breakfast. It was one to be classed with other memorable milestones: starting school; the first long trousers; the first pay-packet; call-up; and the day of capture. That was the day on which we became labourers for the Third Reich, officially on an enemy pay-roll, and began the first term of 'normal' P.O.W. life for other ranks in German hands. The breakfast consisted of nothing more than a plate of polenta, a yellow porridge, probably of maize, with a spoonful of ersatz jam to sweeten it, and of ersatz coffee, but it was a vast improvement on nothing but mint tea.

The working day was to last until five o'clock with a break of one hour for food at midday, when we were marched back to the cabin. The meal, although more pleasantly dished out and eaten in greater comfort than elsewhere, differed little from the inadequate rations to which we had long since become accustomed, but it was normally assisted by a drink of mint tea. One regular variation from the monotony of past diet was the appearance once or twice a week of dubious, tough, dried fish on the plates. Work done, the day was in effect over, for there was nothing to do but carve the bread, as per Stalag formula, consume it with some jam, and plunder any remnants from the Stalag issue of Red Cross parcels to get some sort of weak drink to help spin out the time until lights-out and buckets-in.

Saturday afternoons and Sundays were times of leisure, conforming to the free time of the civilian boss, the Little Man. It was then that dirty, evil-smelling socks and footrags could be rinsed and rubbed in an attempt to get them clean and soft under the icy spout. The sun never touched the camp or its small compound, so clothes, first draped over bushes to drip, had to be brought into the room at night and hung on improvised lines for the rising heat of the stove to dry them out, while their owners lounged about in bare feet, bunched around tables and stove.

On our first Saturday afternoon the guards hauled us out on parade on the road, where the Kommandant, assisted by an interpreter, a middle-aged lady who was probably the village schoolma'am, gave his inaugural address. Sentence by sentence, while Baldy watched the ranks for effect, the rather embarrassed but dutiful lady translated: we were prisoners of war; we were to obey the commands of the Kommandant and his guards; the orders of civilian bosses at work had to be carried out without question or hesitation; no other contact with civilians would be permitted; we had to keep ourselves and the room neat and tidy; there must be no quarrelling amongst ourselves; above all, there must be no attempt to escape, for not only would it end in certain failure, but anyone doing so would be shot. At that point several protests arose advising Baldy to 'come off it'. Baldy put his arms akimbo, thrust his round head as far forward as his short neck permitted, and stared at us with eyes sticking out like organ-stops. As soon as silence was restored, the offending sentence was repeated, to be followed by a threat that any further demonstration would be severely punished.

The subject of escape, except at Salonika, had rarely been seriously discussed, and on the very few occasions when the topic had arisen talk had been restricted to the principles rather than the practice, to the duty of each man to attempt escape if he saw a chance, and to the possible consequences of the almost inevitable recapture. Common sense and the only experience would decide what would actually happen and, Convention might lay down certain rules for both sides, but even then, one or two cases could hardly be taken as a blueprint for all, since our captors would remain the final, and only, arbiters. Salonika experience gave no guide. There sentries had killed men attempting to get through the wires. By and large that was accepted as fair, provided the escapees had been properly challenged. More to the point was what would happen to someone caught miles outside the camp. Presently men would try, driven by boredom, desperation, sense of duty, frustration or simply desire for adventure. Then we would all know.

Baldy sprang another surprise on us the first Sunday afternoon. It must have been about two o'clock, a time when, meagre lunch already forgotten, everyone was finding it hard to get through a boring afternoon, when the passage door opened. Heads turned as they always did whenever the Germans intruded. The guard mimed his order, head leaning sideways on his raised hands, palms pressed together: everybody into bed. When he then showed signs of locking the door to the compound, he was almost bowled over in the rush to get to the 'bog'. No one wanted to be left, bucketless, with already overloaded bladders. We got into bed.

Most of us made a big mistake. Instead of getting to sleep we lay there continuing our conversations or starting new ones. The neighbour to my right, the man who had played the soundless harmonica in Wolfsberg, hailed from Perth, Western Australia, and was that most unusual of beings, or so it seemed to me at the time, a quiet Aussie. Norman Hodgetts was, I am sure, quiet by nature, but it was difficult to judge, since he had unwisely placed his neck in the path of a bullet. Having gone in neatly at one side, it had nicked a vital passage before coming out at the other. As a result Norman shouted in whispers not always easy to catch among the usual hubbub in the Lager. The compulsory siesta provided a rare chance for us to have a quiet chat without too much strain on Norman's throat. Our conversation, like all others on both sides of the room, gradually faded out, and we fell asleep. It seemed no time at all before shouts of ''raus! 'raus!' had us all awake again, struggling to realise where we were and what was happening, whether it was time for work once more. Flopped about the tables, muttering and evil-tempered, we felt worse than if we had stayed up all afternoon.

The Londoner, Edgar Parry, fell easily and naturally into the role of interpreter, his knowledge of the enemy's language far exceeding the restricted vocabulary with which the rest of us had to make do. He informed us that, according to the Germans, there had also to be a Vertrauensmann, a Man-of-Confidence, someone elected by the prisoners to be their official spokesman in all dealings with the Kommandant and the sole channel for complaints either way between captors and captives.

The notion that the fascist, militaristic Germans would recognise an elected spokesman went against all preconceived ideas and prejudices; that they should command that one be selected reeked of a snare, and aroused suspicions that the Vertrauensmann would be a convenient whipping-boy, or at least someone to be played off against the Senior N.C.O. to create dissension and undermine his authority and all discipline. P.O.W.s were still soldiers, and had not lost recognition of rank. On the contrary they looked to their N.C.O.s to look after them; the greater part of the resentment and outrage at Tanky's behaviour in Salonika had been due to his abrogation of the true responsibilities of his rank.

Behind barbed-wire the lot of the Senior N.C.O. was not an enviable one at best. Powerless, he could nevertheless lose neither his crown nor stripes nor responsibility for lower ranks, while at the same time he was used, reluctantly lending the authority of his rank, to transmit the captors' orders. In the many arguments in Wolfsberg about whether warrant officers could be made to work, much had been made of the point that each should decide for himself whether he would decline to work for the Germans (so leaving the men without officers or N.C.O.s or warrant officers when they most needed them) or whether he would work in order to stay with and guide them. In our case the problem revolved around the standing of Sergeant-Major Hodson of the Northumberland Hussars, whose undoubted seniority in rank could not be made to vanish either in fact or in the minds of his fellow captives by a simple order of the Germans, however innocent their intentions.

Our choice was considered, sensible compromise which resulted in our having the best of both worlds: Sergeant-Major Hodson was elected. It was a choice which gave Baldy more than an equal to confront and allowed time to see how the Man-of-Confidence post worked out in practice. The status quo was maintained in line with what had happened at previous camps where the word 'Vertrauensmann' had never been heard. The decision had been rendered all the easier to make by the camp not having been long enough established to have allowed opposing factions or obvious alternatives to have emerged.

Work, not just casually assigned to men who happened to be in the wrong place at the wrong time, but as a permanent occupation was the very *raison d'être* of the Arbeitskommando. From within an hour of our very first breakfast on the day after our arrival, it was to dictate the pattern of the days and weeks, and of our whole lives. A mile back down the track to the village began a routine which, apart from variations imposed by locality, nature of work and idiosyncrasies of overseers, would continue to be the lot of most prisoners until the distant day of release.

Before we arrived at the camp, captivity had reached the length of being counted in months, but work fixed the week as the predominant division. Where, before, life had been a long string of meaningless days to be dragged through, one after the other, it now became a procession of laborious weeks, a slow toil from one week-end to the next. 'Cheer up! You can't call it a week' became a favourite catch-phrase, to be heard at depressing moments, sometimes as early as Monday with just one day's work behind us and an eternity to labour through until the next break.

Had it been possible – but it never was – to overlook the fact that the work was at the behest of the detested enemy, the work itself would not have been the worst means of getting through the monotony of captivity. Most of it took place outside the barbed-wire. It began to toughen men up again, although most would have opted for getting fattened up first. The most salutary effect was on the brooders. They couldn't remain completely unresponsive to work: it got them off their bunks, however unwillingly, and thrust them, not too brutally, into company not of their own choosing; it loosened their muscles, and tongues; and, in spite of themselves, it forced them to swear, sometimes, even, to laugh. Even for the rest of us, work had a similar, beneficial effect, admitted by no one at the time, causing us to rub shoulders and exchange talk with others not normally of our company back in the fug of the Lager.

The work-site could not have been set in more idyllic surroundings: the wide, clear, chattering stream bounded merrily over its rocky bed in masses of spray; narrow waterfalls bounced down the hillsides; wooded slopes rose endlessly to disappear into the bluest of skies; the valley wriggled and twisted to give a fresh view round every bend, and with every time of day and angle of sun. All around was a peace impossible to comprehend after the turmoil and carnage of Crete, enhanced rather than broken by the continuous sounds of rushing waters and the incessant songs of the birds. It might have been Shangri-la, or Utopia, except that we, who did not want to be there, and our guards, made it ugly and broke the divine stillness. Rarely did anyone else do so. Whole days would pass with no sign of people other than ourselves.

According to our flimsy knowledge of the Convention, we were not to be employed on any task directly connected with the war effort. We had great difficulty in finding a reason why the Germans should have gone to the expense of maintaining a Lager of forty men to service a road no one seemed to use, so they were in no danger of being accused of breaking the Convention in that respect. Neither did we, on our side, feel guilty, for not only did it seem absurd that our work could have any sinister effect, it also appeared unlikely that repairs of substance would have been considered in the valley but for a surplus of cheap labour. Remembering the signs for Wintersport equipment, we concluded that the road was used seasonally for that purpose, as well as by the local hill farmers.

In the early weeks of repairing the neglected road, the allotted tasks varied. The Little Man, the engineer with a Hitler moustache, scampered around on short legs, switching his attention from one job to another, assigning men and tools. Most of the time he battled with trying to make himself understood, sorting out holes dug to the wrong depths in the wrong places, timbers sawn off too short, or stones stubbornly resisting all attempts to be split by tools clumsily wielded. It may have been for that reason or because of orders from above that, one afternoon, the Kommandant had us queuing into his office for the purpose of recording each prisoner's occupation.

My place was about halfway along the chattering, curious line. Immediately in front of me stood men mainly from the Royal Engineers. Each man, long before his turn arrived, strained to hear what was being asked and recorded. The whole hut seemed to house no one but engineers, for man after man gave just the one occupation. Rising from his chair, emphasising his words with thumps on the table, Baldy blew his round top. Freely translated, and abbreviated, what he said was:

'Engineers! Engineers! You can't all be bloody engineers! Engineers have papers, certificates, diplomas! They've been to university! Have you all got papers, certificates, diplomas? Has every man jack of you been to college?'

After that tirade, the boys switched the answers about a bit, using somewhat more imagination without encroaching too hard on the truth. The rest of the list showed an unusually high proportion of bank clerks, reporters, salesmen and shop managers, as befitted a nation of shopkeepers. The Kommandant, to everyone's astonishment, did not go back through his imbalanced list and sort out the 'engineers' from the peasants, and so made perhaps his first concession to anything less than complete mastery over his charges.

The unpalatable truth was, however, that the Germans were the complete masters. Unlike the other camps, at which prisoners had been left more or less to their idle selves to while away the tedious hours with little or no interference from their captors, at the Kommando almost every minute of every day was dictated or supervised, indoors and out.

At work, the Little Man, with a contract to fulfil, told us what to do, and the guards enthusiastically saw to it that we did it. Their lot was just as boring as our own, their day just as long. Pinned to us and to the job, they had nothing else to do. Apart from being in poor condition and having no heart for the job, many prisoners had little knack of using the strange tools, especially the awkward, crutchless shovels. That gave the sentries the opportunity first to be amused in a superior fashion, and then to display their Aryan superiority by simple demonstration, which, in turn, was our cue to act admiringly dumb while they handled the shovels, often nearly strangling themselves with their rifle-slings in the process.

All too soon the guards learned to avoid such situations. Instead they contented themselves with looks or words of disparagement, yet continued to see to it that the work didn't flag. A far more satisfying way of easing up was to affect an interest in the job, and involve the guard by pointing to hole or rock and asking him, 'How does your mother like her turnips?' or 'Where does a monkey stuff his nuts?' Roused from his

61

boredom and pleased by the deference to his authority and knowledge, he would pour out incomprehensible instructions and information at which one could nod understanding and eventual agreement. Such games appealed to only a few and to them only some of the time, the hard fact being that most prisoners had as yet little spirit for such humour, and found the time passed more quickly when getting through the motions of the work while minds wandered off over miles of ocean, to Australian beaches, New Zealand farms, England's green and never-so-pleasant land, and to slag-heaped Welsh hills.

In the seemingly uneven contest between the prisoners and their guards-cum-overseers, it was, strangely, but, on reflection, inevitably the latter who weakened first. This taught us an important lesson. In many respects, although the German masters would continue to call the tune, the prisoners themselves could influence the manner and tempo in which it was played. The sentries found the days dragging even more than we did. Their undue interference might have stemmed as much from boredom as from zeal. It was impossible for them to breathe down everyone's neck at the same time, and, since their primary task was to ensure that none of the prisoners escaped up the closely wooded hillside, they tended to separate and gravitate towards both ends of the lengthy site, where there was no one of their kind to talk to.

While the prisoners chatted away and ignored them, the guards became more and more frustrated. They began to find it more companionable to be friendly, and to restrict themselves to their primary function. In addition, the guards knew that, comfortably away from the brass of Stalag and the discomforts of the front, they were in a relatively good paddock. Their charges were in a position to scorch the grass. It was inadvisable for them to provoke anything which might be heard at Wolfsberg.

One of the guards, a sleek, black-haired Austrian of athletic build, claimed to have toured Britain with a professional soccer side, a piece of information which was as good a starting point for conversation as any. It was not long before it was used to elicit the rather more useful information that the nearest club of standing was at Linz and that the journey took the better part of an hour by stopping train. Thus we obtained a glimmering of a clue as to our whereabouts in Austria.

Taken at the more leisurely pace made possible by the

loosening of the reins by the guards, some of the work proved both interesting and challenging as long as the good weather lasted. Just as some men nurture a secret ambition to drive a railway engine, so some of us found it a temptation to fell a tree, split a huge rock or form one of a three-hammer team driving a hand drill. One of the more interesting early jobs which occupied a whole afternoon was the throwing of a lightning, do-it-yourself bridge over the river. We started from scratch by felling two tall pines and lopping the branches. By the time we had finished, a sturdy footbridge connected both banks about a mile below the camp, but why the bridge was ever built remains an unsolved mystery for, except for that same afternoon, I can recall no one ever using it, while the virgin slopes on the far bank carried not even the suggestion of a goat track. A month or so later, a second bridge, constructed by like method at a spot up beyond the Lager, was to find regular daily use as our means of crossing to what was to be the main work site.

Most work, however, proved laborious and of little interest. We dug holes or filled holes in, bent over picks and shovels, trundled and tipped wheelbarrows, prised rocks out of banks or laid stones to support banks, drilled and blasted rocks, or, in truer convict fashion, we shuffled up and down, armed with long-handled hammers and broke stones.

Work couldn't end soon enough. We all became experts at measuring the time, especially the midday break and finishing time. Our valley, or at least that part of it to which our activities were confined, was one huge reliable sundial which, as long as the sun shone, never let us down. Day after day, during the first months, the sun shone brilliantly, but never on us, for it didn't cross the valley. Our side lay in perpetual shade, the shadow of our mountain cutting a bold line across the opposite slopes to provide an unfailing, easily-read timepiece. When the ever-moving shadow descended to touch an outcrop of rock, we knew it was lunchtime; when it rose to darken all save the tip of a prominent conifer, another working day was over. The slight daily adjustment to allow for shortening days was beyond no one's capacity. The hill even indicated the seasons. We watched autumn descend in a broad band of changing colour, and dreaded the time when it would engulf us, winter hard on its heels.

Untravelled as we were in Europe, we still needed no telling that the winter was bound to be tough. But help was coming through from the world we had left. The help came in stages to lighten our lives and the better equip us for facing the certain drudgery of work outdoors and the blank emptiness of the limited leisure in the Lager.

The first break came with the issue of lettercards, a whole month's ration, but marred by the order that all had to be written that same day. This was immediately a point of contention, expressed most vocally by Eddie Hopkins.* Why should they all have to be written that same day? He had a wife and child: they were the only people he was interested in writing to; as for his other family and friends, his wife could pass on the news, and they would understand. He would rather pen her a line once a week than send a batch of four in one go, with nothing to follow for a month. Hopkins's speech, like many another, might have been forgotten with the passage of time, but the unpredictable course of future events was to keep it fresh in most memories. The disputed cards were indeed all written and handed in that same Sunday. Future issues, however, were distributed weekly, and so the grievance did not need to be voiced again.

Just as the contradictory rumours in Stalag about the issue of lettercards proved to include a correct one, so it was with Red Cross parcels. There was to be one whole packet per week for each man. The first ones, hauled from the village by tractor, arrived about a month after us. But nothing could be straightforward and simple, and the distribution brought its problems.

In conformity with the practice of separating prisoners from their clothes at night, the Germans, while fairly and conscientiously distributing the parcels, took good care that no food could be stored in preparation for escape. They kept the parcels securely under their own lock and key. Each parcel was opened in the Kommandant's office, by a guard in front of the prisoner, with Kommandant and Vertrauensmann standing by to ensure there was no underhand work by either side. The contents, objects of as much interest for the Germans as for the recipients, were pulled out, an article at a time, for the prisoner to note. Chocolate and raisins, or any food in paper wrapping, he could take, but the wrappings were first removed or broken. Only two tins were allowed to be taken at a time, or rather

* Fictitious name.

64

selected, for they had to be opened and the contents turned out. The rest of the tins were then counted back into the box, the number recorded on the lid with the prisoner's identity, and the box left in custody of the guards. Next evening two more tins could be claimed for opening.

Confusion began with the opening of the very first parcel. Chaos and anger took longer to develop as full realisation of the imposed procedure slowly sank in. Unthinkingly relying on Stalag experience, we lined up empty-handed, expecting to walk off embracing the boxes. It took considerable time and explanation for the message to get across to the first man that he was to receive only two tins, which, before it then dawned on him that he was in fact to receive only the contents, had already been opened. The front of the queue broke up in dismay and disorder as men went in search of their plates and whatever old tins had not been discarded, while, further back, puzzled mates doubtfully held their ground, asking what was up.

The order that just two tins be collected was an unexpected blow in itself. There were, however, a number of easy solutions, based on combining and sharing. Far more disastrous, and less capable of quick solution, was the edict that only contents leave the Kommandant's office. Surprisingly bountiful as the ration of a complete parcel per week might be, a tin of corned-beef or pilchards still needed to be husbanded to spread over days, and butter, milk, or jam over the whole week. Meat could be slid out of its tin in one slab, with nothing wasted and left in the tin, and what was not eaten that night kept on a plate – but for the fact that the plate would be needed for next morning's polenta and midday potatoes. But what did one do with a plate overflowing with jam, or condensed milk, or treacle? An uncovered plate was hardly the best of storage dishes for anything sticky in a crowded room with no trace of a cupboard. To envisage enough good condensed milk to sweeten a couple of mugs of tea or sufficient jam to colour a slice of bread disappearing into the bin each time a tin was opened was unthinkable.

Proceedings came to a grinding halt while Kommandant, Vertrauensmann and Dolmetscher endeavoured to sort things out. The rest of us stood around in ever more heated debate. Hull stevedore, Freddie Baines, summed it up in one of his favourite sentences: 'If we stand for this, we'd stand for coal breaking on our heads.'

5   65

At first the Kommandant fell back on a repeated 'Befehl ist Befehl'.* The prisoners united on the line that if it was an order from above which had to be carried out to the letter, they would have no alternative but to obey, but would expect provision of enough suitable dishes to make the exercise practicable. The guards could open the tins, but they would be left holding them, for no one would sacrifice his only plate.

It was conceivable that we might hold the stronger cards. We could perhaps exert the same pressure on the guards that the Kommandant at Wolfsberg had often threatened to put on the prisoners when he warned that he'd keep them on parade all day: he was in the happy position of being able to relieve the sentries, but not the inmates. At Stalag that had been a real threat. At the Arbeitskommando the jackboot was on the other foot: the Germans' numbers and free time were limited, and already overstretched. We were going nowhere; we had nothing to read, no wireless to listen to. They did. If the queue were kept going with only a couple of men at a time, each taking minutes to mull over his tins, make his choice, supervise opening and emptying and check the count, Kommandant and at least two guards could be bogged down for most of every evening at the low cost of just about ten minutes queuing time per prisoner.

The discussions ended in a compromise which could be regarded as a substantial victory for us, without inflicting humiliation on the Germans with whom we had to live at close quarters. Solid foods had to be turned out, but 'runny' items would be handed over in their opened or punctured tins. For the next week partly-emptied tins cluttered the shelves; after that the issue of a second parcel ensured each man an empty box in which to store them. With the handing over of the tins came another gain – tin labels to be carefully removed, folded, and preserved as toilet paper. That was what the large patch-pocket on the thigh of a battledress was really for!

The night which had followed the parcel issue in Stalag had been marked by the intermittent rustling of tinfoil in the small hours. I had attributed it to restless, hungry men unable to sleep for thinking of their chocolate. My turn came after the first issue at the working camp. The irresistible craving, not for food as such, but for something sweet, was persistent and overwhelming, permitting no rest. I gave in once or twice in the

* 'Orders are orders.'

night, each time resolving that the square slowly melting on my tongue would be the last inroad into my diminishing stock. Each time I yielded I felt more wretched. The awareness that others were audibly losing the same battle didn't help overmuch. What did assist, however, was the sight of the same man, evening after evening, offering to swop whatever tins he had drawn, be it corned-beef or creamed rice, for condensed milk which he unashamedly proceeded to wolf with a spoon before our very startled eyes. If there is any such complaint as sweet-starvation known to the medical profession, we had it.

A prisoner who had been drafted into the kitchen as a spud-basher was now given access to the boiler in the evenings to provide boiling water for tea and coffee of our own making. Tea, brewed in our giant mugs, became the basic ingredient of evenings spent sipping, smoking and chatting, precipitated another crisis in our dull lives, and resulted in the mass evacuation of the beds at the far end of the room.

Morning had regularly revealed the slop-buckets perilously full and, as often as not, with one or two overflowing. Dark, damp stains had spread inwards along the floor and upwards along the wall. Abuse had been hurled from near-by bunks as, in the cold gloom of the last hours before dawn, a late user attempted to relieve himself, a drop in one bucket, about the same in another, until, wet-footed, he found one not quite full. From the moment when parcels arrived to provide the drinks to help us through idle evenings, the buckets had no chance of seeing daylight before spreading their maladorous surplus, not in a damp patch, but in a squelching, slippery pool through which men had to paddle. Mornings would begin with quarrels as to who would carry the stinking vessels out to the bog, an operation which left a trail the length of the room.

At about the same time another dismaying setback occurred: someone announced he had found a 'chat'. The news was received in stunned disbelief. But there was no doubt of it. We were all experts, with experience too sharp and recent to permit of mistake. Several more cases were found. Whether the finds were Salonika lice or an indigenous Austrian variety seemed a point of no importance until it was realised that if they were the former they could possibly survive delousing. Casting my mind back to the 'actress' in the food queue at Wolfsberg, I felt convinced the infestation had been carried with us, and even more certain that the fellow who had announced the discovery had

67

acquired his parasites from someone else who must have known he was 'chatty' but had kept quiet about it.

Little time was lost in informing Baldy. He was proud of his new rank and uniform, and he and his guards had no chance of keeping their distance. The other regular contacts, the civilians, would also have to be considered. Baldy lost no time either. A tar-machine-like contraption arrived within days, towed by the tractor and supervised by a fat, scented, bespectacled Gefreiter, whom not even a cartoonist could have made to look less like one of the jackbooted Huns stalking terror across Europe. Roadwork came to a dead stop for a day while he cooked our clothes.

After that reverse, the next improvement came from the Germans, once again confirming that among the know-alls at Stalag there had been some who had actually known what they were talking about. There came a monthly pay-day, with the amount, exactly to the pfennig, one of the many figures freely quoted in Wolfsberg – eighteen marks, twenty pfennigs. The wages came in Lagergeld, paper notes like soap coupons of various denominations, for use only in P.O.W. camps. They were meticulously counted out and signed for, the role of pay-master not being entrusted to Baldy but being performed by a civilian pay-clerk making a special sortie into the valley for the purpose.

What on earth use Lagergeld could be in a camp where there was nothing to buy was a puzzling joke until the guards supplied the answer. We had been gradually absorbing the fact that Herr Lemmerer, in addition to apparently owning most of the village, was also our contractor and landlord. He was not only the one who paid our wages; he was also the one who would get most of it back. The guards would take our shopping list to his store. A list of essentials was not difficult to compile, particularly since most articles were either unavailable or forbidden to prisoners. The bulk of purchases consisted of razors and blades, tooth-brushes and tooth-powder, combs, saccharine tablets to eke out the small Red Cross ration, cigarette papers to enable us to spin out the butt-end tobacco, matches, cups, pencils and paper. The Solingen blades were good, also the saccharine tablets. Other purchases were indifferent, with the exception of the tooth-powder which was awful, and grated and cloyed in the mouth. Meagre as the monthly wage was it stretched to cover the few things in most demand, and indicated that future Lagergeld would, very probably, accumulate uselessly. By the second pay-day men were resorting to buying dangling Austrian pipes in order to defeat the feeling of having toiled for nothing.

My first job on acquiring a packet of razor-blades was to get rid of my beard. Tom Hughes devoted a large part of a Sunday morning to snipping my locks, after which, with the aid of a brand-new blade and a mug of hot water from the kitchen, I succeeded in revealing my face without too many scars.

As mornings and nights grew darker and chillier, fears for the winter ahead weighed more heavily and constantly, especially when milling around the watertrough for the early morning wash or when examining clothes and boots suffering from over-work and long neglect. The couple of middle-aged civilians who had arrived to augment the work-force gave more than hints of what to expect when they told us in all earnestness that the turbulent stream, a fast-moving mass of foam, would freeze over, a forecast received with some scepticism. Even without the autumn rains just beginning the stream looked far too rest-less to succumb to frost. More acceptable and heartening was the often repeated assurance that, once the out-door daytime temperature fell to below fifteen degrees of frost Centigrade, outside work would stop. The prospect of enduring a long winter in temperatures of that order in inadequate or makeshift clothing could do nothing but depress.

The precariousness of the position as regards clothing was forcibly illustrated by Earnie Jack's misfortune in losing a clog. It happened while returning from work. Crossing one of the loose-logged bridges spanning the gullies under the road, he slipped to his knees as an ill-fitting log rolled under his weight. When he struggled back to his feet, one of them was minus its clog. Helplessly, we watched it racing away in the middle of the current, out of reach and soon out of sight. Although his dot-and-carry progress back to the Lager was marked by such cheery sallies as 'Some one-legged Black Sea fisherman will be glad of that clog in a week or so', no one under-estimated Earnie Jack's plight. There was nothing in camp to replace even one boot.

Curiosity was hopefully roused on discovering one evening that workmen had been busy in our room during our absence, their activities concentrated at the foully soiled far end. From the amount of timber material lying around in the compound, something big was being attempted by way of alteration or reconstruction. The mysterious workmen were rarely to be seen, but, day after day, the progress of their labours came in for close inspection until the broad plan began to unveil itself. The end of the room was being divided off to add two more small rooms. From then on interested speculation centred on what would be done with them, and what influence they would have in improving our lot. The one towards the back of the hut should, by unanimous agreement, be a washroom to replace the outside trough and to take the slop-buckets from under our noses and bare feet. That was what it materialised into. A zinc trough, with pipes and taps, installed along one wall, remained an ornament for weeks until the outside pipes, fed directly from the mountainside, were linked up and lagged to give us the luxury of a cold wash indoors in place of a cold wash in the compound. Overwhelmingly it was voted a pity that the plans, while providing for an overflow drain, didn't extend to including a funnel on the wall to connect with the earth latrine and so obviate all need for buckets. But as the boys said: 'Where the hell do you think you are? Butlins?' The second additional room, identical in size and shape with the first, seemed to have no immediate purpose, but was to come in handy later on.

The next advance in comfort, sprung on us without warning, came with such nice timing, so unexpectedly and completely filling the most urgent remaining need, that we felt prayers must really be answered. Lettercards, parcels and pay had been anticipated in much prior discussion, especially at Stalag where some men had known the right answers, and were comforts to cause delightful surprise not so much by their arrival as by their scale and quality. What turned up at the Arbeitskommando in a number of tea-chests had not been forecasted by anyone: a complete new rig-out all round, every article new and of British army issue, not booty of war, but a consignment specifically shipped out for distribution to the likes of us. The whole range of clothing – shirts, battledress, greatcoats, boots and sidecaps – was not only enough to kit every man out, there were so many spares to try on and choose from that everyone finished up with a reasonably good fit. The surplus was repacked for dispatch back to Stalag, together with our carefully collected old gear. Baldy, true to the principles of his overlordship and his own thoroughness of execution, took no chances on any prisoner hanging on to spare articles which might have defeated the purpose of his nightly, pre-emptive count.

I saw the last of my green Belgian jacket and my French jodhpurs. We took on the look of soldiers again, in identical uniforms adorned with badges and flashes inherited from the discarded clothes, a transformation which, as well as lifting spirits, gave the camp overnight a newer, much younger look. It must be confessed that, during the long-drawn-out issue, and for days afterwards, no small part of the satisfaction with the new clothing arose from the ill-concealed envy and astonishment of the guards as they fingered the real wool and compared it with their own limp, ersatz uniforms.

The surprise issue gave rise to the last of the great stands against Baldy, from which confrontation we once more emerged victorious. In our pride, we viewed with horror the prospect, a near-certainty, that blouses and greatcoats would be desecrated by the painting of large KGs on the back, as had been the case with most of the old clothing. The letters stood for *K*riegs*g*efangene, prisoner of war, but the Germans, to their own lasting amusement, preferred to regard them as the initials of King George. To the amazement of those of us not present at the actual conversations in the Kommandant's office, after representations had been made based on the argument that a prisoner's uniform should be respected, the clothing stayed untarnished by paintbrush.

The long-delayed arrival at our ultimate destination had eventually confronted us with the hard, previously-unguessed-at shape of the captivity to be endured. The clothing, on top of the food parcels, presented us with the physical equipment to face it. Gradually, mental fortitude and strength of character became the keys to survival, in place of sheer physical endurance. Preoccupation with beards and bowels, food and feet, lice and latrines, and with all the other petty things which in normal, outside life would have been dismissed as trivia, began to give way to ponderings on longer-term problems: how wives, parents, children and sweethearts were faring; how to fit into the new life; how to get fit again and stay that way; and how to adapt mentally to the dull, repetitive days.

The repetitive days were all too predictable, needing an argument, fight or disaster to distinguish one from another. From the time we were awakened by the rapid, machine-gun click-clack of the colour-sergeant's Rolls Razor, stropped in the cold gloom long before the ' 'raus, 'raus' of the guards, right through the long day until the last pair of boots was clomped down in the passage in the shadowy fug of late evening, the only variation was in the moods of the men. Good-tempered and humorous as they were, even in their grumblings, they had no inexhaustible range of repartee. That, too, became repetitive and often unbearably predictable unless provoked by some unusual incident. Even the news-reel act palled by over-repetition.

The news-reel act kept its appeal longer than most diversions, due to the variety of improvisations introduced into the clowning. Whenever a speaker was felt to be 'shooting a line', someone would start the 'ta-ta, ta-ta-ta-tara' of a cinema news-reel signature tune, during the playing of which the screen used to be filled with shots of sportsmen simultaneously bashing balls, punching, jumping, running, rowing and leaping over nets. The moment anyone struck up the tune, someone else would bounce to his feet, stab the air with straight lefts, do a ten-yard dash, swing into a cover drive, gracefully toss a ball in the air and, with a racket as imaginary as the ball, lob over an imaginary net, before parking his bottom on the floor to get in a few swift oar-strokes, all of which was the preliminary to the grand finale of fingering a shot over a crossbar. When hilarious displays of that kind failed to elicit enthusiastic applause it was a sure sign that we had entered the doldrums. Considering everything, unpleasant scenes and stand-up arguments were rare, and, when they arose, it was usually Lancashire wit which led the return to calm and reconciliation.

Sometimes disagreement proved embarrassing when it threatened the possible invited intervention of the Germans in matters which most men instinctively felt should be settled amongst themselves. One such incident bubbled up after Tony Vella discovered a long-lost pair of socks hanging up to dry. Declaring that he would have recognised them anywhere because he had darned them with 'de-greena-de-wool', he was adamant that the new owner had stolen them. The charge was hotly denied, yet, for most of us, the accusation had the awful ring of unpalatable truth. During the argument which followed there developed some backing for reporting the matter to the Kommandant and allowing him to settle the affair. For the majority the idea was utterly abhorrent, far more so than that of having a possible thief loose among their few, vital possessions. In the end Tony Vella recovered his socks, the other party being allowed the benefit of a simple, regrettable mistake, and our jailors were kept out of it. An important, nagging question had been posed: where the British writ couldn't reach and German jurisdiction was taboo, who would enforce what law?

The Germans, unfortunately, could not be kept entirely at arm's length in another episode of a more humorous nature. It began with, and revolved around, a 'pudding'. To vary diet, make an appetising use of raisins, prunes, or currants, and to break away from the deadly sameness of meals, most men at various times, experimented with concoctions, principally along the lines of bread puddings or the 'collier's lump' of my boyhood. The mixture of soaked, saved-up bread or biscuit, mixed with fruit, a little fat and sugar, would be put in a tin in charge of the prisoner kitchen-help at breakfast time. He would be responsible for putting it into the oven, by kind permission of the German cook, and looking after its welfare until reclaimed by its inventor for midday 'duff'.

The creation which caused all the fuss went into the oven, and was forgotten until too late. The expectant owner collected it in a charred, uneatable state. Dreams of days past shattered, he paced up and down the room, hopping mad, displaying his burned offering to all and sundry, and vowing to have the so-and-so offender out of his warm kitchen and out among the boulders before he could say 'essen'. Nothing would shake his resolve. Food still being no trifling matter, he got some support. The careless one was replaced by another prisoner, automatically involving the Germans on the fringes of the dispute; after all, it was their kitchen. Lancashire wit had the last word and put things back into perspective with the words of a ditty heard for weeks afterwards:

With his pud tucked underneath his arm, he walked the
                                        Lager floor,
With his pud tucked underneath his arm, at the dinner hour.
He said old —— had burned it, and —— would have to pay,
He said he couldn't eat it and would have to throw the bloody
                                        thing away,
With his pud tucked underneath his arm, at the dinner hour.

With minds considerably less concerned with lurching from one day to the other, and with gobbling down each meal just to be alive and well enough to queue for the next, we entered one of captivity's most deceptively easy, but dangerous phases, a time when, more than ever, one's inner strength would be decisive. To lift one's eyes and look straight forward into the vista of the years ahead required more resolution and a steadier nerve than to set the gaze no further than on the next pitiful meal. Minds, however dulled, had to fix on something, and their testing time came as day by day they needed to focus less and less on the overriding needs of the bodies in which they functioned. That was when, having so far survived largely by instinct, men began fully to appreciate the true implications of their predicament, and to ask, 'survived for what?'

If our working camp suffered from any particular misfortune, it was that the testing time found us at a small, new camp devoid of recreational facilities and outdoor space. It was also one of the most remote and isolated of those administered from Stalag XVIIIA. None of us even knew where we were, other than that we had arrived from Wolfsberg via a place called Rottenmann, and that a guard had hinted that the nearest town was Stainach. On the permanently shaded side of an Alpine valley, we were assured that we were about to face a winter of a severity none of us had experienced or imagined. The winter was also to be the most depressing of the war, for different reasons, punctuated as it regularly was by news, delightedly fed us by our captors, of disaster on disaster for the allied cause.

That winter taught us how resilient the man in the next bunk could be when it came to the crunch. Most men gave a long, hard look or two down the dizzying vista of the endless years ahead, dropped their gaze before heads began to spin, and got down to the job of seeing each other cheerfully through each day as it came. The place and manner of confinement had succeeded in welding us into a compact bunch, of which the Lancashire contingent formed a solid nucleus. The largest natural grouping, many were from the same units and had unit friends among the rest of our number. This fact providentially combined with their cheerful, extrovert characters to prevent them from withdrawing, as they might so easily have done, into a tight, self-sufficient circle, and to ensure that tentacles reached out to embrace almost everyone.

As the cold weather was closing in, the Lancashire men lost one of their number to Stalag, not so much victim of an accident as of inadequacy of treatment for a trivial graze suffered by a man in poor condition. The incident was just another of the many bumps and cuts incurred in the course of humping boulders and wielding strange tools on jobs to which we were not accustomed. What began as a knock on the shin, and nothing to worry about, refused to heal, grew larger and more painful until the victim was unable to hobble, and turned into a gaping, festering hole threatening to endanger the whole leg. We had no medical supplies or medical orderly: the guards' resources, scanty as they were, exceeded their knowledge in applying them. Not a day too soon the patient started back to Wolfsberg, accompanied, if my memory is correct, by the razor-stropping colour-sergeant, who wisely opted to exercise his 'right' not to work. The latter was, probably, the oldest among us, and, having given the Arbeit a trial, he decided it was a young man's occupation and that he would be better off slowing down to the more idle pace of Stalag. His sergeant-major, Hodson, elected to stay on and continue to plague us with his periodic, unmusical bellowings of:

We're the Royal Horse Artillery, the Right of the Line,
    The first to go in and the last to come out.

The theatre of work had shifted from the track on our side of the river to a point on the other bank some hundreds of yards upstream from the camp. There the real work, planned and more ambitious, for which we had been assembled, waited to be tackled. A new stretch of road had once been started and then abandoned. It was no more than two hundred yards long, petering out into virgin slopes at both ends. The project, whose purpose baffled us, was renewed with a superfluity of forced labour. That side of the valley, overhung in places by huge out-crops of rock, ran steeply down to the water's edge, making every yard of progress slow, laborious and costly. If the inten-tion was to carve a new road, it seemed an enormously am-bitious and pointless undertaking to embark upon for the sake of the two or three pedestrians and hill farmers making use of the old road on a busier than usual day. There had been many days on which no one had passed.

Whatever the task, it was much easier to perform the work than to resolve the conflict it stirred in mind and soul. Ponder the situation as long and often as one would, no conclusion ever emerged to satisfy. At every order, however reasonably given, hackles instinctively rose. It was pleasant to get out from behind the stockade, it was challenging to split a rock or fell a tree. It was exhilarating to strain muscles. Often one got lost in the work, caught in the rhythm of the task, then the horrible truth would rush back, the pace would slow and finally stop. One would be left with the emptiness of sheer futility, savagely determined not to do another needless stroke. To get carried away happily by the most fleeting of jobs guaranteed subsequently remorse and deep-felt resentment, feelings difficult to ignore or dismiss.

It was at work, however, that I got to know a large number of my fellow-captives really well. Work introduced me to men seldom properly encountered indoors where the natural groupings were dictated by past association, nationality, or proximity of bunks. There was Frank Wheatley, a New Zealand newspaper man, with whom I discussed the last All-Blacks as, side by side, we padded along making chippings out of small stones. The Maori, Piwi Pirini, was a favourite with everyone, including the Germans to whom he was both a curiosity and a source of pride. When I was paired with him time rarely dragged. The constant binding of Freddie Baines, the Hull stevedore, who had a girl-friend called Ivy, a poor opinion of Fleetwood trawlers as compared with those of his home port, and a preference for Kingston Rovers' prowess in Rugby League as against that of Hull, concealed a perceptive humour and an ability to sum up any situation in a few dry, complaining words. Gunner Jackie Hart was capable of switching off his play-acting approach and pursuing any more serious topic. Eddie Hopkins, from St. Helens, the man so concerned about his wife and child, turned out to be one of the better talkers with whom I found much in common. Jock Stewart, the purple-faced Scottish sergeant, was always good at raising a laugh, and never more so than when excited and virtually impossible to understand: the shout of 'Dolmetscher'* was a sure sign that Jock was getting worked up and incomprehensible. Without exception the Lancashire men helped the days along, Harold Floyd, George 'Wigan', Barnes, Barlow, and the rest.

Small as the party was, there were some men one only occasionally worked with, but all made their contribution to the formative period of forced labour captivity: Tom Hughes and Bradbury, Mark Jenner and Moffat, Sergeant Hedges and John Cobb, Jock Fraser and Johnson, and, of course, Edgar

* 'Interpreter'.

76

Parry, our interpreter. Those early months were impressionable ones.

But, for me, the most entertaining fellow-labourer was Stephen Brinson,* from Clitheroe. If anyone was racking his brains to recall who played what role in *Abdul the Damned, The Count of Monte Cristo* or *The Three Bad Men*, Brinson was his man. He could reel off dates of premières and of when and where he had seen the films, and pinpoint any actor in any part, however minor. Apparently he hadn't missed any films, and remembered all he had seen. One couldn't start to whistle or hum without him naming show, singer and composer by about the fourth bar, a practice which I, an habitual whistler and complete ignoramus on matters of stage and screen, found more than a little frustrating, sometimes downright annoying. Yet it was for me that he reserved his most astounding performance.

We were lopping the branches off a couple of felled trees. After a slow start, for which I felt grateful, admiration of celluloid heroes and heroines not being a subject for which I could muster much enthusiasm, talk got round to the relative merits of my countrymen, Jack Petersen and Tommy Farr, as heavyweight 'white hopes'. Brinson floored me with a recital of the detailed record of both boxers, with whom they had fought and where, in what rounds the contests had ended and by what verdicts, and even who had been the referees to hold up the winners' hands. From there, to make certain I stayed down, the Lancashire lad subjected me to a barrage of miscellaneous information about the history of boxing in South Wales so wide in variety and so exhaustive in detail that few Welshmen could have stayed in the same ring with him. Facts about the Moody brothers of Pontypridd, historic bouts at the Greyfriars Hall, Cardiff, before it was burned down on a date which just slipped off his tongue, together with names I had assumed never to have been heard outside the Valleys, rained down on my bewildered head.

That brilliant performance was never surpassed, but, on subsequent days, the theme was enlarged upon, even after the sorry occasion when, Brinson having proceeded to practical demonstration of more dramatic knock-outs, I cleverly crossed a left over his guard, and instantly qualified as his least favourite sparring partner. There ensued an icy interlude of

* Fictitious name.

77

days, during which I was just another 'bloody Welsh mountain-goat', before my restoration to grace and to the favour of sharing his nostalgic thoughts of the cosy snug of the Wheat-sheaf, Clitheroe, the haunt to which he invariably returned at the end of each recital.

None of the three Australians in the camp looked the typical, suntanned type of which there had been so many splendid examples in Egypt and Crete. Norman Hodgetts, still very much the convalescent from his throat-wound, was slender and pale. After the departure of the colour-sergeant of the North-umberland Hussars, the other two Australians acquired the distinction of being the oldest and youngest inmates. The older of the two, Seaman Aussie, again of no great stature, was in-deed suntanned, with a leathery skin to match the legend that, although in the Australian army, he had spent most of his years sailing before the mast. Whatever his previous background, he appeared admirably suited for his voluntary role of con-descending, philosophical, indulgent guardian and mentor to the third Aussie, Young Lionel, who, judged by physique alone, looked even less representative of the Australian Division than his two compatriots. But what Young Lionel lacked in inches and tan he more than made up for in ingenuous swagger and bluster. He was, perhaps, alone among us in regarding the whole business of being a P.O.W. as part of a great, continuing adventure, an epic exploit in which he was playing a man's part among men.

When Lionel and I were paired up for work, the only con-versation capable of being pursued for any length of time arose from his persistent and confident assertions that he could, and would, escape, that he only had to apply his mind to the exercise and choose the moment, and the stupid Jerry Huns couldn't hold him in. With the blithe enthusiasm and arrogance of his immature years he swept aside all claim to merit in any German or in anything German. 'The only good German is a dead German' was a motto he repeated with every show of conviction. To him, in spite of everything which had happened and was still happening about him, the world was the same old British oyster, and he was just the boy to open it.

As long as his contempt was confined to German brains, abilities and products he could be argued with and humoured, but when, as invariably happened, he reverted to his theme of

78

escape and extended his disparagement to embrace the puny barriers of the few miles of Austrian Alps encasing us, I felt compelled to play the Devil's Advocate and, even to the point of deliberate exaggeration, to illustrate as starkly as I knew how the formidable nature of the project to which he seemed irrevocably committed. Switzerland, the only conceivable goal, was at least a hundred miles away, and most probably considerably further. Going on foot and skirting all civilisation would involve a walk of three or four times that length, and would take weeks even if not a foot were put wrong; the only safe time to travel would be at night, and that would make progress slow and dangerous; the Alps we could see were only the piddling foothills, and he had never seen the real thing; above all none of us was in any state as yet to face the task, and had no means of feeding ourselves throughout the prolonged period of exposure.

My arguments carried little weight with Lionel. He would get to the valley and 'ride the Rattler', the familiar Aussie expression for hitching an illicit lift on a goods train. The phrase was flung out as nonchalantly as if Lionel had crossed and recrossed the bush as an unpaying passenger all his life. Considering the likelihood that he could hardly have been accepted for military service without stretching his age a bit, his experience in Rattler-riding might very well have been nil. Few things concentrate the mind and assist the marshalling of arguments so much as having to find the clincher to defeat an opponent who, frustratingly, refuses to concede merit to anything which might run counter to his open-and-shut-case. I owe it to Young Lionel that, maddeningly, he parried everything thrust at him, with the result that he caused me to kick around all the pros and cons of escaping, to conjure up every argument I could and to re-run in my mind all the many discussions I had been involved in, or had listened to, in Stalag and in Salonika.

What kept us prisoners was not the stockade, nor the guards, but the sheer physical barriers of distance and mountains in a land where everyone was an enemy and the escapee an outlaw. Switzerland had been in exactly the same place, and neutral, during the First World War, and other nations on the continent had been either neutral or friendly, as well as unoccupied. More than one man in the camp had known ex-prisoners who had worked, unguarded, on farms, yet no one could cite a single case of successful escape. Escape had to be far from impossible, but

79

it would only come after careful planning, and even then only to the man for whom the ball consistently bounced right. It would be bound up with luck, but luck would only run with the careful who fostered it, never with the careless just 'having a go'.

For prisoners who had already found themselves reluctantly transported into the heart of an enemy-occupied Europe there was little sense in engaging in precipitate escape plans. Even for prisoners like us, taken on battlefields separated from friendly frontiers by hundreds of miles of sea, the best chances had been lost by not attempting the break when still strong and fresh, immediately after capture. The double shock of defeat and capture had numbed perception of the possibilities still existing in areas where the enemy effort, concentrated on victory and conquest, was ill-organised for holding men eliminated from the contest. The loss of a few prisoners in forward fighting-zones would have caused no great stir; one single man adrift for only hours in the heart of the Reich would unbalance the books and set in motion all sorts of relentless machinery. Once firmly incarcerated in a Stalag, after the debilitating experiences of transit camps, with the certainty of years of imprisonment ahead, one needed time to assess the increased difficulties with a view to applying the results of such assessment to future developments in an ever-changing war situation. To rush into escape attempts with no true appreciation of the conditions prevailing in the countryside seemed ill-advised; to do so with no knowledge of the consequences of the almost inevitable re-capture might, even in cases where demoralisation was not the result, mean lengthy imprisonment under more rigid discipline which would rule out all chances of success should the overall possibilities improve.

Of all the points put to Lionel in an effort, not to dampen his youthful ardour, but to persuade him to over-estimate rather than dismiss the opposition, the only ones which were in any way fruitful were the advisability of chewing over his project during the winter and having a go in the spring, and of the need to take a companion with him. A simple broken leg in the mountains might be fatal.

The snows were with us early, and, once arrived, clung tenaciously in the hollows until reinforcements arrived in such strength that for two whole days we were pinned to the camp

80

as swirling flakes blotted out the hills. Work was resumed in a fairyland of dazzling white and blue, broken only by the dark scar of the river, its waters suddenly sinister. It was only mid-November.

The postman, the policeman, who paid regular visits, as well as the few civilian passers-by, took to skis, as did also the training plane which on most days wheeled overhead disturbing the birds. The interminable hours of drudgery dragged worse than before, making the return to the stuffy warmth of the Lager ever more welcome as the days shortened and grew steadily colder. 'Bludging',* leaning on shovels, sitting on barrows, and generally dodging work, a skill at which most men daily became more proficient, paid less comfortable dividends. The frequent leisurely strolls to and from the 'bus-stop', the three-sided latrine erected at the lower end of the site, lost their attraction as exposed bottoms got numbed by biting frost and fingers grew feelinglessly clumsier with belts and buttons.

What the winter would have been like but for the incredible performance of the Red Cross, whose supplies not only clothed us in a style to make us the envy of guards and civilians alike but also virtually fed us, it is really impossible to imagine. Some such comfort was an essential for anyone viewing a warring world from the isolation of captivity in our valley. Daylight was spent in snow and frost working for the enemy, a humiliation which deepened as the thermometer fell; darkness found us locked away in an ill-lit hut with nothing to do. What little news penetrated through from outside, doctored by the biased lips of the guards and tinctured by their patent desire to impress on us the hopelessness of our position, told of nothing but enemy successes and British reverses. From the Russian front, news which for months had revolved around astronomical figures of miles advanced by the Germans switched to diminishing, negligible figures of distances still to be covered before bringing about the falls of Moscow and Leningrad.

Most demoralising of all for us, since almost to a man we had been withdrawn from the desert forces, was the stunning revelation that even in that desert, our own stamping ground, the Germans, who had had no appreciable forces there in 1940, were strutting over large tracts we ourselves had captured in our own single, dramatic advance against their Italian allies

---

* Australian expression: a 'bludger' was a scrounger, a dodger, a 'wide-boy'.

only a year before. We could take in neither how the Germans had been allowed a build-up of such strength, nor how such novices in desert warfare could have thrown back forces which had been there for generations, and that at a time when Britain was committed to no active front elsewhere, while the enemy was also locked in a campaign to crush the might of Russia.

The guards lost no time in imparting the one piece of news we had longed, although not expected, to hear – that America was in the war – but they conveyed it with such evident self-satisfaction that it was obvious they didn't consider it the disaster for their cause we imagined it had to be. The reason for their jubilation became shatteringly clear as, day after day, almost, they fed us with details of what was happening at the other end of the world: how Japan had struck at Pearl Harbor; how the American fleet had been crippled; and how the Japanese, having swallowed Hong Kong in a gulp, were pouring down through a doomed Malaysia. Many of the men, especially those regulars who had served in the Far East, felt outraged and would not believe what they were hearing, but for most of us it was all part of an all-too-familiar pattern: with actual, sensational victories such as the enemy had consistently enjoyed, what need had they to invent fictitious ones either for themselves or for their new, aggressive allies? We would do better by looking for satisfaction and healing for our wounded pride, not by discrediting enemy claims but by assessing the value of silences with regard to other areas.

As the Grinner delightedly mimed the Axis successes by walking forwards, raised palms pushing in front of him, and the Allied defeats by pacing backwards, the only solace was to be found in wondering why he never mentioned Moscow or Leningrad, both of which he and his fellows had assured us more than a month earlier were as good as under the jackboot. But at best it was meagre consolation for knowing that what the Germans had done wherever they had turned in Europe, their distant allies were doing even more rapidly over greater areas in Asia.

The spread of the war to the Pacific had the effect of closing what little gap there might have been between the outlooks of the Anzacs and the British. The men from 'down under' had crossed the world to demonstrate their identity with the British cause. It was always a matter for astonishment that they made so little of the ignorant comments of the more stupid British who asserted that Australia, Dominion status or not, was still a colony and that the Diggers had had no option but to jump at Britain's command. Overnight the Anzacs saw their homeland threatened and, for the first time, could view the conflict from the same angle as the boys from the U.K.

The receipt of mail, at first just a trickle, was the first event of fundamental importance not to be equally shared by all. Even memory of later batches when I received nothing far from qualified me to judge the feelings of men who, eyes glued on the diminishing first bundle, listened with ever-sinking spirits for their names to be called out. Some of them, anxiously concerned for their families in the big cities which were regular targets for the Luftwaffe, found the sight of us, wallowing in page after page, a fresh cause for worry, quip as they might:

'If you've finished with the first page, pass it down.'

'If my missus could write, I'd have had one twice as long as your lot put together.'

As Christmas approached, Johnson, a Kentish boy, fell sick of a disease which was obviously not just a cold and which appeared, in fact, to be more than influenza. With a raging fever, he was moved into the little room which had, providentially, been built when the far end of the main room had been partitioned off. There he was to remain for weeks, his condition giving cause for grave concern; a concern, it must be added, which the Germans – to their lasting credit – shared. The village doctor made several journeys to the Lager until Johnson was out of danger.

Our patient was still virtually in isolation when Christmas came. It fell towards the end of the week and so gave a long, welcome break from the penetrating cold outside. The Red Cross assisted us to make it seem like a festive occasion by providing a special, seasonal issue of a food parcel, with tinned plum pudding and tinned stuffed turkey replacing the usual items. The male cook had been superseded by a buxom, middle-aged Hausfrau who did her best to make our Christmas dinner look presentable and appetising with a small slice of meat which might have come from a real animal, and a liberal sprinkling of caraway seeds. Herr Lemmerer, our contractor and landlord, stayed unseen but donated a small bottle of lager per man to help the meal down.

The highlight of the festivities, on Christmas night, was

without question the sound of Taffy Dennis's superb voice ringing through the room to hold us enthralled and draw the guards tip-toeing in to stand silently inside the door. Hard as it was on George Wigan and Piwi Pirini, no mean performers either of them, to follow Taffy's renditions, it was harder still on me. Their styles and voices had at least been different, and contrasting, Wigan's bringing memories of Arthur Tracy, 'The Street Singer', and Pirini's conjuring up visions of warm South Sea islands; whereas mine, a far from good, untrained baritone, must have sounded like the perfect demonstration that not all Welshmen can sing. I must have underrated myself, for not only did I get the applause due from politeness and jolly party spirits, but, weeks afterwards, I was gratified to stumble on a group seriously trying to find the reason why all Welshmen were good singers.

All too soon the return to work thrust us back to face up to reality with a vengeance. The cold persisted so intensely that it was only the sight of the guards stamping around, desperately trying to maintain their circulation during their long, idle hours on sentry-go, which brought any glow of warmth outside the hut. We packed on all the clothing we could, hammered and drilled, trundled and heaved, to keep ourselves tolerably warm and, when feet and hands got too cold to feel, we, too, stamped around cuffing our arms, or took ourselves off to the blacksmith's cramped shanty on the other side of the water. There one could wait while the old, muttering blacksmith put a fresh point on zapin* or pick, conveniently blunted on the iron-hard earth. As he stoked up his trestle furnace, incomprehensibly grumbling all the while, one had a chance to admire his expertise at planting, unerringly, juicy gob after juicy gob of brown tobacco spit on the tall pyramid of clinkers under the fire tray. The pile of ashes was almost as fascinating as his repulsive habit. It rose in such a slender spire and with its peak so near the bottom of the hot fire-tray that one expected it to fall over or spread its base, as ashes should. It never did, for the very good reason that it was held solidly frozen together, caked into a hard, grey-brown mass by the frost and the rich spit sprayed on it. A flying hack at its base would have produced broken toes.

The shrivelled-up blacksmith had surprised us when he first

* A tool with a curved, steel claw on an axe-handle.

appeared amongst us back in the autumn, incongruously dressed in lederhosen and stockings, a garb the livelier, younger Little Man had never adopted. He startled us even more by reverting to that same dress at the height of the winter's frosts, with off-white, long pants bulging out around his knees in the gap between stockings and shorts. We readily understood that the bulges allowed freedom for knees to bend when climbing the steep ground, but it was some time before we absorbed the lesson that a loose undergarment, such as a pair of pyjama trousers, underneath ordinary wear formed a better insulation barrier than tight-fitting long drawers.

Throughout the whole of the first week of the new year, and for days afterwards, the temperature never rose above twenty degrees of frost Centigrade. Hopefully, we recalled the statements that work would stop of its own volition when the thermometer registered fifteen degrees. We gave hints to the Little Man, as well as to the suffering guards, who should have been our allies in that cause, but still the almost impossible work continued as if it were high summer. Long before midmornings the frost gave us the appearance of white-haired men with strangely unlined faces. Warm, moist breath froze on lapels and upturned collars, and rebounded upwards to freeze over eyebrows, eyelids and moustaches, turning them all to a uniform, furry white.

A resentful feeling that the civilians had let us down badly with their assurances about a lull in work, led us to give even less credence to their ridiculous talk of the river freezing over. To our inexperienced eyes, the water, though admittedly less in volume, seemed to flow as merrily and menacingly as ever. The local experts were to be proved right, and we to have had eyes that saw not. Eventually, our inquisitiveness on seeing the Little Man stand daily on the bridge at its lowest point of sag and, using a surveyor's pole, measure and mark the clearance above the surface of the water, arrived at the pitch of asking him why he was addicted to this routine; but by this time the river was well on its way to becoming frozen – not, as we imagined it would, from the top downwards, but from the bottom upwards. The level had been rising for some time, the water threatening to overflow the centre of the bridge, due to rocks literally growing with ice under the spray and then joining together or becoming linked by trapped, quickly-icing branches and twigs. Belatedly aware of the process, we watched it develop rapidly. Rocks and arrested flotsam grew to form solid barriers behind which the water slowed down to placid pools, until surface ice, spreading relentlessly out from banks and barriers, stopped all visible flow, transforming the stream into a staircase of long, wide, shallow steps. The next fall of snow added a thick carpet to match the surrounds, across which the deer left their hoofmarks after their nightly foragings.

The deer, elusive creatures which none of us had ever so much as glimpsed, gave at least a dozen prisoners a welcome opportunity to escape from the claustrophobic confinement of the hut to participate in a strenuous excursion to the top of the opposite mountains. Baldy had been replaced by a new Kommandant, a tall, gangling Feldwebel who, from the very start, applied himself to his task with less regimentation and more common sense, without relaxing the more justifiable precautions of his predecessor. When, one day, this approachable Kommandant asked if we would provide volunteers to get needed fodder up to the deer-grounds, some of us jumped at the chance to test our legs and break away from the restraint of another long, idle Sunday.

After lunch on the chosen day our party trudged - more cheerfully than usual up the valley until, after less than a mile, we found, to our great surprise, an inviting-looking Gasthaus alongside the road. Skis were propped against the wall of the narrow veranda along which we were escorted into the Gaststube, where their owners, four or five young men who must have slid down from the hill farms, sat enjoying their wine around the Kachelofen projecting into one corner. We were directed to wall-benches opposite. The landlady brought us each a glass of red wine to sip while we soaked in the scene and the cosy warmth.

Wine finished, older civilians, guards and prisoners filed out to collect their light but bulky loads, large sacks of fodder, one for each man. After only a further few yards up the valley, the road swung left to cross the river, thus partly explaining why the new road was being built on the side it was. Then began a long diagonal climb up the mountain, through deep snow broken and disturbed only by the feet of the men in front. The Game Warden led the way with measured, even strides. Everyone else followed in his footsteps.

The hidden path continued under the trees for the most part, but when we came to a wide, clear face we were halted

86

and, softly, word was passed back: 'No talking. Beware avalanches!' Sound vibrations could easily start the snow off on a long slide, and we had already cleared enough small avalanches – working parties had often been detached to unblock the road to the village after it had been cut by slides of snow – to realise that the steep, exposed slope on which we were poised could be dangerous, and that an avalanche triggered off there would be anything but small. For most of us, all too glad of a respite after the unaccustomed exertion, the warning was superfluous. Other than to indulge in the odd moan about aching thighs, there was little chance of us chattering. Long before we had recovered, the party was off again. Where the ground evened out after breasting a false crest we reached the racks a little way short of the main ridge.

The journey down was more carefree and took only a fraction of the time spent plodding up the slopes. This time the stop at the Gasthaus lasted barely long enough for us to dispose of the empty sacks and, disappointingly, did not include the offer of a further glass of wine. Back in the Lager, to the disturbance of drowsy mates, most of us felt a tired exhilaration and a definite small satisfaction that, for the first time in months, we had done something we didn't openly and instinctively resent. Weeks later, no doubt as reward for our labours, a midday meal included a small slice of venison, the first most of us had ever tasted.

The daily cycle grew more and more oppressive and, ungratefully perhaps in view of all that had been done for us, a feeling of having been abandoned beyond some lost horizon weighed on all spirits. Lazing on bunks in the evenings and during the weekends – we had reasserted our rights to that indulgence the instant Baldy departed for Lagers new – there was ample opportunity to take stock of what was happening to us. Men were putting on weight, particularly those who, like George Dutton, had been reduced to skin and bone by dysentery or some other ailment contracted in Greece; but it was an unhealthy, pot-bellied recovery, distorting bodies by an excess of irresistible potatoes, cabbage-soup and polenta, plus prolonged swillings of nightly tea or coffee. Have a body like mine on a litre-and-a-half of weak tea! Calmly studied, some men appeared pale, grotesque, misshapen caricatures of the selves they had been on arrival in the camp, an impression which was never more stark than when enhanced by the play of light and shadow from the overhead oil-lamps. Never having had much flesh to start with I had kept my shape, but even I had seen thousands of spots dancing before my eyes and had felt the room spin around me, especially when I stood up quickly. It was reasonable to assume that the impact on more bloated figures was worse.

I had deliberately taken to eating only a portion of my mid-day potatoes or soup. Instead of continuing the meal I had got into the habit of lighting a cigarette to dull the appetite and so avoid the awful, heavy nausea which used to overwhelm me before parading for return to work. A non-smoker until well into my twenty-fourth year, I became a smoker for life just by taking a puff or two to prevent myself overeating the swill distorting so many of my fellows.

In previous camps one had been able to make a sortie into the compound to pace up and down, either alone, with one's thoughts fleeting beyond the confines of the wires, or with a congenial companion of one's own choice to focus mind and talk on topics more fruitful than the superficial, forced banter and back-chat of the barrackroom. Ideal as the inmates were for making life bearable, it was inevitable that, as the winter tightened its grip, banter became irritating to nerves already chafed raw by repetitive sounds and predictable mannerisms, and that the babel of dialects lost much of its novelty. Norman Hodgetts summed up the frequently prevailing mood perfectly one night as, a particularly trying day behind us, he crawled on his bunk beside me and bawled as loudly and feelingly as his punctured throat would permit:

'For Christ's sake, Churchill! Hurry up and win this bloody war!'

The phraseology was as right as the vehemence. We felt we had had about enough. But the significant word was win. Only victory could make the utter waste of our lives worthwhile. But everybody seemed to be taking an eternity about it.

There were periods when a sense of absolute freedom, some-thing which surely could never have been experienced anywhere except in captivity, would sweep over me. The feeling, some-times lasting for days with diminishing intensity, was always a tonic. Its origins seemed to spring from a stark realisation that one had no property, no responsibilities, no family ties or obligations which could effectively be exercised, and it ended with a conclusion that the worst the Germans could do would be to harm one's body or destroy it. In that startlingly straight contest between one man and all others, the prisoner was the one who had never the need to glance over his shoulder to check the effects of his actions or to modify his simple, direct course in concession to any outside influence. While the feeling lasted I felt uplifted and strangely contemptuous of the guards with their constant preoccupations with insignificant discipline and their worries about home leave or foreign postings. It may have been that the whole thing was the first stages of becoming 'barbed-wire happy'. Whether it was or not, I was never tempted to act out the conclusion of the logic, and climb the stockade fence. Superior as I felt, I still kept the realities in view, but I began to understand how easily and willingly one could throw one's life away.

Singapore, the impregnable fortress, fell, and the *Prince of Wales* and the *Repulse* disappeared under Pacific waves, evidence of continuing disaster which was bitterly repudiated by several of the men who had been nurtured on the glories of an empire on which the sun never set. Names like Borneo, Sumatra, and Australia itself, rolled off the lips of guards, to lengthen the list of humiliations we were supposed to just shrug off. We clutched at the straw of Derna. That small Libyan town, insignificant in the overall strategy of the war, suddenly for a time assumed an importance beyond reason. The Germans had claimed it was about to fall, in their excitement overlooking the fact that months earlier they had claimed to be holding it. There was some news they didn't impart! How else could they explain besieging a town they'd not lost?

As an aid to getting through the long evenings, Seaman Aussie set me on the road to emulating one of his many skills. In the line of smoking he scorned two things, 'tailor-made' or factory produced cigarettes, and machine-rolled substitutes. In his bible the only true smoke was the one firmly rolled by hand. Everyone meticulously cleaned and sorted his butt-end tobacco, but Seaman Aussie went further: he broke every one of his 'tailor-made' issue, stored the tobacco shreds in an airtight tin with a moist slice of potato peel, and rolled each smoke as desired. What emerged from a few expert twirls of his practised fingers was a masterpiece of precision, eminently smokable, quite unlike the pathetic results produced by the slow, tobacco-spilling efforts of the majority, some of which took on the shape of trumpets which needed to be screwed up at the end to prevent loss of most of the weed. I became an expert at the art but never achieved the proficiency of performing one-handed.

For weeks no supplies got through, and the food became more unappetising than usual. More serious was the prospect of exhausting the precious stock of food parcels. The ration had already been reduced to half a parcel per week. When a fresh consignment got bogged down in the village, it was decided that we ourselves should haul them the last few miles. Accordingly, the next Sunday morning, half of us slithered and slid our way down to the village, mocked by the sunshine bounding back from the snows of the opposite slopes. It was no surprise to find ourselves ushered into the Gaststube of Herr Lemmerer's Gasthaus. As we took our places around the sides of the room, heated by a Kachelofen of large dimension and gleaming design, those of us who had taken part in the deer-feeding expedition sat back prepared to judge our landlord by whether once again the wine was produced. We were not disappointed, and marked Herr Lemmerer up a notch or two.

Everyone (we were loaded down with five parcels each, four draped like life-jackets from shoulders and the fifth shifted from one frozen hand to the other) was glad to see the Lager come in view. The journey back had been exhausting and treacherous. It was a job well done, allowing a couple of weeks' grace for the road to become passable for the tractor. The weather softened in time to avoid the need for a second trip, and when fresh stocks arrived they were accompanied by a number of personal clothing parcels.

Several men had already received a clothing parcel from their families early in the new year. The sight of the luxurious extras paraded by the lucky ones had served to increase impatience with the never-ending blockade of snow and ice. All articles discovered in the brown-paper parcels, each one opened and checked by the Germans in front of the prisoner, were necessary rather than merely useful, but to the recipients they were luxuries indeed: thick, soft bath towels to make a wash-all-over in goose-pimpling water inviting where before it had been a torture of drying oneself 'wetter and colder than before'; handkerchiefs for noses which had run free and unhampered for freezing months; toothpaste which left a pleasant, tingling taste in the mouth; socks to change; pyjamas and slippers to do away with sleeping in work-soiled underwear and to end lazing around in the evenings in ammo boots; and real soap which smelled nice and gave a plentiful lather.

One of the effects of being cut off from the world and of the receipt of clothing parcels was that Lagergeld, which had always been difficult to dispose of to any advantage, began to accumulate to an embarrassing degree. The Kommandant might have had this in mind when he produced his camera and proceeded to take snapshots of his charges, in groups at the worksite or posed in front of the hut, in each case against a background of snow. The photos were for sale to the prisoners as well as for his own album, and there was no limit to the number of copies he was prepared to produce in return for our money. Although the films were made of 'paper' there was nothing wrong with the copies we eagerly bought.

One of the surer signs that winter was on the way out was the passing of the frost wall, a yielding cover of hoar which had blanked out the long, vertical earth bank facing across the river. Another indication came when the Little Man began to detail detachments to march down to the village for work. Their unusual assignment was to saw and stack ice-blocks for re-frigerator sheds. It was on a day when the ice-sawing party was away tackling the job which made the rest of us curious, that Nature, to dispel all doubts about the turn of the seasons, put on a dramatic display.

I was one of a trio detailed to drill a projection of rock perched high above the river on a bend at the uppermost extremity of the site. On the elevated rock we were enjoying the first rays of sunshine to come our way for months. Only a part of the general site could be seen, but upstream we commanded a fine view of the gorge. Brinson was with me; who the third member was I have long since forgotten. Predictably, Brinson had allowed a long drill to 'stick' by careless sinking and turn-ing, and it was while we were debating whether to call up the Little Man to free it or to try loosening it ourselves that we first became aware of the noise, a subdued, distant roar. Briefly, we divided in opinion as to whether it was the tractor or the training plane, and would have forgotten about it had it not continued to get louder and louder until the roar seemed to embrace us and to throb from every side. Then we saw it. Around the bend of the river came a wide, black wall of rushing water, tumbling and turning, spewing filthy foam, balancing tree-trunks and roots, ice-blocks and even boulders, and crashing through and over every puny obstacle in its head-long progress. Safely balanced on our rock, we just stared. Then reason took over. We yelled, as loudly as we could. Most men were working, out of our sight and out of sight of the danger, on the very edge of the river; some, those trimming the retaining bank, were actually standing in it.

Deafeningly, the wave swept beneath us. We watched it batter its way downstream, past a scattering of prisoners scrambling up the bank. As the noise subsided in the distance we clambered down to the site. Everyone had got clear in time. They stood watching the water level rapidly falling. The only victims had been one unretrieved jacket, the frozen barriers sunk without trace, and our bridge, which, trestle-legs kicking in the air and displaced and tangled, still hung together with some possibility of being salvaged.

Spirits had lifted with the thought that the worst was behind us, successfully endured, when the news began to circulate that we were about to be moved. Rumour had it that Russians would take over. It was hard to conjecture whether the portended move would be a good thing or a bad one, an improvement as most men hoped, or a deterioration as a large number feared. On balance, I believe, most, at that time, would have opted to stay and endure the known captivity rather than face the threatened disruption and the uncertainties of continued captivity elsewhere. We believed, with much justice, that we had 'tamed' the guards and civilians at our camp, and also brought the work down to our own pace. As the Australians put it, it would be 'crook' to have to start afresh at a camp which might prove to be no better, and might conceivably be worse than the one we had got to know the hard way.

In spite of all reservations, on the balmy April day when the column headed back down the valley, through Herr Lemmerer's hamlet and across the flat plain to the railway station, we had every reason for stepping out more briskly than on that morning eight months earlier when we had trudged the same path in the opposite direction. Gone were clumsy clogs, worn-out boots, flapping footrags and ill-fitting, vari-coloured, multi-national uniforms. Instead, Aussie and Kiwi, Turk and Indian, Jock and Taff, all displayed uniform khaki battledress with sturdy boots to clatter in unison over the stones. Nothing could have better illustrated the part the Red Cross had played in our lives than the contrast between our entering the valley and our leaving it. But brave as was the display, hidden in the column was already more than one hint of impending personal tragedy. The neat figure of Hopkins strode along unhampered by kitbag with pyjamas and towel, socks and handkerchiefs. In spite of his devotion to his wife, the few letters he'd received would hardly have caused his pocket to bulge.

We travelled by ordinary stopping train, in a reserved coach at the rear, heavily guarded but accessible by corridor from the rest of the train. At one larger station we had to change. Escorted for security into the general waiting-room, my small group stood within yards of a large, coloured wall-map of Oesterreich, Steiermark and Kärnten provinces. By straining our eyes, without attracting attention, it was possible to ascertain our whereabouts in relation to Linz, Graz and Steier, main towns appropriately printed large, and to get the general lie of the rivers and ranges. The existence of the maps was an important point to bear in mind.

The second part of the journey followed the windings of a wide river which was still with us when, at a small station with scarcely a sign of a village, we were ordered out. We turned our backs on the river and followed a road alongside a small stream which soon brought us to a large straggling village dominated by a mill and stacks of untrimmed timber. The village was to be our home, the mill our work-place.

Chapter 4

THE PAPER MILL

Weissenbach a.d. Enns already had a British P.O.W. camp.
Its inmates had been absorbed into the village work-force, and
that work-force lived on and for the paper mill. The mill
straddled the village between road and stream, while, since its
hungry jaws required vast acres of timber to satisfy its appetite,
timber-stacks occupied more ground than the mill itself. The
huge stacks, spread like the factory between road and stream,
kept the prison-camp, sited on the narrower back road, out of
sight of main village life.

The camp consisted of only one building, scarcely any larger
than the one we had left. It also bordered a road, while its
compound contained an area even narrower than the useless
enclosure of the previous camp. There points of similarity
ended: the new prison was enclosed by barbed-wire on all four
sides, making the hut look what it really was; the compound
was level; windows were positioned so that one could look out;
and the trees and hills did not hem the structure in.

The interior lay-out differed in every detail from the pine
cabin in the hills. The entrance door with its sign 'Eintritt
Strengstens Verboten'* opened straight into a dining-room or
common-room extending the width of the hut, and at the far
end an identically situated door led down several steps into the
compound stretched along the bank of the stream but separated
from it by the barbed-wire. From the right of the common-
room a central corridor passed along the longer end of the
building, with doors opening on either side into small barrackrooms, each with four double bunks. On the left, the common-
room showed three doors. The first was the entrance to the
guards' quarters, which meant that all their comings and goings
had to be an intrusion on common-room activities, and that,
even when out of sight, only a thin wall would divide them from
whatever the prisoners were up to. The second door had two

* Entry strictly forbidden.

different padlocks with two different keys, one held by the Germans, the other by the British, and belonged to a small room used as a parcel store. The third door, against the further wall, took one into a short corridor lined on both sides with zinc troughs serving as wash-basins and equipped with taps for cold water. The outer wall of the corridor contained a window looking out over the stream towards the timber stacks which blotted out almost all view of the village, and, a most welcome sight, a zinc half-funnel, of the very type envisaged but never attained to back in the valley, set into the wall for use as a night urinal. Unappetising as it looked and smelled, its usefulness would be beyond price. The corridor led through another door into the Big Room, a dormitory spanning the width of the hut.

The casement-pattern windows opened outwards for air, but not for short-cuts, since strong, iron bars were set vertically into the frames and strengthened by cross-members. The only stove in the prisoners' quarters squatted in the middle of the common-room, ensuring that most off-work hours would be spent away from the bunks. The great attraction of the stove lay not so much in the amount of heat it threw out to warm the room, but in its versatility, attributable to its large area of hot-plate and to its rear oven, both of which promised that we would be able to brew tea and heat tins whenever we pleased without having to go cap in hand to our hosts. A further, significant improvement in our lot was that lighting was by electricity, in every room. All told, the new quarters promised more comfort and amenities, greater privacy, and greatly reduced feeling both of isolation and of being hemmed in.

Other prisoners (about the same number as our own reinforcing party), some of whom we had passed at the timber stacks, were already in residence. It was mid-afternoon when we arrived and therefore natural to find prisoners at work. Those discovered lounging around in the hut were, however, something of a surprise, but not nearly so much as those fast asleep under their blankets. The explanation took some of the gilt off our pleasure at the visible improvement in our surroundings: the men lounging about had completed a morning shift, while those in bed were sleeping off the effects of a night stint. Most men worked hours comparable with those we had been used to, but a considerable proportion were on a weekly rota of alternating morning, afternoon and night duties.

The prisoners who had spent the winter in Weissenbach, in a

camp which could hold more than twice their numbers, had spread themselves about bunks and rooms and given themselves the maximum amount of space. The intruders found themselves split up and distributed throughout all rooms, somewhat cramping the style to which the original occupants had become accustomed. My bunk was a top one, in the Big Room.

After depositing my kit, I joined some mates for a welcome mashing of tea. While waiting for it to brew I visited the toilet, and made another pleasant discovery. It was a real, running-water job, the first stenchless one I'd seen for a year or more, very effective and not even requiring one to pull a chain. Built on a solid platform projecting through the wires, the latrine boasted the same basic design as the 'bus-stop' at the previous job, with the addition of a front screen to prevent users being the object of scrutiny from barrackroom windows. The platform stood poised over the stream, its back and sides dropping straight down into the water and ending in a tangle of barbed-wire to prevent escape by dropping down the toilet. The wire had caught a jumble of sticks and branches on the outside, while inside, downstream, the high flood mark was clearly defined by a confusion of tin-labels clinging to the wires: Libby's, Fray Bentos, Fry's, Cadbury's, Crosse and Blackwell's, Nestlé's. In through the jumble of sticks and out through the confusion of labels flowed the clear, transparent waters, revealing a shaded trout, but hardly a trace of excreta.

All misgivings about changing our place of residence and confinement seemed to be finally dispelled that same evening. Bunched around the common-room tables in a blaze of unaccustomed light, old and new inmates exchanged news and views over cups of tea brewed at will, while at a couple of tables others were enjoying hands of whist or bridge, or an absorbing game of chess.

Next morning revealed the reverse, the darker side of the change of abode, the work the mill demanded of us. The fact that the mill, a part of the enemy industrial machine, demanded the work, and that its labour-force would have to keep pace with that demand, gave most reason for pause. It had been an uncomfortable feeling back in the valley to contemplate that work meant regular daily toil, but the blow had been gradually softened by the solace that whatever we did would advance the enemy war effort by not so much as an inch. Toiling to produce an essential product, even if it were only paper, was another matter, making one feel one had gone down a notch or two in respectability and patriotism. It would be a long time before any of us would feel we had fitted into a work niche to equal the one we had left, where consciences had been easy. Weeks passed during which I found myself doing all sorts of odd jobs directed by all sorts of odd bosses, all the time feeling I belonged nowhere. The mill was a primitive, ramshackle structure, thrown together over decades of improvisations and extensions, and the odd assortment of bosses fitted in well with the setting.

There was Herr Flemming, with his spindly body, his spindly, flopping arms, his spindly, knock-kneed, pigeon-toed legs and his permanently harassed expression. His eyes protruded in a continual cross-eyed stare going right past one and, when he moved, his head and upper body came forward as if to catch up with them. The deformity of his lower extremities was made more pronounced by his adherence to wearing either tight, black leather gaiters or equally tight-fitting drainpipe trousers. The prisoners, for the most part, felt sorry for him and, while nicknaming him 'Twinkletoes', refrained from hoaxing him too outrageously – even when he asked for it by showing as little control of his temper and emotions as he had of his limbs. There was little of malice in Sergeant Jock Stewart's summary, that 'no two parts of him go in the same direction at the same time, his eyes are like pissholes in the snow, and his head always says "here I am, my arse is to follow" '.

Feelings were not so kindly disposed towards Martin, another past-middle-age order-giver, of small stature and vicious temper; while Reingruber, who was something like second-in-command of the mill and seemed to do nothing but stand around with an empty cigarette-holder in his teeth, never failed to get under everyone's skin, although no one could pinpoint exactly why. Herr Reingruber's only saving grace, in the eyes of prisoners so long starved of female companionship, was that he had two grown-up daughters who gave ample excuse for standing, leaning and staring. In an insipid way they were quite pretty and, since their home was isolated among the timber stacks and also plumb opposite the camp's back door, they couldn't avoid our gaze, home or away.

The mill would have ground to a halt but for the forced labour, of which the British prisoners formed the most substantial part. The Germans and Austrians, mostly elderly, disabled, or both, were simply the bosses. The only able-

7.

bodied, comparatively young natives seemed to be a party of men who turned up every few days for a short while only to disappear again. They went by train to the upper reaches of the Enns, felled trees, made the timber into rafts, and floated themselves home on the results of their labours next day. It was hardly the type of work to be entrusted to P.O.W.s or undertaken by the limp and the lame. So the mill itself depended on British P.O.W.s and deported Slavs from Yugoslavia and the overrun provinces of Russia.

The work-place might have been only a paper-mill but its operation was essential to the enemy, as proclaimed by the banner over the powerhouse entrance: 'Unsere Leistung ist Unsere Ehre'.* We considered that slogan as little applicable to us as the smaller ones gracing the offices: 'Unser Gruss ist Heil Hitler'.† The latter could be ignored, the former was to remain a constant reproach. Out of the mill came wagonloads of paper, not much of which, we suspected, would find its way on to office desks or into copies of *Das Kleine Blatt*, for the paper was thick, off-white cardboard, in huge rolls and sheets, equally suited as raw material for ersatz blankets and uniforms.

There was one day when no one resented going to the mill: on the contrary, men got out of bed when they didn't have to, to ensure not being left behind. It was the one day when the tall chimney spewed no yellow, sulphurous fumes out over the village – Sunday. Sunday morning was bath morning, and the bath was a delightful, hot shower at the silent mill for anyone with energy left to leave his bunk before mid-morning. Everyone simply assembled in staggered parties, with overcoats over gay, striped pyjmas, and with gay, striped towels round necks. The half-dozen showers had to be shared, but the water was both plentiful and hot, and nobody rushed us.

It was spring, men had been cooped up throughout a long winter, the novelty of capture and work had largely worn off, and speculation was rife both about our own futures and about the course the new campaigning season would take. A restlessness began to stir in the camp, an unconscious attempt to challenge the repulsive set pattern into which our lives were being moulded. On the surface it showed when sergeants began to question whether they had the 'right' to opt out of work and to be returned to the idleness of Stalag, when sappers and

* Our production is our honour.
† Our salute is Heil Hitler.

privates started to rack their brains for the best means of 'tossing the quack' and achieving the same ends as the sergeants; except that their malingerings in Wolfsberg, unless their schemes proved exceptionally ingenious, would be shorter-lived. Perseverance and inventiveness gained both sets of aspirants some measure of success. Although most quack-tossers failed and finally gave up for the time being, another valuable lesson was quickly learned.

It was the hirer of the labour who paid for accommodation, food and wages of prisoners. They required a return on the outlay, besides which, with 'Leistung' their 'Ehre', they could ill-afford interruption to output. It was not worth their while to hang on to 'sick' prisoners while there existed a bottomless pool of replacements. When 'Leistung' was at stake, the desire not to be bettered by a 'bludging' Engländer came a bad second to the urge to let the Wehrmacht deal with the headache in its own way.

The ripple of restlessness had hardly died down when a more momentous event shook the tranquillity. On the day concerned, the demeanour of the guards as they roused us at dawn left no doubt as to the nature of the disturbance, and my own reaction was to feel certain of the identity of at least one of the perpetrators. Hustled on parade with barely time to dress, we buzzed the news along the ranks, while the guards, reinforced by the local policeman, combed each room and counted us unbelievingly.

Three men had absconded in the small hours. Not surprisingly, one was Young Lionel. Understandably, another was his guardian, Seaman Aussie; but the third member of the trio I hadn't expected. It was Johnson, the boy who had almost passed away around Christmas. He, least of all of us, would be in any condition for the adventure. By the time the Germans had established the extent of their losses they were still left with the harder problem of discovering which men were light, and even after checking their lists and every identity disc their total knowledge was still only the names and numbers of the truants. What they looked like was another matter. None of the three had been physically conspicuous, if one overlooked the fact that Seaman Aussie was older than most and sported an interesting gallery of tattoos.

The breakout couldn't have taken place under the discipline

imposed by Baldy. The exit had been made through a small window facing the stream. For days the escapees had worked on the vertical bars until a couple had loosened in their sockets and weldings, enabling them to be pushed down to such an extent that a man could squeeze through. The wires had proved no obstacle; they had simply been prised apart. A short paddle through the stream and the men were within yards of the cover of the timber stacks.

The ensuing day saw the arrival of important-looking officers from Stalag, in braided hats and long overcoats almost concealing highly polished riding boots. Long conferences followed in the Kommandant's office, while, on the work sites, zealous guards and civilians left none of us out of their sight as 'Leistung' continued. The highlight of the proceedings came at midday. Crowded into the rear doorway, we looked out over the stream to be treated to the spectacle of an over-optimistic Kommandant attempting to winkle out his lost charges by firing shot after shot into and under the bases of the Winter Stacks. All he accomplished was to bring Frau Reingruber's startled face to an upstairs window and to give one of his men a job for the afternoon cleaning his revolver.

The escapees were breaking new ground for us all. They were wearing uniform, and had probably not dared to move since dawn. We prayed hard they would give the Jerries a good run for their money, and each hour which passed with the Germans obviously still on the search boosted our morale. It was well into the evening when the deflating news came. The patently relieved Kommandant let it be known that the fugitives had been recaptured five or six miles away.

The sudden end reinforced all-too-powerfully what we had always assumed, that it was neither the barbed-wire nor the sentries which doomed us to endless captivity, but the organised defence in depth of a regimented, documented and occupied continent. On one score, however, minds had been made easy: a recent replacement from Stalag had reported unsuccessful attempts from other Lagers, and in all cases the men had been sentenced to three weeks 'solitary', followed by six months in a Straflager. The punishment, though hardly to be shrugged off, was far from the drastic cure threatened by Baldy.

Stalag began to assume an importance it had not had previously. Replacements sent out from Wolfsberg not only kept us up to date with the news and the happenings in Stalag itself, they also introduced us to a standard of comparison with the other camps which they had left for various reasons. They surveyed their new surroundings with eyes which had gazed critically at other jobs and billets, and for the most part seemed favourably impressed by what they saw. The ultimate proof of their satisfaction lay in the fact that they stayed, some of them to express surprise at men wishing to chance the risky business of being flung into working camps which already had unsavoury reputations for hard toil and severe discipline.

Still, a trickle of prisoners, browned off, or in the search for change or adventure, continued to make the journey back to the attractive, temporary idleness of Stalag. One of them, Bert Williams, a lugubrious-looking Brummagem boy, had become the nearest thing I'd yet had to a permanent combine mate. His exit from the scene of our labours was signalled by no advance warning, even to me, his closest associate at the time. The midday meal, never very appetising, satisfying, or plentiful, had not been very much worse than usual. At about one o'clock I had returned to work on the Night Stack. Just about an hour later the party had leaned on their zapins to exchange the usual cross-talk with the approaching afternoon Putzerei shift. Someone had counted: there were only seven men, instead of the normal eight. Who was missing? We recited the names. The missing man was Bert.

'Where's Bert?'

'He's refused to work.'

'What! Why?'

'He wasn't going to work on pig's swill.'

'What's going to happen?'

'He's off to Stalag on a fizzer.'

A little later on, another, shorter procession crossed the little bridge. Bert, complete with greatcoat, kitbag and Red Cross parcel and, some paces behind, a guard with an air of special responsibility. We shouted encouragement and good wishes, and waved. Bert didn't wave back, his arms being weighted down by his packages, but he turned his head and smiled. Somebody said: 'That's the first time I've seen him smile.' That was an exaggeration, but nothing about Bert Williams's stay in Weissenbach became him quite like his leaving it.

Two other departures resulted from more violent causes. One of the original Weissenbach party suffered a broken nose, which caused, not him, but another of the original Weissenbach men, to leave under escort and the certainty of a punitive sentence, for it was the latter's fist which had inflicted the damage. Of all the hooters on the camp the one he had bashed had been the one most likely to crunch under violent impact. The incident was unfortunate, not only for victim and assailant, but also for the record: it is the only instance of violence between prisoners I remember.

The other departure, affecting me more nearly, arose from an accident. On the principle that the best way to avoid unpleasant jobs was to get one more palatable and permanent, I had long since set my sights on becoming a regular member of the Nachtlage Partei. Success came suddenly on the day one of the Lancashire men had his leg snapped by a log. His case is memorable, not only because I took his place among his mates, but also because, since his friends were all at Weissenbach and he had left under no cloud or threat of discipline, I fully expected him to make every effort to wangle his way back, once restored to fitness. He never returned. I interpreted that as a measure of the difficulty of selecting one's own working camp once one had been swallowed up by the soul-less, grinding machinery of Stalag.

The noisy, crude machinery of the mill chewed up rough timber at an enormous rate. Timber arrived throughout most of the day by all sorts of primitive and weird transport, in sufficient volume to keep the mill running during the day, to build up a reserve for the evening and night shifts, and also to stack up a surplus capable of ensuring production through the hardest of winters when wheels couldn't roll and rafts couldn't float. On the bank of the Enns a circular saw reduced the huge rafts to transportable lengths which found their way to the mill by lorry, horse-cart and bullock-wagon. A heavy, weighted lorry worked all day lugging a long, sixteen-wheel trailer loaded with railway trucks which were then pushed on to a short, raised stretch of rail outside the Putzerei. Local woods also supplied continuous consignments which came in by other horse and bullock transport tended by French prisoners or by old men and young boys who suggested a peasant ancestry difficult to imagine.

Iron rollers conveyed the timber, end-on, through a canvas-covered hole in the Putzerei wall, on the other side of which a circular saw screeched the trunks into lengths of about a metre, stopping the rollers at every cut. Loads in excess of the rollers' needs were diverted to the nearby Nachtlage on the opposite side of the rollers to the rail track. From eight in the morning till five in the evening we were kept busy stacking the excess timber to create a stack capable of feeding the rollers during both the evening and night shifts. Towards the end of the day, when the Night Stack was adjudged large enough for that purpose, further consignments not required by the hungry rollers were diverted to the Winter Stacks on the far side of the Reingruber house.

The Putzerei, or cleaning department, held an assortment of ancient, Heath Robinson-like machines for removing bark, chopping and fragmenting wood, and separating knots. What they didn't do at any stage was to remove the need for man-handling the timber, and the one thing they certainly weren't was safe. The wickedest-looking of them all was 'The Chopper', with its massive, rising-and-falling axe-head. To place a wide-girthed section of trunk upright under the vicious axe-head called for the section to be grasped round the waist and tilted so that its base rested on a metal platform directly under the blade. Since the man wrestling with the trunk couldn't see the platform for the timber blocking his view, it only needed the unstoppable blade to graze the top of the timber a fraction too soon for the whole log to be thrust violently aside and downwards on to the sweating worker's feet. The unchallenged expert on the chopper was the huge, canvas-aproned boss, but it was easy to see how he had become a 'peg-leg'.

By contrast with the Putzerei, the open-air life offered by the Nachtlage Partei – where the work was freer and more chal-lenging, demanding nimble feet, deft wrists and sure eyes rather than brute strength – was tempting for anyone with a natural aptitude for striking a moving object, be it ball or log. The stacks had to have a flat, even surface on which to stand and work. That meant placing each log into its own selected place, and that in turn meant turning half of them. When the log to be turned was big, feet needed to be nimble to step over it as it rolled under one, bodies needed to be supple to twist and follow to keep it rolling and wrists needed to be strong and deft to meet the supreme challenge of angling the log with a zapin and spinning it around in an arc just as it was poised to crash over the back of the stack.

When the burden and futility of work became unbearable the Nachtlage showed up well against most available jobs. One could slip away for a quarter of an hour, in winter into the loading department where there was a warm nook conveniently out of sight at the top of a little-used iron staircase, in summer, on the pretext of going for a drink, into one of the innumerable niches of the Winter Stacks, and be sure one's mates would conceal one's absence. But the Putzerei men had to keep pace with the machines; a blockage in the line became noticeable within minutes.

At the upper end of the village, Russians were housed in another small camp. They shared the shift work in the Putzerei as well as manning departments the British rarely entered. Our own replacements had given horrific accounts of the pitiful influx of half-starved Russians into the empty compound we remembered in Wolfsberg. They had arrived after weeks of being shunted all over Germany, weak and exhausted, young and old, fathers and grandfathers, with sons and grandsons on their backs and shoulders. Non-combatants for the most part, they had been roughly uprooted from their homes and steppes. The tales told of a typhus epidemic, of ninety-odd bodies being buried in a crude grave in a short space of weeks, and of the British burning their palliasses to avoid a spread of the infection.

Two young Russian urchins provided a permanent reminder that there were advantages in being born, and captured, British. They might have been nine or ten years of age. Dressed in dirty, black rags, their faces peeping out from under men's black, peaked caps, they gravitated towards the British whenever Herr Martin, their taskmaster, let them out of his sight. Drawn by curiosity as much as by the lure of the odd square of chocolate, which otherwise they would never have tasted, they delighted to have us pull their oversized caps down to their chins or twist their outsize men's boots almost in a circle, so lost were their tiny feet in the improvised footwear. As Jock Stewart joked: 'Half their length is along the ground.' The day Martin was detected cuffing them accounted for the fact that, months later, when his foot was being slowly and painfully crushed between two huge logs forming the base for a donkey-engine which was shifting under its strain, we let him yell and shriek for a minute or so before someone, relenting, performed the simple operation of stretching out one hand to switch off the engine.

The Germans published a periodical newspaper of a few small pages for British prisoners. Printed in English, it gave the news (Berlin version), reported extracts from House of Commons debates (if the extracts showed up the feebleness of the British war effort), and painted the American 'invasion' of Britain in the light most likely to cause ulcers for any prisoner who had not heard from his wife in months. Best of all reading, however, were the consistent publications of 'Awards' or punishments meted out to prisoners for a whole variety of offences against the Third Reich, or, especially and frequently in the case of paroled Frenchmen, against the purity of the Aryan race. The front page bore the heading *The Camp*; its unofficial title soon became 'Bullshit aus Berlin'.

Accompanying the paper usually was a duplicated sheet produced by our own men in Stalag. Called *The Pow Wow*, its purpose was to keep the Arbeitskommandos informed of developments at administrative H.Q., and to draw attention to the supplies and facilities becoming increasingly available for distribution: playing cards, footballs, musical instruments, books, correspondence courses, and the like. Had all prisoners been concentrated in Stalag, there would have been enough books to satisfy everyone, and enough musicians and instruments to form an orchestra and a band; but, scattered as the captive community was among so many small units over such a wide area, distribution with fairness and without favouritism, blunder or waste was no easy task. A trombone would have been useless in a Lager where the only musician was a violinist, and a football wouldn't have been much good in a camp like our previous one, where there was not a yard of flat ground in sight.

Among the leisure supplies reaching us in the summer of 1942, pride of place went to the packs of cards and the tea-chest of books, articles which appealed to most tastes. A gramophone arrived with a small selection of records of old favourites and recent hits, soon augmented by a bundle of discarded German discs presented by a guard whose wife was glad to get shot of them. We found 'Unter Der Roten Laterne von San Pauli' and 'Blumengeflüster' good listening after a surfeit of 'Jealousy' and Bing Crosby.

A guitar, although strummed by various embryonic musicians, soon became the main preserve of Piwi Pirini, but a clarinet turned out to be something of a headache. There were

105

two bandsmen eager to exhibit their prowess, something which, to most simple minds, should have worked to general advantage. It transpired, however, that such instruments have things called reeds, and that one of the experts, to the great astonishment of everyone else, considering all we'd gone through, had an unshakeable objection to sharing a reed polluted by another – good player or bad. The ensuing debate, ended by a formula no doubt not quite acceptable to either party, proved equally as entertaining to the rest of us as any tune subsequently to emerge from the non-reed end of the disputed instrument.

Stalag also supplied a football which seemed fated never to be kicked until the bright idea struck us that, if the colossal, blackened trunks forming the base of one of the not yet rebuilt Winter Stacks were levered back against the adjacent stacks, there would be a long ribbon of earth suitable for a kick-around. The Kommandant obtained reluctant permission from the mill, and we toiled like beavers through a long evening, shifting the trunks and levelling the troughs caused by decades of enormous loads. For a few weeks we made the most of the elongated, narrow pitch whenever guards could be spared to watch over us, returning each time filthy to the thighs from inches of bark soil. Then the mill reclaimed its own. The loss was made more bearable by the base-trunks being restored to position during normal working hours. The only further chance for a game was engineered by our Kommandant who got his head together with his counterpart at a camp some miles along the Enns, and arranged a match between their respective charges, the venue being a sloping meadow in the hills, equidistant from both Lagers. As proof that the encounter took place, I still have a photo of the combined teams stripped for action in an assortment of underpants, shirts and pullovers.

The football gave us our first and last chance for contact with fellow-prisoners. The hope that it might have been the precursor of several similar get-togethers was quickly dashed, and the ball went into the store, never to come out again during my stay. To make things worse, a second football arrived to join it, provided by the Germans. The only article of leisure equipment to originate from that unusual source, it stayed unused, although we were longing to give it a trial. It was the first ersatz football we had seen, with no trace of leather or rubber, and with simulated laces. We wondered what was used for air to keep it inflated.

106

In spite of that setback, our limited expectations had been exceeded. The one thing we still badly needed was toilet paper, which was ironic considering how we spent most of our time. The factory product was entirely unsuitable, more akin to cardboard. The situation had certainly improved since *The Camp*, the *Pow Wow* and the occasional copy of *Das Kleine Blatt* had augmented the few packs in the food parcels, but when sudden emergency compelled one request to a loan of the needful it was still only granted in accordance with the formula, 'one up, one down, no polishing in wartime'. Conservation was all the more necessary since one of the signs of increasing austerity back home was that labels on tins were disappearing in favour of description of contents being stamped on the bare metal.

The improvement in our lot was in no way better illustrated than by a nice practice which had gained currency, started by no one knew whom. We were still at the stage when it was a great disappointment to discover that none of the parcels collected at intervals from the village Post Office was addressed to oneself. That disappointment, linger as it would, was most pleasantly softened by the discovery, on returning to one's bunk, that luckier, thoughtful mates had each dropped a packet of ten cigarettes on one's blankets, as well as on each of the surrounding bunks. The practice soon became the norm in every room.

Life was further enriched by the acquisition of two young kittens who, in total ignorance, sported about the common-room when not curled up on a bunk or against the warm stove and, later on, when they grew bigger and more adventurous, sallied out through the wires with never a thought for the guards, only to return unfailingly as if to the cosiest hearth in Weissenbach. Just as the kittens ignored the 'Eintritt Strengstens Verboten' notice on the gate, so did the prisoners so far forget the order to keep the sacred wires clear as to plant sweet-peas at the base on both sides of the gate. In season they made as splendid a display as any in the village.

Progress was not continuous. An event which truly shattered us was the way we lost Brinson. No one expected the bombshell which burst in our midst one dreary midday. It was lunchtime. Someone rushed into the Big Room where I was gathering my eating-irons. He flung it at us: 'Brinton's gone round the bend.'

It was a crude accusation, often levelled at everyone and

anyone at the least (and sometimes without any) provocation. This time it sounded different, with no trace of the usual pique or amusement at some outrageous prank. The voice betrayed shock, excitement and an element of disbelief tinged with apprehension. Brinson had strolled up among the laggards. At the Lager entrance he had continued ambling on up the road. His companions, by now turning in at the gate, had stopped and stared, wonderingly, then unbelievingly. The sentry had yelled, been, equally astonishingly, unheeded, and had then challenged. Brinson's companions, taking in some part of the incredible drama, had raced forward, overhauled Brinson and grabbed him. They had propelled him unwillingly back.

The speaker reported that Brinson was sitting on his bunk, the object for study of numerous uncomprehending eyes. Someone came in and asked me to try my luck at rousing him. I found him, as reported, sitting on his bed with a small bunch of friends around him, all of them, like the couple of guards staring in from the corridor, baffled and helpless. When I tried to get him to talk or even simply to notice my presence, he gave hardly a sign that he knew who I was or, indeed, that anyone was there. Wherever he was, he was certainly not in the Arbeits-kommando.

That same afternoon he trudged to the station under escort. That was the last I saw of him.

The receipt of mail was not always the joyous event it should have been for all recipients. Only the most insensitive and smug failed to note that the world was leaving them behind; indeed the more regular and detailed the letters, the more obvious it became. Seemingly lesser men who had set no foot outside Britain were gaining the promotions in industry and on the barrack squares; the girls left behind were getting married and reducing the delights of still distant repatriation; while children were growing up with allegiances to all kinds of people other than their fathers. For some men letters got fewer as their girl friends found companionship elsewhere and the true implications of having a prisoner for a sweetheart sank in, and a few began to feel their wives slipping from them as correspondence dwindled and grew cooler. Outstanding among the latter was Eddie Hopkins.

'The List' was mythical but its therapeutic effect was impossible to measure. It began after it became known that one or two girls had jettisoned their captive sweethearts. Someone waited for the mail to be read, and then called out 'anyone else for the List?' From that moment on it was there to stay, an important feature of life in the camp. To put one's name on the List guaranteed bantering, often very hard to take when emotionally upset, but for most men it was a small price to pay for the consideration and friendship, the unsolicited sympathy and warm, clumsily-disguised protection which followed to keep them from brooding on what they couldn't cure. In much lighter vein was Jackie Hart's reaction to the most often repeated advice scribbled at the end of the greatest proportion of letters, 'keep your chin up'. After reading each letter he would raise his chin a notch; if he'd received quite a bundle he'd get through the last one by holding it between his upturned face and the ceiling.

Late in the year another list, real and covering many pages, made its slow round of the camp. Supplied by the Red Cross and accompanied by a thick bundle of appropriate questionnaires, it served to remind us that, though our mail might give the strong impression that everyone we knew outside of captivity was either about to arrive on leave, on leave, or just returned from it, hundreds of men had met a fate worse than ours: they were missing without trace. Any information which might pinpoint the fate of a luckless one was being sought.

Only after the list had passed into other hands did it occur to me that two names, those of Ash and Ashford, had not been listed. The omissions had to indicate that their fates were known, so I began to assume they were known to be either dead, alive and prisoners, or alive and free. The more thought I gave to the matter, however, the more I realised that, subconsciously, I had expected their names to have been mentioned. One thought more than any other nagged in my brain: when had the bulk of us been officially reported and recorded as P.O.W.s? If the two men had been registered as prisoners before going into the drain, had that alone been deemed sufficient for an entry of 'fate known', and would such an entry hold good after a lapse of eighteen months with nothing further heard from them? Someone, family, friends, would surely have enquired about them, as month after month went by with not so much as a postcard. One man could have been an orphan, and single; surely not two.

However unsatisfactory my ponderings on the fates of Ash

and Ashford, there was some satisfaction to be derived from unravelling a more personal riddle. Both my brothers were also in the Services, the elder in the Navy, the younger in the R.A.F. The latter was at that time enjoying a 'good war' in Canada, a bit of luck I by no means begrudged him. The riddle, or the first part of it, arrived in a couple of letters from my sister. The first told of my elder brother being home on leave, the second of his being interned in Algeria. Using my detective powers, I decided, rightly as it later transpired, that his ship* must have been one of those sunk on a Malta convoy. My main reaction was to feel sorry for my sister. Having started the war with three brothers at home, she was having to battle on with all three scattered around the globe. To cap all, she now had to send parcels to two of them!

At about the time Young Lionel and his friends had made their break, the same thing had been happening at camps throughout Austria. Dozens of men had chanced their arms and tested the German defences. There had been no record of reported successes but, in spite of that, the Spring Handicap, as it was aptly termed, set others planning for the next round of attempts in the autumn, when trees would bear fruit and the earth conceal roots. Weissenbach had no runners entered. Then, one afternoon, three prisoners arrived from Stalag with no intention of working in or around the mill except for as long as it might take them to leave, and their departures were provisionally fixed for the very next day.

They spent their evening sounding us out about the local layout, and informing us that their plan was simply to try a fast run for Switzerland. Strong, tough and determined, they looked as likely a trio as any to get success. They talked of the Escape Committee which had backed them and directed them to Weissenbach as a suitable jumping-off base. I suspected I detected a growing doubt as to whether the camp was as ideal for their purpose as they had been led to believe. As for the Escape Committee, according to our informants, it made no plans itself: it merely vetted schemes and, if satisfied, gave approval and assistance, such as cooking the German lists of replacements to working camps and delving into its small stock of hard-won escape aids.

Next afternoon the trio took their places around the Nacht-lage while three regulars, including myself, slipped away to

* H.M.S. *Manchester*.

avoid making the site look overcrowded. A little later the escapees, zapins purposefully over shoulders as if off to another task, strolled openly up the main road. We resumed our places and, seemingly intent on our work, watched their calm walk until they became lost to sight behind the stacks. The Germans, by fragmenting the work-force among different guards and bosses both inside and outside the mill, contributed considerably towards increasing the chances that the men would not be missed until final round-up at finishing time. The absences remained undetected until the end of the shift, with only a couple of hours to go before dark. The impact on the prisoners was not nearly so overwhelming as it had been when Lionel had decamped. A more mature Kommandant declined to take it as the personal affront his predecessor had made of it: the men had got away from the job, where his authority had been diluted, and not from under his nose; and it was very obvious who the missing men were, the recruits of only a day earlier. If the Kommandant had been outwitted, so too, to an equal extent, had been Wolfsberg. No word came till late the following evening: the fugitives had been recaptured in the hills, among the hunting grounds, and one of them had been wounded.

My German was improving with the increased and more varied contacts with civilians, and even more so from reading. Conversation with the civilians was usually limited to the job in hand, but even that had the merit of impressing often repeated words and phrases firmly in the memory: after a morning of being told you were apparently putting vinegar on everything, and that every now and again you were 'basta', you were neither likely to forget the words nor omit to find out from some source that vinegar wasn't a condiment and that 'basta', far from having anything to do with your origins, was actually a form of praise.

There being no German text-book or novel in camp, reading of German was at first confined to a daily perusal of the factory notice-board. The notices were hardly the best beginner's material, the officialese used being of an exaggerated kind. The composer must have been of the old school, still living under the k. and k. of the departed Hapsburgs. Every single notice was prefaced by 'Arbeitsbetriebsgesellschaftangehörige', for 'employees'. Gradually I learned to break down even that monster into its component parts and, by constant reference to

Edgar Parry, found some sort of meaning in a good part of the lengthy instructions issued.

The breakthrough came with the discovery of an unattended copy of *Das Kleine Blatt*, the local paper circulating among the older civilians. Newspapers were forbidden to prisoners, but civilians sometimes got careless. My main supplier was an elderly gentleman who formed the fat half of a Laurel and Hardy pair. They were indispensable wherever a consignment of timber was being unloaded. Every log had to be measured and recorded. Hardy, draped in a green-with-age Dracula cape, stuck a gauge around the waist of each log, measured the length with his eye, and sang out to Laurel, standing by with pencil and record sheets: 'sieben, achtundzwanzig; sechs, einunddreizig; sieben, neunundvierzig.' Alongside the stack was a small room, a shelter from the rain, and in that room Hardy often left his paper, with the result that one only had to wait until the popular double-act had to be performed over a load wanted directly by the rollers to be able to 'borrow' a section of the paper. Emboldened by success and the apparent lack of concern displayed by Hardy, the day soon arrived when the whole newspaper found its way into my patch-pocket.

At first *Das Kleine Blatt* increased rather than diminished the difficulty of mastering the language. Printed in old gothic type, it gave the added headache of deciphering the strange symbols which seemed cunningly designed to put off pilfering prisoners. Initial slow progress with the language was mitigated by a feeling of successfully struggling with the peculiar code in which it was printed. The extra time and trouble taken over individual words impressed them all the more deeply.

Although, on the whole, it had been a bad year for the Allies, at the end of 1942 spirits rose with the news from the fronts. When, after the defenders of Tobruk (of whom we had felt so proud) had been forced to capitulate, Rommel's thrust had carried the Afrika Korps past El Daba and on to El Alamein, the protracted confrontation looked as if it might end with the Germans celebrating Christmas among the brothels of Sister Street,* and New Year sampling the comparable delights of Cairo. Although the Russians had miraculously clung to both Moscow and Leningrad, the enemy penetrations towards the Caucasus, in conjunction with the threat from the Nile, seemed

* In Alexandria.

to forebode a strategic disaster equal to any that had gone before, and the very one we had smugly assumed our own ill-fated efforts in Greece and Crete had at least helped to avert rather than just postpone.

Suddenly came the victory of El Alamein. However often our memories might tell us that the Eighth Army was still far short of the point we had ourselves reached eighteen or more months earlier, the prevailing impression that Rommel had shot his last bolt only to see it fall short, was the greatest thing to happen to us since capture. Elated, we thought we understood the matching depression of our captors. Only gradually, as the civilians seemed to be taking this isolated setback to heart, did we begin to realise that they had more on their minds than the fate of their beloved Afrika Korps. The importance of Stalingrad, and the scale of impending disaster for the Wehrmacht being enacted there in the snow, were matters we learned of from the words and behaviour of Herr Pilsener, the sawman, and of Herr Flemming. Both had sons on the Eastern Front.

As our second Christmas behind wires approached, a new enthusiasm accompanied the words of the jingle, A Trooptrain Was Leaving Old Lavamund, especially the lines:

> Onwards to Moscow they crawl,
> Up to their buttocks in snow,
> Digging slit-trenches in six feet of ice,
> Living on sauerkraut and tortured by lice,
> And they'll never get rid of them all,
> As over their bodies they crawl . . .

The boys prepared to make Christmas an event to remember. With wood and paper from the mill, music-stands were knocked up, each with the legend 'Busty's Rhythm Boys'. Natty white jackets were cut for players of clarinet, guitar, drums (the renowned Busty Arden himself), paper-and-comb and spoons; stiff, black bow-ties were added as a final touch of rare elegance. An Entertainments Committee sprang into existence to enlist volunteers to provide anything in the way of a play or a song or dance.

The heart of the festivities was to be a dinner ambitiously designed to test the full capabilities of the stove. A levy of foodstuffs was extracted to enable Geordie, assisted by anyone else laying claim to being a bit of a cook, to prepare a three-course banquet. Canadian biscuits, more easily ground down for re-baking than the usual British issue, provided the basic ingredient for what we hoped would be a substantial Christmas cake, while American milk from tins graced with dainty 'Betsy, the Borden Cow' would produce an appetising sauce.

Christmas Day found everyone in suitable mood to make the most of the festivities. The meal, to which all had looked forward with a mixture of doubt, expectation and a little trepidation, was ceremoniously served, with few allowing themselves to be put out by the need to swill plates in cold water between courses. We had managed to persuade the Germans to accept Lagergeld in exchange for a couple of bottles of lager per man and, in the event, the cooks had far from disgraced themselves, the stove having stood up well to the unprecedented demands made on it.

The evening's entertainment was lengthy, and consisted of a procession of solos, duets, and choruses, interrupted by a play and various other diversions such as the entry of hula-hula girls in paper skirts, who, ill-matched for size and shape, bore remarkable resemblances to Jock Fraser, Percy Webber and big Jonah Jones. The last-named kept his best act for the finale when, in company with another whose name escapes me although his features don't, he performed a stark-naked belly dance, no doubt perfected in the back streets of Port Said or Alexandria. I vividly recall that his partner, whether for effect or for safety, had removed his dentures before entry. The real stars, however, were again Piwi Pirini and Taff Dennis. One of the guards, a middle-aged character who spent his spare time manfully struggling to master a miniature accordion with the aid of simple music (printed in black for push-in and red for pull-out), treated us to a rendering of his favourite piece and, for encore, his musical repertoire being exhausted, put heart and soul into a heel-slapping dance.

So intoxicating were the effects of the celebrations, coming at a time when the war was at last showing signs of turning in our favour, that some men entered a state of exaggerated euphoria, unsupported by cold facts. Not many days after Christmas I was lying on my bunk at the far end of the big room, reading. At the other end of the room a conversation took the startling turn of assuming that the Christmas just celebrated would, most probably, be the last of the war, and of captivity. I deliberately refrained from chipping in, although distracted from my book. I saw no grounds for their optimism, but had no wish to dampen spirits which would in any case be gradually restored to normality by the months to come. It was unfortunate that one of the speakers, swept away by the theme, sang out:

'What will you be doing this time next year, Taff?'

'Lying on my bunk, I expect, reading a book.'

Then came the question which shouldn't have been asked: 'Why, don't you think we'll be home next Christmas?'

It was too blunt to be avoided or turned aside. All conversations stopped, pending my answer. One or two men looked at me as if I had two heads. There was nothing for it but to explain that, in my view, the war could hardly end without an invasion, and that I doubted if one could be mounted in 1943 with any chance of success, and that the one thing we couldn't afford was a failure. I ended:

'We'll spend another two Christmases here.'

The words, received with such unbelief as to make me instantly regret having spoken them, proved unwittingly prophetic: I had no idea of it at the time, but the only man in the camp they didn't hold good for was me.

As a personal heartener, 1943 started off well for me. The very first letter of the year, from my sister, spoke almost casually of my sailor brother being home on leave, of his having lost weight and gained an infected eye. Reverting to my game of detective, I found it easy to conclude that the American advance through French North Africa had brought a swift end to his sojourn behind barbed-wire. That was one of us out of the bag.

The spirit of comradeship and well-being engendered by Christmas could not, in Weissenbach any more than elsewhere, be indefinitely sustained once the routine of drudgery and confinement closed down again. Yet it was natural to expect that, against the background of Allied victories and enemy doubts, morale would settle at a level higher than before. That was not the case. It was difficult to analyse the causes, other than to speculate that the very resurgence of hope had automatically lessened the need for prisoner to cling to fellow-prisoner as the only solid rock in a shaking world.

In the camp itself, facilities had never been so favourable for getting away from irritations and irritators, neither had there ever been such a variety of diversions. However easy it still was to compile an impressive list of the things men had to do without, the catalogue of goods and amenities which no longer needed to be foregone had definitely lengthened. It may have been that segregation into groups according to room in the Lager or shift at work, accompanied by a dilution of old friendships as more and more familiar faces departed, contributed to the formation of cliques, although with no sign of cementing according to nationality. It may have been that many were suffering from post-exuberance depression, brought on by the realisation that even Stalingrad and El Alamein couldn't alter the need to get up and out on bitterly cold mornings to roll logs for the enemy. Whatever it was, weeks after Christmas, dissension, fostered by a few, not only stubbornly resisted the normal, salving quips and banter of the majority, but steadily proceeded to infect it. And, ironically, the chief cause of the friction was traceable back to the Christmas spread which should have had the reverse effect.

Whether the whole thing started as a result of a casual remark falling on the wrong ears or whether someone had done mental arithmetic was unclear. The rumour started and gained ground that there had been a surplus of biscuits from the levy after all cakes had been baked. A campaign was mounted to call the 'Inner Circle' of Senior N.C.O., Vertrauensmann and cooks to account for the alleged discrepancy. The sheer persistence of the agitation for accountability staggered most of the men, but it couldn't be killed. It would subside for a day or two only to re-emerge more strongly than ever, sometimes from a different and unexpected quarter, until, finally, the stage was reached when only a showdown could disperse it.

A meeting was called in the common-room, and everyone attended: no one was going anywhere, apart from which the uninvolved mass looked forward to an evening's good entertainment, and to seeing fair play. The Inner Circle members being in the hot seats, there had to be an independent chairman. To my surprise, I found myself immediately nominated and seconded, unopposed. Thrust unceremoniously into the chair with no chance of marshalling my thoughts, I had to react quickly. It was no case of chairing a meeting where there was a platform putting a case either to be approved or flung back in their teeth; my handling of the meeting could mean all the difference between a bust-up and peace ever after.

Endeavouring to gain time while holding the attention of the captive audience, I went to some lengths to convey that, although it was regrettable that we were assembled for a purpose none of us relished, the only truly astounding thing was that through all the long months of captivity – and we would soon be mourning our second anniversaries – no such occasion had arisen before. That was a remarkable fact from which we could all derive satisfaction, and for which we could all take credit. At the same time, we must have known that it was inevitable that dispute would eventually arise. The only matter for surprise was that it had not happened sooner. Now that it was with us, at long last, like the sensible people we had already, a thousand times over, proved ourselves to be, we had decided to sit down and thrash the matter out of our systems.

As for our get-together, it was not for the purpose of passing resolutions or making decisions, nor to find scapegoats, but to discover what had gone wrong and to ensure that future dissensions would not be allowed to get out of hand to poison the atmosphere in which we would all have to continue to live. None of us had chosen to be where we were; neither had we any choice as to the company we kept. We were likely to be cluttered up together for a long time yet, so it was up to us alone to learn to live together. The past had proved it could be done.

The very first speaker, one of the men who had been most vociferous in innuendo and direct accusation, while extending the range of grievance by bringing forward more than hints of un-British conduct on the part of the 'accused', did so in a manner much more restrained than had been expected, leaving me in doubt that my long-winded address had spiked one or two of his most lethal guns. The biscuit charge was answered by an admission that biscuits had indeed been left over, but they had been so few that no useful purpose would have been served by trying to distribute them among the donors at a fraction of a biscuit per man, and that to have hoarded them against the possibility of another feast would have made no sense. They had been eaten, and not in secret, by men who had found them on their hands.

The main issue and the most probable cause of the animosity had stemmed from other suspicions, in particular that a guard had gone on leave with British chocolate, and that a German woman, living opposite the Night Stack, had come into possession of a tin of British food. It was at a point in the debate when

117

the biscuit issue had been almost disposed of in a manner hardly compatible with the heated talk of the past weeks, and the more serious subject of the food tin and the chocolate was threatening to become a source of bitter argument, that Sidney Biffin, a man who up to that time had been relatively inconspicuous, rose to his feet. Speaking slowly and deliberately, seemingly pondering every word, he dampened down the heat and slackened the tempo of the wrangle by his evident difficulty in selecting the right words. But the words he found soon gained the attention of the accusers, to whom he seemed an unexpected ally, and of the majority, who, for the first time, were hearing someone apparently dispassionately summing up the prosecution case in words devoid of malice. Encouraged by the readiness of his audience to listen, Biffin warmed to his theme, which was that people back home, all sorts of people, those who could afford it as well as many who couldn't, had contributed towards the parcels, the food and the cigarettes we had received. They had done so willingly, at some sacrifice, in order to help prisoners, not German enemies. Wives, many with hardly any income other than the slender service allowance – and everyone knew how far that would stretch – had sent all they could afford to have their husbands back in the best condition possible.

Just as the agitating faction was leaning back lost in admiration of their advocate and wondering where he had been during the past weeks that he had not declared himself, Biffin, like a latter-day Mark Antony, selected the right moment to gently turn the tables. The sense of timing, the choice of phrase, and the restrained gesture, were all faultless. Above all, he was the supreme master of the pregnant pause. The periods of silence as he stood with his bare, upper torso swaying slowly to take in his full audience were not there because his tongue could not find the words: they enabled the impact of the last ones to sink in and allowed the next ones to be anticipated, usually wrongly. Having made it clear what was the purpose of every bar of chocolate and every tin of corned beef, he proceeded to demonstrate, pithily and with a dry humour which threatened to have men collapsing on the floor in stitches, that if a bar of chocolate could procure a weekly roll in the hay with a luscious German blonde, to the physical and mental salvation of the donating prisoner, be he husband or not, then that was a bar of chocolate well spent; if a tin of meat could cause a guard to

118

turn his back rather than commit a man to the bunker, then that was a tin to be treasured.

The previously disgruntled section were so taken aback by the new twist of the debate, and so overawed by the dramatic change of atmosphere, that not one of them jumped up to point out that neither chocolate nor meat had produced benefits so tangible as those so picturesquely described. Biffin's oration was in full flood, and the audience, loving every second of it, would not have taken kindly to interruptions. He added much more in amplification of his theme, but that only added to the entertainment. He had not simply stolen the evening; he had saved it.

There were further speakers, but the outcome of the meeting had already been assured. Little remained for me to say in conclusion. The discussion had ended on a merrier note than most would have imagined possible, and two unsuspected reputations had been established, Biffin's and, to a lesser degree, mine. Moreover, a new phrase had been coined, 'a clear-the-air meeting'. As I strolled to the stove, an Aussie passed me a mug of tea, and remarked, 'You handled that well, Taff.' But the real honours had to go to Biffin. No one would gaze on him with the same unseeing eyes again.

That winter was less severe than the previous one. There had been short periods when, from a slippery, treacherous Nachtlage, we had been able to glance across to the slopes beyond the main road and watch the village youth practising their skiing. (There, too, in the summer, office girls and shop assistants had draped their seductive, tantalising, sun-bathing lengths during their lunch hours, so causing us to understand the true significance of the 'ultimate offence' placards back in Wolfsberg.) At work we had spent more time in the poncho-like capes issued to the loggers to ward off the rain than in our own greatcoats. Laurel, struggling to keep his record sheets dry, seemed to have taken permanently to wearing an open umbrella with the handle jammed down the back of his neck. To further distinguish that winter from its more protracted, tougher predecessor, the moist chill presented a number of us with colds, which the crisp frosts had not done.

I fell a victim. Nose and eyes streaming, sneezing my head off, and with upper lip blotted out by herpes, I staggered back from work one day, and took to my bunk, determined to stay

119

there until fully recovered, a resolution strengthened by the fact that my indisposition had caused me to become careless enough to allow a log to take the skin off every toe on my left foot. After a long sleep I awoke to find Kommandant and Vertrauensmann standing over me, and registered the fact that the Kommandant agreed I was really krank.

Sergeant Collins, the Vertrauensmann, had himself been waiting for medical treatment which only Stalag could provide, and the actual day of his departure was not far off. The impending departure was unique in that it was his declared intention to return to Weissenbach at the end of his period of treatment. Our valley party had arrived in Weissenbach with a warrant-officer, Sergeant-Major Hodson, who was senior in rank to any N.C.O. already there, and he had automatically continued as Senior N.C.O.; the other, elected role he had filled in the pine cabin was as automatically dropped, since the resident prisoners had their own Vertrauensmann. With the imminent departure of Sergeant Collins a new man would be needed for the post, and I, for one, assumed that the men from the valley, numbering about half the effective voting strength, would opt for a return to the old arrangement which, since there was no obvious alternative candidate, would probably appeal to most of the remainder.

On the first day of my absence from work, I was roused at midday by Earnie Barlow, a Manchester boy, bringing my lunch. I had more or less resigned myself to staying put on my bunk until overwhelmed by the urge to get up and forage. There was no reason why Barlow rather than anyone else should have taken it upon himself to act as nursemaid, but he did, and saw to it that I received both food and a plentiful supply of hot drinks. This routine had lasted some days when he informed me that a meeting had been arranged that night to elect Sergeant Collins's successor.

Getting up from his perch on the edge of my bunk, he asked, 'Would you stand, Taff?'

'Me? A buckshee private? But why not?'

That evening as I dozed, the sound of voices from the common-room reached me only as a distant buzz, unable to compete with the muffled music coming through the wall alongside me from the guards' radio. As I listened to the singing of 'Lili Marlene', I heard the meeting break up and the previously ordered sounds give way to a cacophony of separate outbursts. Footsteps hurried along the corridor and in through the door at the other end of the Big Room. Most stopped at their respective owners' bunks, but a couple advanced to pause alongside me.

'You're the new Vertrauensmann, Taff. Congratulations!'

The job of Vertrauensmann at that time involved nothing very onerous, just acting as spokesman for the prisoners, ensuring that opportunities existed for spending hard-earned Lagergeld, conveying complaints about food, and safeguarding the distribution of tins. The camp had reached the stage of almost running itself under a set of accepted rules of passive confrontation, warily agreed to by captors and captives. The most frequent area of contention lay in the relationship with work bosses, and there we had long since learned that capital could be gained by skilfully playing on the obvious disparity of aims and interests of civilians and military in respect of P.O.W. labour. But the boys had done me a great honour.

The camp supplied no candidates for the Spring Handicap, something which caused one or two men to assume the role of statisticians, partly as a gesture to defend the Lager's record, and partly to knock the escape business into some sort of perspective. The figures projected from the few facts at their disposal were astounding. Starting from the known figures that the camp held no more than eighty men, and that in 1942 six of those had 'had a go', and from an assumed figure – of Stalag registering 5,000 British prisoners – the mathematicians arrived at conclusions which indicated that, assuming our camp's performance was average, in 1942 breakouts had been more than one per day, with a large proportion of days doubling up on their quota. If the average time at large had been only two days, and the bulk of attempts had been concentrated in the two most favourable and favoured months of spring and autumn, the average number of prisoners unaccounted for in Austria during four months of the year would have been at least six per day.

Stimulating as the projections were as proof that men were not lying back waiting for release, their very magnitude was, on deeper reflection, dismaying. One figure was missing: there was always one 'nil' return, the number of successes. No one had any knowledge of an escapee making it to Switzerland: the projection from nought was still nought! For a long time we had assumed there must have been successes from so much effort, and that news of them would patently take longer to filter back than the reports of recaptures which the Germans always hastened to impart. By the summer of 1943 it became increasingly difficult to believe either that there had been any or that such a thing was possible. True as it might be that each and every breakout would upset the enemy, not everyone was prepared to face three weeks' 'solitary' and six months in a punishment camp to attain no more than that limited objective, quite apart from the consideration that, if too many were to jump on that second-best bandwagon, the Germans might decide to change the rules, so making life more onerous while at the same time diminishing opportunity for future genuine escape attempts.

It was inconceivable that anyone with the ingenuity, determination and luck to get home would find difficulty in, or baulk at, the simpler problems of getting word back to former mates and conspirators. Nor could any prisoner understand how a man who had got away could so forget those he had left soldiering on as not to bother to get in touch. The successful escaper would know that mail got through, how long it took and how much it was anticipated. He would be in a position to assess the impact of his tidings, and to recognise that, in most cases, success had depended on the assistance of men who had had to stay behind to put up with the extra inconvenience his absconding had caused.

The Red Cross sent further supplies of boots and uniforms. This time, the Germans, perhaps as bucked by their proven ability to give prisoners a week's start and still return them to the net as we were depressed by it, made no effort to collect the old clothing, with the result that everyone acquired a best uniform and a best pair of boots. It was a far cry from when Baldy used to insist on a nightly surrender of every rag. The immediate effect of the new issue was to get men stitching. Old trousers lost the better part of their legs and showed up at work as the shortest of shorts, to enable thighs to obtain the same benefit from the sun as upper bodies had done. The still hot-blooded women in the village of old men, cripples, and ragged Ukrainians, slowed their walks even more as they took in the views of the timber stacks.

Neither before my capture nor after my escape did I ever see a Tommy sporting a camera, whether touring the sights of Cape Town, Ceylon, Bombay, Alexandria or Cairo, or on duty round his station. Never had I known it suggested that a unit photo be taken. It was vastly different in the Wehrmacht. Every parachutist among the dozens whose papers passed through my hands on Crete possessed a group photo but, since the Führer himself was seated in the centre of each one, I had naturally assumed the photos to have been a mark of favour accorded only to elite troops. After the tables had been turned, and it was I who was the prisoner, it became clear that for a German soldier to wield a private camera was not regarded as the activity of a crank or traitor. In Salonika, the off-duty German soldier without his own camera was as rare a sight as a Tommy on Salisbury Plain would have been with one. Back in the valley, the guards had not only snapped prisoners but had also supplied as many prints as Lagerleld could purchase, while at Weissenbach the kittens, the sweetpeas round the door and my shaven pate had all been recorded for posterity, and a professional had been engaged, with no restrictions on the number of individual and group shots for sale to prisoners.

Sergeant Collins returned after an absence of about two months. Against the wishes of many of the men I relinquished the job of Vertrauensmann in his favour, taking the view that I had been elected only as caretaker. It seemed unlikely that he would have returned had he not been under the impression that he was a recovered Vertrauensmann reporting for further duty. He had kept faith with the camp; the least I could do was to keep faith with him. My appointment had resulted from no feeling of dissatisfaction with his handling of his post, while — an important point in assessing my own position as a private — any narrowing of the gap in rank between Senior N.C.O. and Vertrauensmann could only lead to greater harmony, as well as weightier authority vis-à-vis the Germans.

A New Zealander arrived to take up permanent residence in a capacity hitherto non-existent, that of medical orderly. Quiet, conscientious and extremely likeable, he was a valued acquisition. Another Kiwi appeared on a much shorter visit, to perform an even more unusual function. He was a padre who spent no longer than a day in our midst, but his arrival was no mean event. Squatting on my bunk, we discussed Wales and talked about books, in particular about *How Green was My Valley*

123

which, with a fine sense of timing, I had only just finished reading.

Our surplus earnings secured us the rare treat of a visit to the cinema in St. Gallen, a village a mile or two further upstream. The programme was unchanged from that advertised for the public, but ours was a private showing. The two insipid feature films left no lasting memories, but we should have been warned that a newsreel was to be shown. It was a peculiar experience to be sitting in an enemy cinema, surrounded by enemy guards, while on the screen the Führer received the ecstatic acclaim of enemy multitudes, together with numerous bouquets from blonde, national-costumed Fräuleins, or while Messerschmitts made rings round, and mincemeat of, sluggish Spitfires and Hurricanes. The reel was half over before we regained sufficient self-control to suppress the instinctive urge towards ironic, derisive cheers. The latter half of the reel gave little cause for concern: torpedo boats fired off tracer-shells all over an otherwise empty Black Sea, and soldiers at Odessa hosed themselves down amid immense jollification. The most memorable part of the evening for me was the trek back to Weissenbach: the way was lighted by thousands of glow-worms twinkling under the hedgerows.

Midsummer saw the beginning of a programme of outings, a direct consequence of our protests against being penned in with no proper exercise compound. The outings started with an escorted Sunday afternoon walk for one half of the camp, the other being held back until the following week. Once clear of the village there were no orderly crocodiles, although enough restraint was exercised, we hoped, to prevent the guards vowing never again to get themselves involved in such an unrewarding enterprise.

Thanks largely to a sympathetic Kommandant, the outings eventually led us to going for a swim in the Enns. Only those who had trekked to the 'quack' with ailments actual or feigned had ever sallied over the imposing Franz Josef bridge to the other side of the wide river. Under a protecting bank lay a pool large enough for a party to swim without danger of being swept away by the main current. Walks and swims came suddenly to an abrupt end as the Kommandant found them making too many demands on the limited off-duty time of his men. The breaks from routine had been gifts we had never expected, but that made it no easier to reconcile ourselves to doing without

124

them on afternoons when the sun blazed down on the narrow, dusty compound, and we were reduced to once again watching a world at leisure parading past our barred windows.

Relaxation in the severity of confinement was matched by a corresponding, gradual change in the attitudes of the civilians. Stalingrad, however Goebbels might present it, was to them a catastrophe. Herr Pilsener's son had escaped death and capture, but was in hospital with frostbite: not for some time would he spend his leave back at the circular saw. Others had been less fortunate. Behind the actual, personal tragedies, loomed ominous shadows of doubts which had not existed earlier. From first one, then another, of the older natives came hints of a fear greater than that of losing a war they had been so confident of winning. This additional anxiety grew out of bitter experience of what it had been like for some of them after the earlier war had been lost. Born and reared under the broad shield of the mighty Austro-Hungarian Empire and nurtured on its glories, the collapse of the Hapsburg dynasty in 1918 had left many of them prisoners in far-off, revolution-torn Russia. They had had to make their own ways home to an impoverished, dismembered land. By the time some of them saw their homes again, as many as six or seven years after hostilities had ceased, their country and its government had forgotten them. For them there had been no gratuity and little rejoicing. The spectre beginning to raise its ugly head was that a second defeat would not only leave their sons captive in Russia, but would also bring those same Russians into occupation of their villages.

During a lull in work on a cold, damp morning, the Nachtlage party had trooped into the civilian shelter room and spread themselves over the benches. In addition to Laurel and Hardy, one other civilian was present. A load of timber having arrived, the double-act left the room, leaving us to follow. I was last to leave. As I passed out of the doorway I became conscious of what the remaining civilian, still seated on his bench, was whistling: the Internationale! He was answering me. As was my frequent, annoying habit, I had been whistling to myself, and the last tune I had whistled before getting up from my seat had been the one taken up by the civilian. That was the first active sign that there were sympathetic natives.

Another sign came in more practical form. It was Easter. Frau Pilsener, an elderly woman who, like many others, brought her husband a hot lunch in a partitioned, blue enamel container, was picking her way between the rollers and the back of the Night Stack. She had to pass close to me to avoid the logs I had positioned for the rollers. I felt something being pressed into my palm. Without looking, I could tell it was an egg. My first reaction, apart from surprise, was to wonder what to do with it. It was hardly the recommended article for a logger's pocket, but when I glanced down I saw it was painted blue and suspected it was a festive egg, hard-boiled.

By late summer such furtive gestures were being accompanied by equally furtive questionings: did we think the British and Americans would get there before the Russians?

The invasion of Sicily and the downfall of Mussolini caused me, for the first time, to consider escape a distinct possibility. In all previous ponderings on the subject I had invariably been driven back to posing the question, 'Why has no word come back from anyone, confirming an escape?' The only reasonable answer I had been able to give myself had been 'Because there hasn't been one'. If word had arrived at only one Arbeitskommando, it would quickly have got back to Stalag, and then from there, after a short delay, simultaneously out to all other camps. The lines of communication between Weissenbach and Wolfsberg had been almost continuously open in both directions and, in spite of our experience of isolation in the valley, it was difficult to believe that Weissenbach was especially favoured in that respect. After recognising the unhappy fact that hundreds of escapees, including the most determined and dedicated, the most ingenious and confident aspirants, had ended up behind Straflager wires and not a single one, as far as we were aware, in the safety of Switzerland, we were compelled to ask why.

The physical obstacles were obvious, but there had to be other related reasons. Each assumed failure served to convince me that Switzerland was too narrow and predictable a goal. Recent news from Wolfsberg tended to indicate that others, elsewhere, were drawing similar conclusions, for among reports of failures were a few stories of men being picked up in Italy and Hungary. The most intriguing statistic one would never know was what proportion of the recaptures were of men who fell into traps set to catch other escapees trying their luck from other camps along the chosen route. The fact that so many were having a go from so many different places at the same time, with no co-ordination of effort, might have contributed considerably to reducing the chances of any single man getting through. The best bet was to start from the fringe of the camp concentration.

The weeks continued to slip by with nothing but conflicting reports of the Italian situation. It was impossible to guess what was happening, and *Das Kleine Blatt* gave no guide. Only when a fresh arrival from Stalag brought first-hand information about Italian units marching into captivity as if into their own barracks did it become clear that the Italians, with all their own forces largely concentrated in their own country, had been unable to prevent their former Axis partner taking control.

The Austrians, mostly a Catholic people, confined their swearing to religious words and phrases. Where the prisoners resorted to the obscene and the lurid to express their feelings, the civilians fell back on outbursts more akin to blasphemy, the favourite expletives being 'Kruci*fix*' and 'Sakra*ment*', with the stress heavily on the last syllable. When it had been established beyond all doubt that Il Duce had been toppled from the exalted position he had occupied throughout most of our lives, they would pull us aside and retail a joke which they considered tremendous:

'Why did the Pope send for Mussolini?'
'I don't know. Why did he?'
'To give him the last Sakra*ments*.'

September, 1943, was the decisive month of my captivity. Confirmation that the Allies had landed on the Italian toe came not only at a time when optimism as to the duration of the war was higher than ever before, but also, in my case, when I had never felt so unsettled, and had in fact made up my mind to quit Weissenbach as soon as I could toss the quack.

A graph of the moods of any prisoner would show that it rises and falls according to the impact of three main, interacting factors: the progress of the war, conditions of immediate confinement and, above all, especially when the first two factors are relatively stable and satisfactory, the news from home. Assuming always that the prisoner survives – and all soldier on with that assumption – both war and confinement will end of themselves, whereas the home will remain, a simple, indisputable fact giving the home an ever increasing importance the longer captivity lasts. The prospect of ultimate reunion with family and friends remains the one constant feature with hope, but the reverse side of the coin is the growing knowledge that the longer incarceration persists the weaker is the P.O.W.'s ability to influence events and the stronger his feeling of impotence.

The heaviest jolt since my capture came, suddenly and all unsuspected, from the one quarter in which I had placed complete confidence, from the person who had done most to make life bearable and future hopes attractive, from my girlfriend. The one thing which could be guaranteed during both my period of overseas service and, once the link had been re-established, the years of captivity, was that whenever mail arrived there would be several long, heartening letters from my sweetheart. Her support had not been restricted to words; my brown, cable-stitch, polo-neck sweater had been knitted by her hands, and she had kept me regularly supplied with cigarettes. She had been a real trump.

The batch of mail which arrived in the summer of 1943 brought the usual quota from my girl. Anticipating a delightful spell of reading, I had arranged the letters in order of dates and stretched out on my bunk prepared to drift blissfully back to the only world worth knowing. Lost to all else, I devoured the letters one by one. They in no way took second place to previous letters; the assurance, the nearness, the love were all there, as they always had been. With a feeling of regret that all good things come to too swift an end, I found the last letter before my eyes. I had no need to read it to realise the best of all good things in my life – and simultaneously it rose over me that they were not that many – was violently juddering to a halt. What I was staring at was not the usual, introductory endearment, but 'My Dear Elvet', a stiff, formal harbinger of the very worst. Hollow-stomached, absorbing each word while sheering away from all pursuit of what lay behind what I was reading, I steeled myself to read on.

In my own private war Hitler had won his supreme victory: I had been asked to release my fiancée from our engagement. Numbing as the request was, there lay not a moment's doubt in my mind that I had to comply, and that in such a way as to convey that I felt my fiancée's position more than my own. That was true, prone though I might have been to wallow in an occasional wave of self-pity. During the years of separation she had done much more for me than I had for her. I had been sustained by more than romantic imaginings; in addition to

128

letters vastly outweighing mine in length and frequency, there had been practical assistance and unlimited encouragement. Of two things I felt certain: that no one at that moment could influence her happiness more than I, and that, were I to resort to pleadings or hoisting distress signals, I might possibly succeed – to my own eternal shame and regret, and to the peril of any real joint happiness.

More than one prisoner put interest into his dull life by playing chess by correspondence against someone back home. Having made his move the player sat back and waited twelve weeks or more before knowing what counter his distant opponent had worked out. Puffing cigarette after cigarette throughout the long, restless night, I felt I had been drawn into a similar game, with the frustrating handicap of knowing that my opponent's pieces might be moved a second or third time before I had countered the first move. The problem was insoluble: my engagement meant more to me than a game of chess.

The following morning ranked as the most desolate and hopeless of the hundreds I had spent cooped up behind wires, including those plagued by rats and lice or endured amid the snows while enemy victories were reported with such regularity that it had seemed as if the war must last for ever. At midday relief came with a timely reminder that others had much more to disturb their repose and tax their sanity. Eddie Hopkins's bunk ran at right-angles to mine, lined up along an adjacent wall, its foot pointed directly at my head. We found ourselves alone together at the end of the long room as we collected our dishes.

'Bad news from home, Taff? I saw you smoking most of the night.'

I gave an affirmative answer, without divulging details.

Hopkins continued: 'I'd bad news, too. I was awake and saw you had a problem.'

'Compared to yours, mine's plain sailing. But it's a hell of a life, Eddie.'

We sat a while, talking across the narrow gap between the two sets of bunks. He brought me up to date with the continued saga of his tragic difficulties. His wife and child, objects of his undivided concern, had apparently disappeared from effective contact. Months earlier he had, in sheer desperation, taken the reluctant step of writing to a friendly neighbour, begging for information. After agonising weeks had come a reply offering little enlightenment and even less soothing comfort for his wounds. I caught myself wanting to strangle his wife, and shrank back from examining the origins of those feelings.

My reply went off at the next issue of lettercards. There had been ample time for composing the sentences in my mind. Having carried out the first part of my resolve, I took the precaution of guarding against subsequent waverings in my determination not to write again except in answer to some future letter. As 'the List' had grown so had the number of unwanted lettercards put on the market for the use of men who couldn't lay hands on enough of them: I had been one of those. I chose not to become a seller in a market where I had previously been a buyer. My cards, other than the few required to maintain regular contact with home and to thank considerate friends – including my old school, Bedwellty Grammar School – who had sent me cigarettes, were made available to two other prisoners, free of charge.

Naturally depressed by the prospect of a bleak, featureless future, and convinced that the tormenting break would never have come about had I not been a captive devoid of all hope of repatriation until after the war was won, I took to toying more and more with the idea of escape. It was not too late to participate in the Autumn Handicap soon to be under starter's orders. That thought had no sooner entered my head than it was rejected. The only goal would have had to have been Switzerland – which experience had confirmed many times over as virtually unattainable. However much I might have desired to show Hitler that, in our private war, his was not the last victory, my desire to avoid dividing the winter between 'solitary' and a Straflager was even stronger. Were that to happen, it would put me out of the race in the spring. And it was the Spring Handicap which interested me.

A capitulated, unoccupied and neutral Italy seemed too much to hope for. An Allied-occupied Italy was a remote possibility, and one which, since it would turn every Alpine pass into an overworked supply line and every peak into an observation post, would almost certainly rule the country out as one to aim for. The more attractive picture conjured up in my mind was of the hard-pressed Germans being forced to make their stand south of the Po, with, to their rear, an Italian population prepared to make amends for past follies by sheltering odd escapees for as long as it might take to drive the Huns into the Alps. It would help enormously if the intending escapee were already poised for the 'off' well to the south, around Lavamund or Unterdrauberg, on the very edge of the concentration of working camps.

The first move was to be sent back to Stalag. For that purpose I called my psoriasis to my aid. Should that fail me, a persistently simulated slipped disc might do the trick, or a knee swollen by heavy bashing with a wet towel. The season was the worst possible for relying on my skin complaint as alone sufficient to persuade Herr Doktor Jacks to class me sick and send me packing. Under the influence of the large daily doses of sunshine absorbed while working in only shorts on the Night Stack I was far from being the blotchy figure I otherwise would have been. That was something which had to be remedied. Only weeks earlier I had overheard Edgar Parry, our interpreter, bemoaning the fact that with all the lovely sunshine going begging he daren't strip off and get himself a tan. He had spoken of his envy every time he glanced up at the bronzed figures towering above him on the Night Stack. His last remark to the effect that he wished he 'had a body like Taff Williams, all gleaming brown bone and muscle, like a Greek god' almost had me putting down my book in order to offer him a cigarette. The gleaming tan would take months to wear thin, but I set to work right away to make myself look anything but a Greek god.

By coincidence there occurred almost immediately two chances of getting away from the daytime, outdoor work I had previously sought and clung to, the one almost forced on me by my own stupidity, the other of my own seeking. One afternoon I had left the work site and strolled up to Herr Reingruber's house to quench my thirst at the horse-trough outside his front window. That had been accepted practice on hot afternoons such as that one had been. What I did next was not exactly unusual, but far from accepted by the Germans. There being no one in sight, I had slipped among the Winter Stacks, perched myself comfortably in a shaded niche, and let my thoughts wander for half an hour. When I returned to the Night Stack there was no one to be seen but Herr Flemming and a French prisoner with a wagon of timber for unloading. 'Twinkletoes' pitched into me straight away, yelling at the top of his reedy voice. Actually the torrent of incomprehensible words hurled at me was meant to include the other absent members of the party. Be that as it may, Twinkletoes caught me on the raw, and I answered back:

'Wenn Sie schreien wollen, schreien Sie auf Englisch!'*

The storm abated, to be followed by a disbelieving silence.

That evening, before I'd had time for a mashing of tea, a small deputation of Herr Reingruber and Herr Flemming laid complaint about me before the Kommandant. The subsequent altercation took place on the steps of the Lager, Edgar Parry doing the interpreting and the Kommandant acting as judge. Much as I wanted to get back to Wolfsberg, I wanted to arrive there neither as an inmate of the bunker nor as a sacrificial offering to appease Twinkletoes. My blood was up and, sensing that the Kommandant, perhaps remembering my Vertrauensmann days, seemed inclined to play the incident down, I seized the opportunity presented when, turning to Parry, he asked:

'Doesn't he understand German?'

He knew very well that I did. Seeing the opening, I took over from Parry. Speaking in German as precisely and grammatically as I could, I addressed myself to the Kommandant: that was just it; I had taken the trouble to interest myself in the language; there was no point in bothering if one was to be subjected to incomprehensible abuse; if I couldn't understand what Herr Flemming had shouted in temper, how could the others be expected to understand? I played on the dignity of the soldier: correction and discipline were for the guards to enforce, not the civilians; if Herr Flemming had had grounds for complaint he should have turned to the military before shouting abuse, not afterwards.

In the background of the common-room a voice said, 'Just hark at Taff giving it air!'

I hoped the effect on the Kommandant would be somewhat different.

The two irate bosses were dismissed with an assurance that I would be suitably dealt with. The verdict, pronounced a day or two later, was that I must do a couple of weeks on 'the ashes' a job no one was keen on. That I declined to do, vowing I would walk off on the very first night. My reaction was neither particularly brave nor stupid. The sentence, and my reply to it, were both conveyed via Parry as intermediary, and there was at

* 'If you want to shout, shout in English.'

the time a solution to hand most agreeable to me and most probably acceptable to the Kommandant; one which, if presented in sufficiently severe terms to the aggrieved bosses, would appear to confirm that firm justice had been done and appropriate punishment meted out. I was to be given night work, neither on the ashes nor in the Putzerei, but on the Night Stack where a convenient vacancy had unexpectedly arisen.

The proposed job fitted in with my plans. It required someone skilled in doing the reverse of what I had been doing for at least twelve months – dismembering the stack so laboriously built up during the daytime. It would keep me out of the sun, allow me plenty of time to think, and assist the return of my blotches, every single one of which I endeavoured to preserve by assiduous scratching as soon as it appeared. I dug my nails into every itch. In a matter of weeks I had penetrated as far as Doktor Jacks's surgery, way up on a hill beyond the Enns and the Franz Josef bridge. Further progress seemed to be exactly nil until, having returned from my third or fourth visit under the impression that it might be quicker and more effective to slip a disc, I was informed I could pack my bags for Wolfsberg.

It was strange to contemplate that I was actually about to leave the men amongst whom I had lived so closely for over two years, and with whom I had shared the deepest depths of humiliation, depression and near hopelessness. They had been the only real family I had known since capture. Both in the valley and at Weissenbach there had been a close-knit community around me, with a feeling of comradeship hardly affected by the intermittent arrivals and departures. In Arbeitskommando terms Weissenbach was perhaps as green a paddock as one was likely to find under any Stalag. It seemed certain that the majority of the men I was about to leave would see the rest of their barbed-wire days out working at the mill and mashing their tea in the common-room. Except for one man I was not to see any of them again, but the break was not yet to be final, for they were to hear from me again in what I hope was, for them, a manner as heartening as it was unexpected.

At the local station the sentry handed me over to a military escort already in charge of a number of prisoners who had boarded the train at various points higher up the line. Almost every time the train stopped more prisoners were handed over, until, by the time the party had ceased to grow there might have been as many as thirty of us, all, for a variety of reasons,

genuine or concocted, heading for Wolfsberg. A few were sick
and in need of medical attention; a larger number were facing
punishment for an odd catalogue of offences and misdemeanours; but the majority, like myself, were trading on
simulated or exaggerated ailments. Quite a number, again like
myself, were about to see Stalag again after an interval of over
two years; whereas others left no doubt that they were habitual
returnees used to commuting between Wolfsberg and any working camps the Jerries might sling them out to sample. Among
the latter were several who obviously enjoyed the role of
patronisingly initiating men of the former group into the
pleasures and pitfalls of life in the 'big city' of Stalag. In the
reserved rear compartments which we occupied, a separate section had been set aside for a few Italian prisoners, the first I
had seen since those I had encountered long before in British
hands.

It was October and the days were noticeably shortening. The
tedious journey required that we change twice, the second time
involving a long wait at St. Michael. By that time it was already
quite dark. The Germans seemed to have altered little in their
habits since my last train ride. From the top of tall standards
exterior lights blazed down on tracks and sidings. In view of the
admitted intensity of American and British air-raids, it was
still hard to reconcile the German and British attitudes on how
to conduct a war. One was left with an impression either that
the latter, with their total black-outs right from the onset, had
over-acted, or that the former were slow or stubborn in adapt-
ing to a rapidly deteriorating situation. Judging from the
apparent indifference to danger, one could have had doubts
about the effectiveness of the bomber campaign against Germany until one reflected that the heart of Austria was still just
about the most distant target the Allies could reach.

Chapter 5

STALAG REVISITED

The perimeter lights showed in the sky long before we came to them, at first a glow reflected back from low clouds, and then a glare of light framed by the blackness of the surrounding forest. There was the delay in the administrative compound, just as of old. The knowledgeable ones, those for whom sorties from Stalag had become a way of life, enlightened us on what to expect: there would be no British compound that night, no brew-up, and not even a bunk, just a hard kip on a cold floor. Information was not limited to initiating the ignorant and unsuspecting into the changed conditions to be encountered. Alert eyes kept close watch on the comings and goings of the Germans, for much would seem to depend on who would be responsible for giving us a going-over next morning.

When finally the party shuffled forward through the second gate, it was only to be carefully shepherded into a hut just inside it. The night was to be spent securely locked up with our belongings in a large, bare room, pending search and documentation. It was all part of the constant battle to prevent prisoners from regarding Stalag as a desirable residence. Word circulated that the search officer would unquestionably be a character well known to the regulars as being methodical, meticulous and excessively zealous in seeing that nothing 'verboten' got any further than those four bare walls. With his zeal for turning up smuggled articles went an enthusiasm for ensuring that offenders had ample time to reflect on the rules during a spell in the bunker. Men got into a huddle to work out how to conceal contraband, especially letters.

I had three letters. One I had slid into a slit in the outer casing of my cardboard Red Cross parcel; a second, still in my breast pocket, was destined to be rolled round the cord of my kitbag and worked slowly into the cord-sleeve. The operation couldn't have been performed earlier while the cord still had to be drawn and the kit-bag carried, for the ruffling of the sleeve

135

and the pull and rub of the cord would have combined to wear away the paper and obliterate the writing. I put the rolled letter into position, leaving the cord only partially drawn: the bag would serve as my pillow almost up to the time of the search. It appeared that neither letter was likely to go undiscovered if the officer of the search was up to his reputed form, but I was concerned to keep my promises given in Weissenbach and hand them over to the proper recipients if I possibly could; in addition to which, like every man in the room, while long past resentment at the thought of next morning's proceedings, I considered it a challenge to win the accepted game of who could outwit whom.

The third letter was the one of least importance. Its contents were known to me, it was only intended in the conscientious mind of the medical orderly as a guide for the doctor, and I'd tagged along with my complaint for so long that I expected no treatment. To safeguard the letters which mattered it might be wise to sacrifice the third in such a way as to impress on the officer that he was dealing with one of the biggest nitwits of a fly ever to get himself entangled in his sticky web. I tucked the letter into my breast pocket, allowing the white end of the envelope to peep out like the suggestion of a neat pocket handkerchief.

True to the gloomy forecasts, next morning found the room invaded by a posse of soldiers under the command of the very officer about whom so many unpleasant tales had circulated the night before. The prisoners, each separated off with his own bits and pieces, were spaced around the sides of the room. A knowledgeable Glaswegian occupied the space to my right and gave me a running commentary as the thorough searching worked its way towards us from the left. My searcher had hardly had time to begin before Eagle-eye himself pointed to my breast pocket. The soldier took out its contents and passed the envelope to the officer. He opened it, glanced at the notepaper and barked: 'It is forbidden to bring letters into the camp. Bunker for you.' The English had scarcely a trace of accent. He hardly deigned to give me another glance, although, while he devoted his attention to Jock, the soldier continued a perfunctory poking about of my uniform and kit. The parcel was not even lifted off the floor and, although I had to tip out the contents of the kit-bag, I was left holding it, empty and upside down, with no German hand laid on it.

My mentor commiserated with me about the bunker which, privately, I felt I had a good fifty-fifty chance of avoiding.

'Why didn't you hide it, Taff? Or pass it to me?'

'Nae panic, Jock! Big-head missed the real sweeties.'

Apart from having had its boundaries extended to include part of what had been No-Man's Land and huts erected on the additional area, the British compound seemed to have altered little. Even the football had to be punted about between the same two huts. Superficial impressions, however, were misleading, for life inside the same old wires had changed enormously. The prisoners had erected an organisation which in most important respects ran their lives smoothly and efficiently, whereas the Germans, with all outward panoply of power as much in evidence as before, seemed to have lost the initiative and retained only a vestige of effective control.

No sooner had we been conducted through the gate than British military police took over and ushered us into a room strategically placed in the near end of the first stable. There, details of name, number, unit and Kommando were recorded, a type of documentation which would have been invaluable back in Salonika where it would have turned up particulars of missing men.

My bunk was in one of the newer huts. The room was heated by a small central stove around which most of the occupants spent most of each day, arguing or playing cards, the weather outside being for the most part cold and damp. The company contained the usual assortment of Aussies, Kiwis and Pommies, augmented by the presence of a Yank, and of a Mexican, who, permanently blue-faced and generally goose-pimpled, rarely moved from his perch on a top bunk, from whence, while lying on his stomach, he could gaze directly down at the stove. By the time I had settled in, the whole compound began to reveal that it was no longer safe to assume that every Anzac and Pommie was part of the left-overs from Balkan defeats. A good sprinkling had been taken in the desert, some of them survivors from Tobruk, and had spent most of their captive months in Italy, from whence they had been moved into Austria on the collapse of Mussolini's regime, bringing their erstwhile jailors into bondage with them. On two things most of these men were unanimous: that the Italians were kaput and lacking the will to defend either their own land or their own prisoners; and that Italian bread had been wonderful compared with German pumpernickel.

With the threat of imminent bunker poised over my head, one of my first tasks had to be to get rid of my letters. Contacting the engineer to whom the one was addressed presented no problem. Police information took me straight to his bunk, and from there an interesting trail which brought me face to face with men I had lost track of since Piraeus and Salonika led right back to my own hut, where the object of my search was warming his backside in front of the stove.

Delivery of the second letter proved far more frustrating, since a peculiarity of the camp guaranteed an even tougher job in slipping a letter from the British compound into the French one than in smuggling it into Stalag. All contact was blocked by strong British pickets. Tom Bowman had entrusted me to deliver an envelope to a mate on the staff of the French enclosure. What should have been an interesting, easy matter turned into a cat-and-mouse game of trying to persuade or outwit my own countrymen.

Having learned from experience that, in times of scarcity, fellow-prisoners could reveal all the hogging, hoarding and racketeering characteristics of any other type of society, a rigid control of barter prices had been introduced. The French were in the doghouse for violation of the rules, and pickets kept a stranglehold on the approach to their quarters. Argue as I would, appeal to the police office as I did, there was no begging, blustering or barging one's way through the gate. After a couple of days I gave up, and, fixing the envelope to a piece of firm cardboard of the same size, I tossed it under the slouching feet of a passing Frenchman, on the other side of the fence. He picked it up, glanced at the address and gave a 'V' sign. Next morning, around stoves, on Appell, and in the water queue, the British rocked with laughter over a huge joke: during the night, the pickets had got dead drunk on some potent home-brew, and had had to be withdrawn.

The threatened spell in the bunker did not materialise. It was obvious that there were no empty bunkers to spare. Offenders already convicted and sentenced for crimes and breaches of discipline more serious than innocent letter-smuggling were tea-drinking and card-playing in almost every hut, while they waited, far from patiently, for others to move out of 'solitary'.

The previously empty neighbouring compound consisting of the remainder of the stables was crammed to bursting-point with Russian prisoners. There was no access between them and their British neighbours, from whom they were separated by a formidable barbed-wire fence. On the Russian side, especially around the square doorway of the nearest huts, knots of men waited patiently for the tins and packages tossed over by their more affluent neighbours. The Russians being in receipt of no regular mail and parcels, there was no danger of unfair trading and pickets bedevilling the relationships through that fence. Familiarity and long practice had produced a traffic more akin to charity than trading.

Pleasant as it was to hang on to one's bunk until the very last moment before dashing for morning Appell with a greatcoat hastily thrown over pyjamas, and to return to it as soon as the parade was dismissed, Stalag was in some respects a harder place to live in than an Arbeitskommando. It was true that there was much more of interest than there had been two years earlier, and that the company was much more varied, comprising a cross-section of the most interesting people from scores of working camps as well as from Stalag itself, where many with entertaining and unusual talents had been retained. One heard news of camps one was unlikely ever to visit, learned of characters one would never meet; one talked to men who had still been free, in America, Down Under, and in Britain, long after one had forgotten what freedom was like, and listened to tales of battles not long fought. But the one ingredient which was missing was the one Arbeitskommandos could supply as a compensation for work, a sense of belonging to and playing a part in a settled community with daily problems to overcome. Whatever common interests might bind the inmates of Stalag, they could not override nor remove the knowledge that almost everyone was a bird of passage, that each man would soon, in his turn, as dictated by the Germans, leave to pursue his individual life under very different and unforeseeable conditions in once more strange surroundings.

Most of my time was spent stretched on my bunk reading books borrowed from the extensive library which fed all the tea-chests sent to working camps. When I got bored I joined in the never-ending discussions, which always seemed to end in arguments, around the stove. One of the chief debaters was an Aussie with an impediment in his speech. One morning the debate, about the apparently chequered career of the Australian cruiser *Sydney*, reached the heated stage and was narrowed down to a straight confrontation between several men on the one side and the big, dark, curly-haired stammerer on the other. Being outnumbered and unsupported drove up the Digger's temperature and aggravated his difficulty in shooting out the words with which to blast his opponents. It might have helped if the ship had been christened with a name beginning with any other letter but 'S'. Every time he came to the word, and he made no effort to avoid it or to find a substitute, there was an agonising pause while he struggled to hurl the word out. Finally came a stage where everyone, disputants and bystanders, could stand it no more, so certain did it seem that the man would collapse. He stood there, quivering lips distorted, head tilting farther and farther back, with veins standing out like whipcords on a neck and forehead literally purple. We stared at him helplessly, afraid he would burst. He made it, and we breathed again. His head came forward, the swollen veins subsided, and the colour slowly ebbed from his face. Uncomfortably, his adversaries left him to his double triumph of clinching argument and victory over his impediment.

That Digger was a character in the compound, quite apart from the obvious distinction of his handicap. Whether he noticed me, just another passing hut-mate with another unusual accent, is doubtful, but, had either of us been able to read the future, we would have studied each other with some interest. We were to meet again, far from Wolfsberg or any Arbeitskommando, under circumstances neither of us could have anticipated or considered possible.

Understandably, since the German aim was to reduce the resident population of Stalag to as low a figure as possible, and to curtail the stay-over time of passers-through, nothing appreciable had been done to improve comfort during my long absence. Hot water for tea could still only be obtained by queuing with tall, enamel jugs outside the boiler house in the far end of the last hut, in exactly the same way as on the memorable night of the first food parcel issue. Each hut sent a couple of men to bring back hot water which could then be brought back to the boil on hut stoves. The issue was supposed to start after morning Appell had been stood down. That never happened. When the guards cleared each hut for parade, the water-carriers, almost to a man, set off with their jugs, not on to the parade ground, but across or past it, to line up at a door situated in the end of the very hut against which the Kommandant would stand to survey his charges.

The assembled parade had no need to resort to the old tricks of ducking and dodging to defeat the count. Everyone knew that as many as twenty men would be missing, tightly bunched around the corner of the building framing the dignified figure of the Kommandant, together with his entourage and the British 'Inner Circle'. The substantial discrepancy seemed not to detract in the least from the Germans' ability to dismiss the parade with apparent unconcern. In addition, it was not uncommon to return straight to one's hut only to find a neighbour still soundly sleeping.

One morning we had better than normal entertainment when the water queue was taken by surprise. The count had actually begun. A bored guard walked a little too far for the security of the carriers. Warned by their lookout, the truants dropped their jugs and scattered. What followed was pure pantomime. Guards disappeared at the double around both ends of the hut and through its central archway in an effort to cut off the watermen. Just as in the liveliest of French farces, khaki-clad prisoners and field-grey sentries, pursued and pursuers, burst into view and vanished from sight, the prisoners belting along as fast as their legs could take them, the guards competing with each other in yelling out instructions which no one heeded. Apart from several who managed to submerge themselves in the by-then disorderly ranks of the parade, the panting watermen were eventually cornered, one by one, and lined up against the opposite hut.

All pretence that the Kommandant knew how many inmates he had in the compound was openly abandoned a day or two later. I cannot swear that the words attributed to the Kommandant were actually spoken, for, as usual, he addressed the parade through the interpreter, with words audible only to the dignitaries in his immediate vicinity, and my place was at the end of the lines. What the interpreter caused to be announced, and there was ample evidence that he didn't invent the announcement, was that the Kommandant would be pleased if anyone getting out of camp would kindly let him know and not keep him guessing. The parade was in an uproar, with men hanging helplessly round each other's necks in their anguish. Alongside me a wrinkled Kiwi who had omitted to put his teeth in was unashamedly licking in the tears from the corners of his mouth. The Kommandant stood composedly surveying the scene, as dignified and unmoved as ever. When the noise had subsided sufficiently for his voice to be heard, the interpreter continued:

'The Kommandant means, of course, after the man has gone, not before.'

The afternoon of that same day demonstrated the truth that the prisoners, though unable to escape, were, to a large extent, in charge of their own compound. Three men had been released from the bunker and escorted to the compound to collect their kit preparatory to the obligatory journey to a Straflager where they would serve the second, longer part of their sentences. Foolishly trusting, the escort had released them from close custody at the compound gates, and optimistically waited for them to return. When the prisoners didn't show up, the Germans made a search of barrackrooms and compound, without success. Calling in every available guard, they went through the place with a fine tooth-comb, ordering everyone out of huts and marshalling them into the narrow gulley alongside the wires. Fortunately for the game the afternoon was mild and sunny. The prisoners were not averse to fresh air and, just in case things became a bit dull, took not only themselves but also a fair supply of raspberry-blowing instruments along.

While banjos strummed and trumpets blared, tables were brought out and arranged just inside the gate. Long lists covering many pages were laid on the tables. One at a time we filed past, displaying our discs for checking. It was a slow business as officers examined each disc and turned from page to page to verify and tick the numbers. Sometimes proceedings came to a halt as a disc was produced clearly bearing a number already as clearly ticked off. A conference would then ensue, for there was obviously no way, apart from starting from scratch, by which they could check whether a wrong number had been marked or whether they were seeing the same disc a second time. 'Helpful' prisoners called out their own numbers in passing, in their enthusiasm not infrequently getting them the wrong way round, something easily done when using the German formula for reading off four-figure numbers. Other men were naturally clumsy, while others again were understandably nervous in face of such an impressive display of Wehrmacht uniforms, so it was only to be expected that discs

142

were dropped and occasionally kicked under tables by shuffling feet.

After passing the table check the prisoners were let through another gate past sniffing dogs into an empty enclosure where, years earlier, the reception marquee had stood. Leaving us to our own devices, our music and our chatter, the Germans concentrated on a renewed onslaught on the empty huts. It availed them nothing. Before finally giving up, they repeated the list-checking exercise as they fed us back to our billets.

The ease with which the Germans could be outwitted, in spite of the heavy concentration of troops, watch-towers and fences, made for an interesting life and served to raise our spirits. What it also did was to highlight the sheer futility of any serious attempt at escape. The enemy could well afford to allow us our frustrating pranks. Every time we witnessed the humiliation of our captors and gloated over the wounds to their pride, every time we listened to the innumerable tales of men who had been at large for days and rejoiced in their achievements, we imbibed the truth that in each last resort the Germans were the final victors and that the most the prisoners could attain to was causing the maximum amount of annoyance and diverted energies before inevitable surrender. Memories of an afternoon the guards had wasted trying to unearth three men who were still in their midst might entertain us long after the war was over, but prisoners were still prisoners even when an embarrassed Kommandant couldn't produce them at will.

It is doubtful if any of the hilarious cat-and-mouse games in Stalag had any direct connection with a single genuine attempt to escape. The camp was bulging with the biggest concentration of schemers among the thousands of men belonging to Stalag XVIIIA, but the range of schemes played out in Wolfsberg was unlikely to contain many concerned with breaking out of Stalag's defences as a preliminary step to freedom. More probable was that a fair number of men had arrived there as a necessary prelude to finding their ways to Arbeitskommandos which might prove better and nearer launching pads than the ones they had left. Why break out from a Stalag when the Germans were only too eager to transport one in comfort to a camp forty, fifty or even sixty miles nearer the objective, and there to take one outside the wires daily on pain of punishment for non-compliance? The hub of the forced labour system, Stalag, was the one place in which to gain knowledge of the whereabouts and prevailing conditions in the widespread network of camps. Information collected from the hundreds of men briefly passing through was available about the location, type of work, recreational facilities, scale of food, attitudes of Kommandants and employers, and escape prospects of almost all working camps.

My ambition was still to obtain a move towards or into the Alps and on the edge of the camp concentration and, provided the reputation of the camp were not too awful, I had no great reservation about the nature of employment. A friendly Australian, with a staff job in Stalag and in a position to ferret out advance information of exit-lists, undertook to look out for my interests.

Meanwhile I stuck my nose into books, joined those discussions which roused my interest, and roamed the compound. The Two-Up schools were no longer the distinctive feature they had been, football was still played in the same fashion on the same elongated pitch, and a new, daily attraction was the open-air practice of a small banjo band, led and drilled by one Artie Albro. His short, dark hair was close-cropped, with a central parting painted on in white paint. He would stand his sweating team in line facing him and put them through their musical drill like any sergeant-major, and with as little respect for their feelings – barking orders, handing out abuse and the occasional compliment, and displaying a wide repertoire of colourful language. The music, of no mean standard, was still but a minor part of the whole show.

One half of the first hut had been converted into a theatre. The resident company, deliberately built up over the years by their retention in Stalag where their talents might be enjoyed by representatives of all camps, put on a show each Sunday evening and, since the hall couldn't hold everyone, priority of attendance was given to the new arrivals passing through on what in most cases would be their only and last visit to the sophisticated life. The music, singing and sketches were of high standard, with sets and costumes wonderfully contrived from almost nothing; and the shows were geared to an audience as capable of appreciating the aesthetic as of lapping up the bawdy. They ended with two items which, for me, provided the best entertainment of the evening: 'Confessions' and 'Forecast'.

144

For the 'Confessions' programme the speaker told of his own experiences. As often as not, the experience was that of an unsuccessful escapee, the lecture being a good opportunity to enable as many would-be escapers as possible to hear at first-hand the nature of the hazards of fugitive life. Such a speaker had been due to give us the benefit of his experiences on my first Sunday in Stalag. Unfortunately, our hosts had other plans for him and he was unavoidably detained.

The substitute, pressed into service at short notice, filled the breach admirably. His claim to fame was that he could speak with more authority than most on the relative drawbacks of life in a military glasshouse, a civilian jail, and a P.O.W. camp. In between the many unscheduled breaks when he buried his head on his arms and shook with uncontrollable laughter, which overflowed among the audience, he let us into the secrets of a past extending back through World War I and, for his pains, poverty and imprisonment for debt in the inter-war years. For the record, he graded the different types of incarceration in the following order of undesirability: civilian jail, glasshouse, and then P.O.W. camp, with the reservation that P.O.W. imprisonment was in a class of its own, there being no fixed sentence to serve. At my second concert the confessions were those of a New Zealand radio announcer. Nothing could have provided a greater contrast to the preceding lecture.

Somewhere in or around Stalag, the 'Inner Circle' had access to a secret radio capable of picking up B.B.C. broadcasts, and it was news from that source which formed the basis of the 'Forecast' programme. With look-outs posted to ensure that no Germans interrupted, a large map was shown on the stage. After bringing us up to date with the war news, the speaker assessed the strategic implications and then, sticking his neck out, gave his forecast of what the next moves were likely to be. Far more important than whether his crystal ball was clear or misted was the rare chance it gave to study the cumulative effect of the innumerable nibbles the Russians had taken out of the huge bulge of the peak German advances. The previously incomprehensible bites began to make a pattern. Since, long before, names such as Moscow, Kiev and Rostov had dropped out of the news to be superseded by unknown places, all perspective had been lost in the ceaseless effort to understand the importance of battles waged in the vast expanse of Russia.

10

On 11th November I left Stalag. My number had come up. My contact had assured me I was bound for a paddock where the prospects were reputedly not too black, and roughly in the desired direction. The new camp was at Marburg, on the Yugoslav border. I recalled the stretcher cases removed from the prison-train.

On the journey a knowledgeable Stalag regular attached himself to me. In a short space of time he was threatening to become what I had never had in all my captive days, a regular partner and combine mate. That suited me, for, although I was instinctively inclined to choose my own mates, and even to do without one rather than endure one not of my own selection, he was an earthy character with an obvious flair for coping with the immediate present.

There was a long walk in the dark from the town of Marburg, the major part of the way following the railway track well after it had left the town. Unlike my two previous working camps, our destination was lit by perimeter lights, picking out buildings and wires – an unwelcome sight, too reminiscent of Piraeus, Salonika and Wolfsberg and holding out small hope of the relatively cosy, intimate conditions of Weissenbach. We continued along one side of the lighted square. Where the lights ended the wires proceeded on indefinitely into the darkness. An armed guard stood at a gate leading through the unlighted stretch of wire. He bore a rifle but his uniform was black and not of the normal military cut. The oddness was accentuated by the presence of a Wehrmacht sentry in regulation field-grey gazing down at us from his tower at the corner of the illuminated square. The unusual-looking sentry checked us through the gate. We trudged the length of another side of the brightly lit square and ended up turning left again into an enclosure with the third side of the camp on our left, and, on the right, a long, wooden building comprising the separate guards' quarters.

Chapter 6

THE FACTORY

The camp bore little resemblance to either of my two previous Arbeitskommandos, for, in lay-out and organisation, a better comparison would have been with Stalag. Not only did it really have a compound, but the three buildings it contained took up less than half its space, although the two wooden barrack huts were each twice as large as the one at Weissenbach. Those two huts were side by side, close to, and parallel with, the wires facing the German quarters, which themselves, simply by virtue of being outside the compound and under a separate roof, provided a novel departure from anything I had known before. The considerably smaller toilet hut, lying at right-angles to the end of the second barrack building, was a vast improvement; in addition to the expected taps and troughs, it boasted hot water and a simple shower, while the latrines were separate compartments with flushes.

The design of the big huts was simplicity itself. A wide, central corridor ran the whole length, terminating at either end in double doors leading to the compound, while on both sides doors opened into square rooms accommodating twenty-four prisoners each. The double-tier bunks ranged round the walls left room in the centre for two tables and a number of stools. As I took my place on the only vacant bunk, an upper one, in the room allocated to me, two things struck me: it felt very warm in spite of the open door, and the number of men sprawled about their bunks or grouped at the tables must have been about a full complement, something which would have seemed very odd in the Big Room at Weissenbach at that time of evening. The explanation for the heat was not far to seek. Just inside the door stood a square-sided stove.

Since I was the only one of the new intake billeted in the room, I had the undivided attention of the men for the rest of the evening. They were eager for news, whether of the war, of Stalag, of my previous camps, or of long-parted friends, for none of them seemed to have seen the skies over Wolfsberg since they had passed through Stalag two-and-a-half years earlier. I would have preferred to have learned something of what I had let myself in for by joining their company but I had to be content with gleaning stray items of information dropped in the course of answering the questions flung at me.

'Which Arbeitskommando are you in?'

I stared at the questioner. He had been in the place a couple of years, so why did he ask me, a newcomer?

'There are three Kommandos here, 64/GW, 65/GW and 66/GW. Which is yours?'

The business was beginning to make a bit of sense. Every working camp had a number, but I'd never heard of three with three different numbers all under one roof or behind one set of wires. In the room were members of all three Arbeitskommandos, just mixed up together with no means of telling one from another. As for myself I had no inkling of which party I was meant to reinforce. Three firms of contractors, each based in Graz, employed prisoners from the camp: Beiers, Heigl und Schwab, and Koschak. Apart from Beiers's work being largely concerned with maintenance of the railway line, all three firms seemed to have fingers in a variety of odd-jobbing or construction pies connected with a factory, within whose perimeter the Lager was sited.

I had not been snuggled down under my blankets very long before my hands started to scratch at my neck. It took about ten minutes for me to arrive at the revolting truth. Sitting up suddenly, I flung the blankets back in one movement. Scuttling across the pillow, or rather, across the striped towel I had lain over it, were a couple of red bed-bugs.

'You've got bugs in this place.'

"You've said it, Taff. There was no point in telling you. It's always funnier when they find out for themselves.'

Bed-bugs are not in the same league as body-lice, at least not in my experience, and I'd had plenty at Mustapha Barracks in Alexandria, where, after a first night spent racing them along the barrackroom table with the aid of straws, it had been routine to draw a blowlamp from the stores twice a week and burn out every joint in the dismantled iron bedsteads. Drastic as that treatment was, it served only to keep the pests under some sort of control. Unlike lice, bugs do have the decency to leave one alone in the daytime, off one's bed, and don't resort

148

to riding around in clothing. Their unendearing habit of favouring the neck for their nibbles, makes them relatively easy to repulse, but at the same time serves to emphasise their nauseous nature. The neck normally lies not far from the nose, and men are inclined to turn in their sleep; the smell of a squashed bed-bug is distinctive and revolting. There were some drawbacks to not having Kommandant and guards under the same roof as their charges. Recalling the haste with which Baldy had brought in the delousing unit, I suggested:

'Why not collect a box-full and dump them in the Jerry compound?'

'I expect they've got their own.'

I doubted it.

Wherever men had had access to bread and to a stove some few slices had always been transformed into toast, the number depending on how many men had both time and patience to take their turns on a homemade toasting fork in front of the red glow inside the small stove door. In Thesen, as the camp was called (after the nearest surburb of Marburg), things were managed much differently, and better; in the scramble to get breakfast in time for morning Appell, the toast looked after itself. The infallible invention of an unsung genius catered for everyone in every room, never ruined or blackened a precious slice, and gave an automatic announcement when each individual piece was done to perfection. The only thing it couldn't do was to brown both sides at once. If a round of soggy bread was pressed firmly against side, back, or front of the stove it stayed there until the side being toasted dried out to an even, appetising brown. Then it dropped off leaving the untoasted side in perfect state to receive the same treatment. The toaster never broke down, and there was only one simple rule for operation: never place your bread under a slice already on the toaster, otherwise that one, being cooked first, would knock yours to the floor. If the toaster was fully engaged, the lower half of the round chimney-pipe gave equally good results.

At Appell, the prisoners in Thesen got the worst of two worlds: they were messed around on parade just as in Stalag while the Kommandant assured himself he'd got all the men he was supposed to have, and then they had to turn out for work. Both in the valley and in Weissenbach counts had been more frequent throughout the day, but they had been informal affairs normally lasting only minutes. At Thesen the Kom-

mandant would keep us waiting and then would follow a somewhat less interesting and less stimulating, small-scale version
of the fun and games at Wolfsberg, as guards discovered there
were men still in bed or in the toilets. On cold, wet days, after
a day's cold, wet work, it wasn't funny.

The first morning's parade was an overcoat one, with a
persistent drizzle. From what I had heard the previous night, I
fully expected the prisoners to be drawn up in three separate
sections, corresponding to the appropriate Kommandos. That
was not so; there was just one long column of three, comprising over two hundred men. Outside the wires, on two sides,
black-uniformed guards, one accompanied by a dog, passed
on patrol or stopped to study the parade. Straight ahead, a
passenger train disgorged its entire load of men and women to
be checked through the same gate by which we had entered the
night before. The disembarked passengers hurried down past
the wires to our left. But even after the last of the passengers
had disappeared somewhere behind us, the path alongside the
railway still held a steady stream of pedestrians.

The parade was finally dismissed and we were ushered out
through the compound gate and into the enclosure dividing the
prisoners' quarters from those of the guards. Awaiting us, in
addition to soldiers, were a number of civilians with yellow
armbands. Men milled around in total disorder as, one by one,
parties were assembled and marched off, some by guards,
others by civilians. My new-found friend of the train and I
were among the last to leave, in charge of a civilian, and
accompanied by four others of the new intake. Outside the gate
of the enclosure we joined the thinned-out line of civilians, and
turned left. The dirt path turned into a concrete road after
only a few yards. To the right were low office buildings, pre-
fabricated structures, behind whose windows clerks and
draughtsmen were already at their desks and drawing boards.
Rising behind the offices, the valleyed roofs of larger sheds left
no doubt that there was a factory of some importance.

Our boss conducted us on to the muddy verge some thirty
yards short of the end of the offices. A little farther on the road
was blocked by the main factory gate, at which a knot of black-
uniformed factory police scrutinised the passes of everyone
entering or leaving: the factory had indeed to be of importance
to warrant such vigilance. We had arrived at our work site, the
rubble of a demolished brick building between the road and the

150

parallel factory fence, behind which tall conifers, stretching into a dark distance, cast a gloomy, dripping shade. We had to clear the rubble and sort the bricks, a job which, at the rate we set about it, could last for weeks.

Through the trees on the far side of the wires, the works police passed on their frequent patrols, armed with rifles like our own Wehrmacht guards. More often than not the policeman would stop and watch us through the wire grill. Instinctively, without a word said, we would stop work and stare back. The civilian boss vanished once or twice, and that was also a signal for work to stop. At the main gate, a huge man, obviously the chief of police, with a uniform carrying enough braid and medals to do credit to at least a rear-admiral, paid us more staring attention than we considered necessary, so when he stared at us we also stopped work and stared deliberately back. It was cold standing about, but the consensus of opinion was that if they expected us to work unsupervised or supervised by works police it was well worth a cold from standing idle on the squelchy ground. When the boss next returned it was plain there'd been a conference, for he stayed at his post. Across the road, clerks, who had taken more than a passing interest in the situation building up outside their windows, dropped their eyes back to their ledgers.

The camp was in the area of a factory which, from the number of workers of both sexes to-ing and fro-ing, the imposing apparatus for ensuring that no one, not even our guards, got in or out without careful scrutiny of papers, the size of the recently constructed buildings, and the heaps of coiled-metal shavings strewn around, could hardly have been turning out anything so innocuous as pots and pans. The factory fence formed the camp perimeter on two sides, from which the other two sides were visible for every yard of their length, and that, in effect, meant we were guarded day and night by two separate lots of armed sentries. It had never been pleasant to be held in a compound by the Wehrmacht; to be patrolled as well by armed civilians employed by our bosses was an outrage.

Even more disconcerting was the realisation that, in the event of an air raid, we would be a helpless part of the target. That thought was not unnaturally followed by another: that the camp, contrary to our collective past experience, was lit up at night and might have been deliberately placed where it was for the very purpose of deflecting bombers.

Before the morning was over my friend had more or less made up his mind to get back to Stalag, by hook or by crook, and was labouring far harder at trying to persuade me to do the same along with him than either of us were at slinging slimy, cold bricks. His hut had bed-bugs, too, and he'd seen all he wished of Marburg. He'd go over the wires, if there was no other way. By lunchtime he had me wavering, and had not the location of Marburg fitted into my rough plans it is certain that lunchtime itself would have convinced me to set my back on the place.

The camp had no common-room or mess-room, a fact which accounted for the presence of so many men in my room on my arrival, for it was the only place they had to spend their time and eat their meals. The lunch, when it belatedly arrived in one large container, was dumped on a low platform between the near ends of the two huts, and abandoned. There was no queue for the contents, a ladle and a mess of soggy, pulped potato. Other than the bread ration, that was the only food supplied that or any other day, the total contribution by the Germans towards the feeding of their prisoners, yet the inmates, most of whom seemed to have inhabited the camp for years, appeared unconscious of anything lacking.

My friend translated his intentions into action and his persistent frequenting of the sick parade produced the desired result. His zeal in campaigning for me to join him in trying our joint fortunes in Lagers new stayed unabated. There was no sign that his allegiance and friendship might grow cold and be transferred to another more amenable subject among his new room-mates. In spite of being thoroughly depressed and revolted by the place, I felt reluctant to throw away the distinct advantage gained by the move to Marburg in the context of my plans. Had the sole criterion been, as it would have been some months earlier, that of physical comfort, I would have fallen in with his schemes. Not all my feeling of being unsettled could be laid to the account of the bugs, the food and the factory; their contribution to my mood lay in the fact that they offered the wrong climate for someone beginning to feel the horrible, yawning gap which would go on for ever in the correspondence with my ex-fiancée. I had learned the worst: she had married another.

On the evening before his departure my friend tracked me down in my room to say his farewells and to renew his persuasions and pleadings: he would wait for me in Wolfsberg; he would be there for three weeks in any case; should he get slung out, he would leave word where to find him, and smooth my path to his new camp. A plain refusal to follow, or an evasive answer were things he would not take. I was sorry to see him go, and for a time I missed him. It is debatable whether Heigl und Schwab felt the same way.

Whatever else the camp lacked, it had a library; not a mere tea-chest of books as at Weissenbach, but half a room of closely-packed shelves, presided over by a short, thin, bespectacled Kiwi keen on revealing his treasures to any kindred soul. He, pursuing his congenial occupation with missionary zeal, and *Rogue Herries*, did most towards reconciling me to staying in Thesen. *Rogue Herries* was followed by *And Quiet Flows the Don*, by *The Don Flows Home to the Sea*, and by *Stately Timber*. Closing eyes and mind to all else, I did my best to make up for the years the Jerries, the lice, the bugs and the Arbeit had eaten. The peculiar set-up in the camp, whereby all indoor activities were normally confined to one's room, around the fire and tables, or one's bunk, enabled the most insatiable bookworm to get away with it without being considered unsociable.

Heigl und Schwab shifted the scene of my labours right outside the factory wires to a more congenial setting deep in the forest. I became part of a small gang leaving the factory each morning, in charge of a civilian overseer, through the main gate. Outside, the road continued on for a couple of hundred yards before joining the highway leading left to the town of Marburg, and right to Celje, a fact easily verified by the blinds of trailer-towing buses depositing workers at the junction. After ambling along for about a mile in the direction of Celje, with dense woods of conifers flanking the road on both sides, we turned right along a rough track which went, for half a mile or more, into the forest between main road and main railway line.

There was a large clearing with positive signs that trees had only recently been removed. Part of the open space nearer the factory already held a number of huts, many of them with occupants – Russian, both men and women – and showed evidence that family life was being resumed under enemy direction and supervision. It was the nucleus of a village, a

Slav community brought into being in a remote setting well out of sight of the local population. Our labours were required for clearing more of the site, digging trenches for drainage and holes for electric poles, and preparing foundations for new, prefabricated, wooden huts. Both work and surroundings were a pleasant change. Most of the time one was left more or less free to tackle the allotted tasks at one's own pace, and the invigorating, interesting walk had to be undertaken four times a day, since the party returned to the Lager for the midday meal. My mood began to take a turn for the better.

Christmas came and went: my third behind wires. I hardly remember anything of it. There was the obligatory concert but, since the only place it could be held was in one of the draughty corridors, with the best will in the world it could hardly be a suitable event for infusing the sort of festive mood enjoyed at Weissenbach a year earlier. The winter itself, by no means severe except in bitter patches, left no great mark on the memory other than that two prisoners attempted an escape through the wires and the snow, and were recaptured the same day.

My own excursions outside the factory perimeter, as well as those of other working parties with whom I came in contact, served to increase my information both about the immediate locality and the location of Marburg in relation to the Alpine ranges and Northern Italy. The town had another name, more suggestive of its true position on the map than the one used by us and our captors. Its other name was Maribor, a name which at first hearing brought to mind Derby winners rather than a key garrison town. It was in fact the Yugoslav name for Marburg.

In 1938, the Nazis, with the active support of a large, vociferous, Austrian party, had annexed Austria by the Anschluss and incorporated it into the greater Third Reich, thus making it an integral part of metropolitan Germany. Later in the same year, using other methods and bringing Europe to the verge of armed conflict, only averted by the appeasement of Munich, they had added the Sudetenland of Czechoslovakia and 'liberated' another concentration of German exiles from alien domination. When, in 1941, Yugoslavia had been overrun, a section of Northern Yugoslavia with a large, vocal, German and Austrian minority had also been returned to the Austria from whose empire it had been lost in 1918. Maribor

154

lay in the area taken back into Austria and, for the first time, into the German Reich.

By the best reckoning I could make, the town lay about a hundred miles east of Trieste, the Adriatic port which had been the centre of agitation and contention similar to that which had smouldered in the Danzig area on the Baltic, and which had ostensibly provided the spark to set alight the whole conflagration. Profiting from the successes of their allies, the Italians had settled the running sore of Trieste by extending its hinterland as well as grabbing other slices of the Adriatic coast, just as the Germans had confiscated Maribor and its surrounds. If the Allied invasion of Italy followed the course I hoped it would, only a hundred miles at most would separate me from an area where both Italians, anxious to appear in good light with the invading forces, and Yugoslavs, keen to demolish Italian claims to the land, might be not averse to sheltering escaped British prisoners. That hundred miles, for the most part an extension of the Alps, would not be so inaccessible as farther west between Austria and Italy, and yet was sufficiently rugged to offer a possibility of evading recapture.

The width of the valley at Marburg gave a clear idea of what was immediately in front of one, exposing the options from which one would have to choose, both for the first move and for hiding up afterwards. Yet the more one studied the obstacles to be faced, the easier it was to see why escape attempts without aids such as disguise, papers, money and some little outside help, had to have only one ultimate result – recapture. At earlier camps what lay beyond the near-by hills had to be imagined. At Marburg one saw not only the hills but also a concentration of what things could lie in the valleys between them: rivers, railways, roads, villages, towns, glider fields, forced-labour camps and barracks, each one a hazard to the escapee and an ally to the pursuer.

The run of the valley was from the north-east to the southwest. Close under the hills to the east flowed the wide river Drava, its whole length easily watched and patrolled. From the river bank, meadows ran towards us for a couple of hundred yards without cover, right up to a high ridge which, following the river, seemed to run for miles in both directions. At the top of the ridge began the forest which blanketed the valley's width until it came to an abrupt halt two hundred yards short of the railway line. The foothills on the other side of the track were separated from it by a further half mile of meadows, several of which had been joined together to make a glider training field with half its length immediately over the railway from factory and Lager. The forest was also bisected by the main Celje–Marburg road running equidistant between river and railway. To the north the whole width of the valley was blocked by the town and its sprawling suburbs. Only the south-east showed no obvious obstacles or traps, and for that very reason one felt an instinctive reluctance to probe in that mysterious direction. The barrier in view, however high and disheartening, is at least capable of study and assessment. Acceptance of the tempting invitation to make for the shelter of the forest continuing down the valley from Thesen would still leave the problem of crossing railway and meadows at a point unreconnoitred, and might lead to a trap should road, river and railway converge.

Regular receipt of clothing parcels over a period of two years had resulted in my being well-stocked with underwear, night attire and toilet gear. Accordingly, I asked my sister to send nothing more unless specifically instructed. Success or failure, it was prudent not to leave stuff in the pipeline.

The days continued to lengthen and the weather grew milder. The time was approaching for food to be smuggled out in dribbles and hidden in the woods. The signal never came. The American and British armies stayed maddeningly bogged down around Naples, seven or eight hundred miles away, their progress stubbornly blocked in the narrow passes. Not only would the distance to journey be far too great; the enthusiasm of the Italians to shelter anyone would also be reduced.

Outside the main factory gate a paperseller took up his stand every morning as we came out to work. Newspapers were forbidden to prisoners, and civilian money, also forbidden, was needed to buy one. The sight of the papers within arm's reach was tempting; I was eager to catch up, and to keep up, with the news, and to extend my German reading now that Laurel and Hardy were no longer available as suppliers. The normal boss, of Slav origin, and inclined to be overawed both by his responsibilities and by his self-willed charges, at first resisted all my attempts to persuade him to buy me a German paper, even in spite of the bribes of an occasional cigarette; but tobacco finally induced him to part with some small coins. By getting through the crush at the gate in the van of the party I found the time spent waiting for the others to arrive could be usefully employed by pushing into the mêlée around the paperseller, sticking out an arm with my pfennigs, and saying 'Beobachter'. The newsman never let me down, the works police were too busy to notice, and our overseer turned his back.

The *Völkischer Beobachter* was the official organ of the Nazi Party, an imposing-looking paper which served as the mouthpiece for Hitler and Goebbels. Week after week, a study of the bulletins under the heading of 'Das Oberkommando der Wehrmacht Gibt Bekannt' showed no appreciable alteration of the front in Southern Italy. Frustratingly, although small maps of battle sectors were printed, the Germans refrained from ever relating the area of fighting to the whole peninsula or even to its foot. Part of their news technique was to tell their readers most of the truth, but at the same time to render it impossible for them to know whether that truth was good or bad, a victory (which they always claimed or implied it was), or a defeat (which they never admitted). The maps rarely showed a prominent place, only a jumble of unknown names, so that one only gained a clue as to which way the battle was swaying when close examination showed that a village to the bottom of a map was one which had figured towards the top a week earlier. As winter gave way to the spring on which I had set my hopes, the sketchy maps showed that there was little prospect of an Allied surge forward to Rome and Florence, and the imminence of the fall of the latter city was to be the signal for me to start my preparations. Even the anticipated breakout from Anzio proved a dud. The *Beobachter* did not depart from the truth in describing the pace of the Allied advance as snail-like.

The air forces did their best to make amends for the ground forces. Beginning with an isolated raid of some strength which passed within earshot, attacks on targets to the north of Marburg became a once- or twice-weekly feature of life. Up to that time, with the one exception of the sight of Ruhr refugees passing through Weissenbach after the dam-busting raid, we had seen nothing to indicate that bombardments of British cities were being repaid in kind. Suddenly, on cloudless mornings, the earth would begin to vibrate with the rumbling of engines throbbing their way towards Vienna and Wiener Neustadt. If one could light on the right spot in the sky one could pick up momentary glints of reflected sun as each plane passed. It was impossible to count them; they were too far away and almost impossible to detect without the tell-tale glints. The vibrations sweeping the valley, coming as they did from this invisible source, magnified the impression of the numbers and might of the craft involved. Sometimes, long after they had passed and all sound had died away, vapour trails would be left drifting towards us, and, if the wind was right, the forest would seem to sprout silvery tinsel.

It was a peculiar sensation to reflect that several times a week hundreds of men who had never looked at the world from inside the wires of a prison compound were passing almost over our heads and in a matter of only hours would be eating their steaks in the same mess where they had enjoyed their breakfast eggs. The sound of the planes did much to reconcile me to the abandonment of my plans. For a time it seemed as if the decision not to get out of Thesen at the persuasion of my short-term friend had been a wrong one; but that line of thought didn't persist long, for, as the weather improved, so did life in Thesen.

Batches of replacements had begun to contain prisoners moved in from Italy. Many had first experienced captivity as long before as I had myself; others had been taken in more recent fighting, including the not-too-distant battle for Sicily; while one or two could even speak of having been in England after cigarettes had risen to the astronomical price of half-a-crown for twenty. Shoulder badges of red cloth with titles picked out in white began to mingle with the brass and bronze of Greek campaign days. Some of the new blood had fought in battles which had been victories for their armies, if not for them personally, and even those taken long before in the desert had behind them the experience of being moved by their captors first to Italy and then to Austria, before the tide of our own advances. With the appearance of the bombers, such men felt they were once again entering just another stage of retreat into an ever-shrinking Reich. Their general attitude to imprisonment was somewhat different from that of the majority of longer term inmates of Thesen: to them, Thesen was little more than another staging-post, and they would make the most of it while they were there, ignoring or bypassing most established P.O.W. tradition.

One or two of the 'Italian' prisoners formed part of my gang, first Sergeant Rose of the Leicesters and Sergeant Honeywell of the Indian Army, followed shortly afterwards by a number of Aussies who seemed to bob up and disappear in a baffling manner. The disconcerting habit of being of the gang one day and nowhere in sight the next was attributable to two causes: they had been conditioned to captivity in Italy, where, apparently, regular daily toil had not been the rule; and also they were taking advantage of a very welcome change in our lot.

Our employers, Heigl und Schwab, had the numerically lowest quota of prisoner labourers of the three firms of contractors. There had been rumours of them pulling out from Thesen in favour of new contracts elsewhere, and of their labour force being distributed among the two remaining firms. However someone in the hierarchy at Graz had decided to spread the available work among the reduced labour force still on the firm's books, and to extract a reasonable amount of work out of us by allotting each man a fixed contract to fulfil. Whatever the original reasons or ultimate reactions of the instigators of the scheme, the new arrangement suited us admirably, for it reduced the working day to only about three hours. Jobs previously spun out all day were completed in less than half a day on the firm guarantee that we would be taken back to camp as soon as every man was finished.

A natural consequence of the new programme was the splitting of the gang into two, one half working till midday, the other in the afternoon, both escorted and supervised by the same overseers, who had not been accorded the new privilege. The contract arrangement was confined to a comparatively small number and in no way affected the vast majority in the camp. It thus became possible to swop from one gang to another and even to work only on alternate days provided one found a willing partner. Guards and bosses at first displayed obvious concern at the constantly changing faces, but soon became inoculated with the idea that all they had to worry about was that they returned the same numbers to camp as they had taken out. Time and repetition convinced them nothing was very much amiss. Gradually the composition of our small group stabilised at eight men, most of them Australians.

Life in camp differed fundamentally, and for the worse, from what I had known in my two previous camps. In both of the former the entire restricted set-up had been geared to community living, with everyone knowing and mingling with everyone else. Not so at Thesen, where there was no common-room or common living quarters, and little reason for the whole complement to meet except at Appell. At work, which occupied most of the day for most men, the small parties had no contact with each other and were often literally miles apart; one larger gang left by train each morning immediately after roll-call and was not seen again until well into the evening. I doubt if any inmate knew half his fellows by name.

The compound of brown earth was hardly used in winter, most men having had enough of fresh air and exercise at work. With the advent of spring, and assisted by a combination of factors, the dull routine of work, to barrackroom, and so to bed, began to give way to a broadening of interests, especially sport, for which the camp, probably because of its larger size, had a greater variety of equipment than had Weissenbach. Ingenuity and resourcefulness, perseverance and bribery, ensured that the sports gear had maximum use.

Up to that time, the only seriously-indulged, regular pastime had been 'perving',* an exercise which devoted adherents pursued en masse twice daily, at lunchtime and in the evening, when the factory girls paraded their unpainted charms past the perimeter fence. In anticipation of their passing, the further doorways of both corridors became blocked with prisoners taking up position for the sport. Most were regulars whose enthusiasm showed no sign of waning despite the fact that works police kept the girls from dalliance with the forward, would-be suitors. For many a man the perv. parade provided a real compensation for being penned inside factory wires.

The passage of planes heading north to strike at the interiors of Austria and Hungary roused the authorities to set us to work constructing shelters. For a short period of intense activity, prisoners normally employed inside the factory area were joined by other parties, including mine, in order to open up large ditches into which concrete could be poured. In addition to giving us the opportunity to bury shovels, picks and even upturned barrows in large numbers, the crash programme focused our attention on an area of grass within the wires capable of serving as a full-sized football field. At the same time scheming minds began to concentrate on another plot of ground nearer the camp itself, an enclosure somewhat larger than a tennis court. A protuberance on the square of the factory

---

* Perv. v. (Eng. pervert): to ogle the opposite sex, gaze lustfully on unattainable members of the opposite sex, gain sexual stimulus from imagined contact with members of the opposite sex.

perimeter, it had stood unused although, since its only gate connected it with the work assembly area between guards' and prisoners' quarters, it may have been originally intended as part of the camp. The Kommandant found himself under continuous pressure to permit escorted parties to use the bigger ground for weekend sport and to make the smaller enclosure conveniently situated under the eyes of sentries already on duty, accessible most evenings. After an initial display of reluctance he yielded, and so we entered on a new era of sport.

It became a regular feature, on Sunday afternoons, for a game of soccer or rugby to be staged under the watchful eyes of sentries pressurised into sacrificing off-duty hours. The games, at first scratch matches between any bundles of men with energy and interest to spare, soon became organised and competitive: England played The Rest, Hut One challenged Hut Two, or, if the game was rugby, it was Anzacs v. Britain. As was only fitting for one whose regiment had produced the then Army Rugby Champions and who had played his last game in front of a three-quarter line which included two Welsh internationals and an Irish sprint champion, I revelled in the sport. It was a perfect complement to the more intellectual pastime of wading my way through the books the Kiwi librarian continued to bring to my attention. The two contrasting, compensating forms of recreation were, for me, ideal, stretching both mind and body at the very time when, thanks to the contract work, life was otherwise not the exhausting affair it had been previously. For men from the North of England, as well as for those from some of the Australian States, rugby meant Rugby League, not Rugby Union, and it was not long before a number of games were being played under the Northern code. For a South Walian even to mention Rugby League, except in condemnation and disparagement, had been a sin more deadly than doing the washing on Sunday, but my nonconformist background availed little and I adapted to the 'forbidden' rules with the best of them.

At work at the Ukrainian village, my Australian colleagues, particularly gunner George Cotter and Sergeant Poidevin began to take a proprietary interest in a delicate piece of work which they had obviously commissioned civilian plasterers to undertake. Two large, rectangular frames of battening, a couple of inches deep, with fine wire mesh nailed taut across the undersides, were being painstakingly filled in, fine layer after layer, with concrete. By the time I noticed that something was afoot, the fillings had set strongly enough to be carefully moved out of the shed where they had lain concealed. The answer Cotter gave my curious questions convinced me he'd gone barbed-wire happy. They were making a two-leaved table-tennis table out of concrete! As a table-tennis addict I wished all power to their elbows, but the very conception seemed impossible and outrageous, especially since the Lager where the table was to be set up was a good mile away, on the other side of doubly-guarded wires.

There was not the remotest chance of securing the services of a lorry or even of a bullock-wagon for transporting the heavy, bulky slabs, so we 'borrowed' one of the cumbersome, iron wheelbarrows strewn about the site. When the slabs were carefully laid across the barrow, face-to-face to avoid scratching and scoring, just about enough of the handles protruded to provide a difficult grip. With one man straining on the handles and the rest of the party bent double around the load to take the weight and prevent shifting, we staggered off over the tufty grass, avoiding tree-stubs and cunningly concealed potholes, and steered an erratic course along a forest track so rutted that both barrow and load had frequently to be lifted bodily over the deeper, muddier hollows. Once we had gained the tarmac of the main road the going became easier. The chief of works police studied us hard and long as we toiled up the approach road to his fortress, the smell of sweat and sweet victory in our nostrils. We could imagine the acid comments passing between the braided giant and his underlings as they watched the strange, heads-down, bottoms-up huddle of khaki. In spite of disparaging looks and vituperative words directed at our shuffling overseer, the police opened up. After that it was child's play to pass the less intensive but curious examination of sentries and Kommandant as we were checked into the compound.

The plasterers had played their part well: not a crack developed. Pieces of slate and plentiful water and elbow-grease, applied for days on end, produced perfect surfaces which were finished off with green paint, edged with white. Mounted on two tables cut down to the regulation height and set up in a room already cleared for the purpose, the slabs gave yeoman service.

Meanwhile other men had been at work making a net for

volleyball, a new-fangled game imported by a group of replacements. The court was set up in the small, unused enclosure and immediately became the daily rendezvous for the energetic. Bare-footed and clad only in shorts, Cotter, Poidevin, Jennings, Adams – the latter two, like Poidevin, Australian sergeants – and myself, thumped the soccer ball over the net until wrists began to ache and swell.

As the weather grew warmer cricket took over from soccer and rugby, the sessions culminating in a series of three Tests between Australia and England. I held my place, without disgrace, as opening bat for England, but the Aussies took the series without defeat, mainly because of the superb performances of a young Tasmanian who, with perfect timing and balance and an incredible eye for the ball, effortlessly lifted anything, fast or slow, overpitched or long-hopped, off toes or chest with complete impartiality. It was the sheer consistency of his batting which drove the nails hard into the coffin of British hopes and not, as some English supporters insisted, the persistent, vociferous croaking of the Australian 'crows' perched round the boundary intent on putting us off our strokes. The Aussie 'crows' barracked, bellowed and appealed whenever it suited them and whenever they could sense advantage, and were liberal in such unrestrained comments as, when a batsman missed a ball, 'you're swinging like a pub door at six o'clock', an allusion to their own licensing laws.

Soccer, rugby and cricket on Sundays, and volleyball for daily fare, did not complete the list of sports in which we could indulge. Cotter and his mates persuaded a civilian factory worker to turn a baseball bat, while boxing enthusiasts spun rope to encircle a ring for staging a tournament in the compound.

It had been a subject for wonder that so many rational, enterprising men had so long endured the bugs and starvation rations without more protest and more numerous attempts to work their tickets back to Stalag. The summer brought part of the answer. Some working parties, particularly the Beiers' rail gang, were on to a nice, profitable line in black-market food – mainly, of all mouth-watering items, in eggs and tomatoes – willingly parted with by nicotine-starved civilians who had also a sweet tooth for chocolate. Thanks to Paddy Roachock, a huge, bush-travelled Digger with the same brown-leather face as Seaman Aussie and George Cotter, I obtained more than my fair share of the goodies. In purely practical terms our combine was as one-sided as it appeared ill-suited: although a natural for ball games, I was a browser and bookworm; an enthusiast for chess, I had no time for cards other than to hold a hand while a player disappeared to attend to the impatient demands of nature. Paddy, on the other hand, was an avid card-player and, in the words of one of his compatriots, a rough diamond: yet he could eat his way through two books while I was savouring one. There could have been few more I-give-you-receive partnerships in Thesen, but it worked. At least once a week Paddy would return in the evening and unpack a haversack of eggs and tomatoes, whereas the sum total of my contribution was part of my chocolate and cigarette ration to augment his barter currency.

The most dramatic stir in our reawakening lives came suddenly and violently from outside. It had been transparent that whatever was being produced in the production sheds by the civilians was of direct importance to the German war-machine, and the more knowledgeable, longer-term prisoners had no hesitation in giving the product a name – propeller-bosses for all types of aircraft. That, if correct, could only mean helping to put Messerschmitts, Junkers, Dorniers and Heinkels into the air. There was resentment that our presence could be used to divert Allied attention from a vital target, and fear that the target might attract a hail of bombs. We were well aware that next-of-kin had been supplied with maps showing the location of Stalags, but it was pure speculation whether American and British High Commands knew the position of Arbeitskommandos, and to men who had long felt that they had already been used as expendable material in the pursuit of victory it seemed ill-advised to assume that any important enemy factory would be spared just for fear of casualties among a handful of prisoners.

Towards the end of a brilliant morning, we in our small party were kicking our heels on the Ukrainian site, impatiently awaiting return to the Lager. The first faint droning was subdued and suggestive of a small detachment of raiding planes making for home by the shortest route. The surrounding trees obstructed our view and baffled the sounds. the planes came in from the south, on a course bringing them directly over our heads. They were markedly lower than any seen before, the bulges of the engines clearly visible to the naked eye. We were still counting the close formation, arguing whether there were twenty-seven or twenty-eight planes, and whether they were Fortresses or Liberators, when the earth gave an almighty heave and all other sounds were obliterated by one terrific, prolonged explosion. In seconds it was over, the planes disappearing over the enormous cloud of smoke billowing up from the direction of the factory. Excited birds rose, calling wildly, and an old woman, apron to her praying face, scuttled past.

'Christ! The bloody factory! The camp!'

There were always men in the Lager, cleaning orderlies, the sick, the Senior N.C.O., the Vertrauensmann, shift workers. And the camp had no shelters. We hurried the boss along, hardly daring to imagine what we might find.

As we approached the factory the spreading pall of smoke darkened the sky, and the once-too-familiar smell of cordite tickled our throats and nostrils. The factory police, rather white about the gills, checked us in. The office buildings looked a shambles of broken walls and caved-in roofs, but over them the large area of roof of the nearest production shed still reared up, intact, not a single hole visible in its expanse of grey. We quickened our steps: the fewer hits on the factory, the greater the chance that the camp had suffered. Weaving through the curious, agitated civilians studying the damage, we came in sight of the guards' hut: intact, but for shattered windows. The bombs must have landed somewhere! The debris we had passed could have accounted for only a fraction. The camp came into sight. Behind the wires, a few prisoners were standing, hands in pockets, straining little more than their eyes to assess the effect the bombs had had on the factory.

The raid had wasted a fortune in expensive bombs dropped to little material purpose. The effects were negligible and production was not halted even for a day. But closer analysis revealed that the raiders had failed by only the narrowest of margins to carry out a feat of almost miraculous precision. Directionally the aim had been perfect and, had the release been made a split second earlier, not only would the bombs have wiped out all production sheds and administrative buildings with one sharp blow, they would also, incredibly, have done so while leaving both our camp and a similarly situated French prisoner compound in the diametrically opposite corner of the factory unscathed apart from the effects of blast. It was to be regretted that the Americans had so marginally failed to bring off the impossible, and it was too much to hope that a future raid could cleave another such clean path between the two defenceless prison camps contained in the target.

At next morning's Appell the Kommandant replied to the strong representations by Vertrauensmann and Senior N.C.O. concerning the vulnerability of the camp. He told us that in this war everyone was liable to be bombed, and as for our claim that the Geneva Convention was being flouted by siting a P.O.W. camp inside a war factory, he pointed out that the nearest front was at Naples, six hundred miles away. His only concession was that, in the event of future raids, prisoners in camp would be escorted out over the railway and the glider field towards the hills. The parade was dismissed and work parties sortied out to their usual toil.

On returning at midday it was no surprise to discover figures moving stealthily among the trees outside the perimeter fence, opposite the blasted offices and on the far side of the volleyball enclosure. All morning bombs had gone off. What was startling was that the figures glimpsed through the trees were colourful pyjama suits with broad stripes. The majority of bombs, having overshot the target, had fallen in the dense, close-packed pines. The Germans, with pragmatic, simple logic, evidently considered it not worthwhile to call in skilled, distant bomb-disposal units while local jails held a supply of expendable humanity. We wondered what types of offenders were handling the unexploded bombs – ordinary felons, political prisoners, deserters or captured partisans – and under what threat or bribes they had been induced to undertake the risky business.

The windows of my room faced directly towards the scene of the activity, and some of the explosions were so near that, prepare oneself as one would for the next bang, they invariably made us jump. Fortunately, the raid itself had disposed of all save one of the twenty-odd panes of glass while no one was in the room. One of my room-mates became the centre of unbelieving attention as he set up a mirror on the window frame and lathered his face for a shave with a cut-throat razor. We were all imagining variations on the same theme: he would be at the stage of tackling a tricky area of stubble, perhaps in the region of his Adam's-apple, when the next explosion would come, and we would be fishing his severed head from under a lower bunk. He was allowed to get no further than lathering-up: he saw the wisdom of the advice and abuse, and abandoned his plans.

A more ironically funny incident occurred a little later. Had the window remained intact, it would, at that time of a pleasant, warm morning, have been wide open for fresh air, and anyone finishing a mug of tea within arm's length of it would, from long habit, have tossed his dregs out through it into the compound. The window having been reduced to one, obstinate pane of glass, it needed no conference to decide there was no point in opening it that morning. There was a communal brew-up. The man sitting with his back to the window automatically swung his mug over his left shoulder, to shatter the only pane of glass which had resisted T.N.T. Habit dies hard!

Other, longer-lasting consequences of the raid soon began to show themselves. A substantial shelter was constructed, outside our wires but within the confines of the factory, batteries of 88s were moved in and mounted on the railway together with supporting searchlights, and Fokker-Wulf fighters began daily patrols on a triangular beat in the skies to the north.

The 88s, deadly as they had proved themselves to be at long range, both against ground and air targets, were impotent against the swarms of raiders which continued to penetrate past us following the mountain ridge to the east. They were well out of range. The fighter planes, although able to intervene, seemed to have negligible success. The gradually diminishing strength of the patrols suggested casualties and lack of replacements.

That all casualties were suffered in the air was refuted by the evidence of our own eyes. Even after the construction of the shelter, the camp continued to be evacuated, in accordance with the Kommandant's promise, during daytime raids. One morning we were being escorted back from the foothills when the fighter patrol approached down the valley, flying low in single file, unmistakably intending to land on the glider field. One by one they swiftly dropped from view. In anticipation of a close-up view of the squadron we quickened the pace. What we saw on entering the end of the field whetted appetites enormously. Two planes had crashed into each other, with no great benefit to either; another lay on its back; and a fourth, having failed to clear a gap in a hedgerow, stood delicately poised on its nose. The guards, sensing that our stares and comments would find little appreciation on the field, diverted us from the direct path back to camp and compelled us to make a detour. By so doing they treated the prisoners to the best sight of all. Halfway down the runway a column of thick smoke was rising from a plane which had shot across the road and struck a telegraph post. Both plane and pole were blazing merrily, while the disconsolate pilot paced up and down, helplessly slapping his thigh with his open palm.

Most days were still carbon copies of the hundreds which had dragged their courses before, but deadly routine was disintegrating and a sense of anticipation sweetened the air. The *Beobachter* made frequent references to the Atlantic Wall, and showed copious photos of Rommel inspecting impressive, impregnable parts of it. Replacements from Stalag reported that southern England had been sealed off and declared a forbidden zone. The words 'invasion' and 'Second Front', which had been bandied about in arguments for two long, weary years, even before Dieppe, gained new significance.

Waiting for the invasion made the last weeks of May and early June extremely nerve-racking; but for the sport they would have been unbearable. In Austria the weather persisted dry and warm; we were not to know the calendar of tides in the Channel. The fear that undue delay could make the difference of a whole year in the length of captivity was in the forefront of most minds. When the landings finally took place we learned of them the very same day, and no one doubted the tidings. Who actually received the news first, and from what source, was hardly worth enquiring: it had to be true, in much the same way that, in the disastrous winter of 1941–42, German claims that the Japanese had destroyed the American Pacific Fleet, had overrun Singapore and had sunk the *Prince of Wales* had been taken as gospel.

Being indifferent to the source of the news was not the same thing as being unmoved on its receipt or impervious to its implications. I will always remember exactly how, when, and where the joyous tidings reached me. It was after lunch and we were still within the factory on our way to work. A dinkum Aussie, tall, blond and suntanned, thrust his way through a group of civilians on the other side of the road, paused on the kerb and held his hand aloft to attract our attention. In another setting he could have been hailing a taxi.

'We've landed. The invasion's on.'

'Where?'

'Normandy.'

In the weeks which followed we prayed that the Channel would stay calm, and closed our minds to the insidious propaganda about the Vergeltungwaffen, the V1 already bombarding the south coast, and the V2, which, if the *Völkischer Beobachter* was to be believed, would be far more destructive and incapable of interception.

While all thoughts were concentrated on the happenings in the west, other news even more significant for my own personal plans arrived from the hitherto sluggish Southern Front: Rome had been taken and, at last, Florence was in the headlines. My cue had arrived. It was time to stir myself and resurrect my old plans for the Autumn Handicap. Opportunity might be about to knock. It did knock, but it was a far different opportunity from the one I'd imagined.

One occupied country had never stopped actively fighting its invaders. That country was Yugoslavia, and I was squatting on the edge of it. Even from that vantage point the situation seemed unreal, but the Germans had never succeeded in concealing that throughout their three-year occupation they had been troubled by partisan activity, or, as they preferred to express it, had been incessantly plagued by 'banditen'. If one had had the luck to select the right editions of the forbidden *Das Kleine Blatt* or *Völkischer Beobachter*, one would have spotted the occasional, brief reference to the 'banditen' of General Mihailovitch and, later on, to those of a certain Tito. The Germans had not been able to resist recording the fractricidal struggle and it had been possible, roughly, to follow the course of the clashes which had resulted in the elimination of Mihailovitch and his followers – remnants of the royalist army defeated by the Germans in 1941 – by the communist-backed adherents of Tito. There had been more than one report to indicate that the pockets of resistance rested on a wider base than that of frustrated citizens setting out after dark with home-made bombs. The Germans gave wide publicity to reprisal executions and arrests carried out in Yuoglslav towns and, every now and then, a brief item would reveal that Russia, America and especially Britain had fingers in the mysterious pie called Yugoslavia. A classic among the items was one which stated baldly: 'Major Tom Churchill has been captured in Yugoslavia.' While our reaction had been to ask 'and who the hell is Tom Churchill?', the Germans, perhaps, felt that an event no less historic than Hess's flight to Scotland had taken place.

Not many weeks after I had reverted to thinking of escape to Italy, another short, single-sentence news item, part of the bulletin issued by Das Oberkommando der Wehrmacht, brought me up with a jerk, and shifted the whole direction of my plans. Leaning against a tree in the forest I read and re-read the sentence over and over to make sure I'd got it right. Then I called Cotter. If any man had a right to know, it was Cotter. The sentence read: 'In Yugoslavia a British plane was captured before it could take off after landing supplies to the partisans.'

We had always assumed that Britain dropped supplies and agents to all resistance groups in Europe. What we had never dreamed of was that the open, mountain-based Yugoslav resistance ran to an airfield, however casual or improvised. If a plane, one of our own, could land with supplies, it could also take off, with prisoners. All we had to do was to find the place and get to it; or rather, get far enough into Yugoslavia to be led to it.

George Cotter had never revealed, in the many conversations we held at work, whether he had actually been captured in Greece in April, 1941, and had then escaped, or whether he had evaded capture. Whichever way it all started, the history of his imprisonment up to the time I came into contact with him had been far from run-of-the-mill. With twelve companions, a store of water and a bag of dubious potatoes, he had crossed the Mediterranean in an open boat in a bid for freedom. Fifty-nine days on the run had ended on the Libyan coast. Landfall had been made in the region of Derna about midday. Encouraged by the waves and shouts of bathers on the beach, the starving, sun-blistered, exhausted boatload had put their backs into one final spurt and were soon being helped ashore – by Italian soldiers. The ordeal by exposure, the marathon journey from Greece had been for nothing but unbelievable disappointment. Had they only known or suspected that the desert battle had swung so violently in favour of Rommel, they could so easily have made certain of staying free by steering a longer course for Egypt. It would have tried their endurance to the limit, but success would have been theirs.

Cotter tried once more in the desert and, having been

shipped over to Italy after the collapse of the Axis forces in North Africa, renewed his attempts on the mainland. There was no boastfulness about his references to his outstanding failures and nothing obsessional about his pragmatic approach to future opportunities. He was no more likely to allow scheming for escape to interfere with designing a baseball bat for the use of the moment, than to permit a game of cricket to thwart a suddenly presented escape chance.

But Cotter had two special ambitions, either of which, when analysed, added up to the same thing – successful escape. His greatest immediate aim was nothing less than to be in London, at the heart of the victory celebrations, on the day the war ended. His other hope was to improve on his previous best of fifty-nine days on the loose, a target which, if achieved, could only bring with it permanent freedom. In all our discussions only one thing struck me as being not quite in accord with the character of the man: that was his resolve never again to commit himself to an escape venture in a party totalling thirteen.

For some time prior to the opening of the Second Front our small party had been shifted to another clearing in the forest, on the far side of the Marburg–Celje road in the direction of the long ridge, and had stabilised to a group of just eight men. Heigl und Schwab had plans for a development similar to the Ukrainian village. Other than that the site was already littered with stacked sections of pre-fabricated wooden buildings, virtually no work had been done towards erecting another settlement to house more forced labour (once again to be Russians).

Almost from the first day on the new site I found I was able to add a new pleasure to my routine: I began to take a daily stroll. At first, on the pretext of responding to nature's calls, the exploratory excursions rarely exceeded ten minutes; even so, the work boss, the same one whom I depended on for my newspapers, appeared a patently relieved man each time I returned to his care. The odd cigarette and assurances that he need have 'keine Angst' gradually induced him to accept the situation. The leisurely strolls grew longer and longer until it was possible to be absent up to half an hour without undue comment.

The area of forest between work-site and main road was intersected by innumerable paths dividing rectangular plots of comparatively new plantings in various stages of growth from acres of old, mature trees. Here and there one came across a section lying fallow around the stumps of trees felled a year or

171

so earlier. It was a delight to meander through the dapples of sunlight, alone with one's thoughts. Snakes sometimes slid across the path, squirrels scraped noisily around trunks or performed aerobatics to skirt a clearing. When one was lucky, turning a corner could disturb hares gambolling. No company could have been more ideal for anyone indulging the luxury of longed-for privacy.

In the latter half of July, just about the time when the Americans were bursting out of their Normandy bridgehead, the prisoners awoke one morning to find the Lager agog with the most unlikely rumours – rumours which, if true, would swiftly put an end to regrets about missing boats (the British having just announced that all men would be repatriated on completing four-and-a-half years' overseas service, a qualification that would have applied to me and to most of my mates in only a matter of months). Hitler had been assassinated! Hardly anyone dared hope the news could have substance: the Führer's hand seemed to lie as firmly as ever all around us. The morning's Appell, while leaving us still in doubt as to his fate, dramatically confirmed that all was no longer well in the Third Reich. The Kommandant, with words which showed through translation as studiously leaving all options open, informed us that a mysterious something had happened in Berlin which might hasten the end of the war, and warned the assembly that, in view of an uncertain situation in the countryside, we would do well to attempt nothing foolish and to remain with the protection of his guards. Within days clarification came: Hitler was alive, if not well, and still firmly in the saddle.

My fourth birthday behind wires had passed when, one morning at work, Cotter approached me. He and Poidevin, together with a couple of his mates, had decided to make a break in the autumn, heading for the partisans. As we talked I felt that he was expecting me to ask 'Got room for one more?', but that was a question I couldn't have put. A man's escape plans were his own, as long as he had due regard for the plans of others and queered no one else's pitch. There were always men ready to jump on another's wagon. As yet no one had been told of my own plans for Italy, partly because I wanted to avoid the chance of having unwelcome company thrust on me and partly to escape having to parry such another request as I couldn't make to Cotter. The stage would soon come when I would have to reveal that I, too, would be in the autumn list of runners; but that information would be better released later rather than sooner. It was hard to refrain from responding in like form to Cotter's confidences, particularly since I felt strongly that I was one man in whom he had neither need nor obligation to confide, but it was clear that any revelation of my own thinking at that time could only have been taken as the crudest of broad hints.

It was almost a fortnight after that conversation that Cotter once again reopened the subject. This time, however, he came out with a direct question, to which an equally direct answer had to be given. After telling me that his party would be breaking from the job, in daylight, and that, to that end, his companions would be infiltrated on to our small gang of eight men in readiness for the combined 'off', he said simply: 'That only leaves you, Taff. Do you want to come along?'

To Cotter I could give only one reply: he would never have asked me along if they didn't want me, and he was most probably the only man I'd met in the whole of my imprisonment for whom I would unreservedly have considered abandoning my own schemes.

'Delighted, George. But isn't the party already a bit bulky?'

'One more won't make all that difference. We've already got an interpreter in Cable. It'll do no harm to have another, in case things turn sour.'

The matter was settled: when the big day came the entire working party would decamp to a man. The whole idea seemed absurd. Odds against success would be enormous, if calculated on the basis of eight men getting home in one bundle – and that was unanimously understood to be the aim – and would still be long if success was simply to be measured by only one of the eight making a clean break, with the other seven acting as decoys or stooges. None of us had any illusions about the slenderness of our chances, yet the escape was to be a serious attempt to put barbed-wire behind every man-jack for all time. At the same time, being realists, we would be content to establish the odd morale-boosting record en route to the bunker, such as beating Cotter's previous best, a feat which in itself was dizzying to contemplate. Too much browsing over the difficulties in our path, other than to evolve methods of defeating or circumventing them, was an idle pastime once the final resolve had been made, so thinking fastened on the facts and theories likely to be made to work in our favour. And there were several.

By far the most inspiring factor was that we would be departing from the too-often-tried, well-worn path which had always petered out long miles short of Switzerland. Our ultimate goal, hidden in mists of speculation and hope, might be more vague and less clearly defined, even, perhaps, non-existent, but the path would be broader and more likely to provide assistance and refuge. Every escapee gave himself as a hostage to fortune, and the pickings in Yugoslavia promised to be better than those we would have met with in Austria.

The Australian members of the party had arrived at the same conclusion as myself, not only about the futility of making for the oasis of Switzerland, but also in realising the fallacy of the fast slog. Granted that the essence of escape had to be movement and progress towards home and that the urge to keep going was aggravated by the need to get within sight of the goal before strength gave out, as well as by fear of dying of starvation and exposure, nevertheless, experience tended to indicate that preoccupation with miles recorded was a sure recipe for carelessness and recapture by a pursuer who had learned not to pursue. The Germans, simply by sealing off the area of escape as reinforcement to their permanent precautions, seemed to have a proud record of ensuring that escapees ran into their arms, and the consequent moral for men like us was to move only when cover was available and, whenever possible, behind rather than through or in front of the hunting packs lying in wait. It was better by far to hole up right away and stay put as long as possible, even until food ran out, rather than try to run the gauntlet of closing traps.

The toughest obstacle in the way of implementing theories of such splendour, and the greatest inducement to opt for the fast slog, was that insurmountable problem of feeding oneself. Even in the improved war situation of August, 1944, Switzerland, over two hundred miles away, was still the nearest known refuge, while the closest fronts by our rough reckonings lay more than three hundred miles away to the south and east, sobering figures which, conservatively, could be at least doubled for a wary escapee skirting danger and hostile civilisation. Such a stop-go journey would take weeks, during which time the escapee would have to eat or be tempted out of cover and away from predetermined routes and routines. Our forest would provide excellent spots for the provisioning of a food cache prior to the day, and autumn fields and orchards could attend to much of our needs en route.

In the run-up to the breakaway our two immediate objectives were to lull the Germans to sleep and to build up a food-cache sufficient to sustain us for two weeks or more. The enemy success in containing or recapturing their prisoners undoubtedly contributed to the way in which we were able to achieve both objectives. It could never have happened so easily under Baldy's regime in the far-off days back in the valley. Our captors had grown slack and complacent on unbroken success. Those working parties which remained out all day did a steady trade in black-market food, unchecked by the sporadic, half-hearted searches and confiscations. For such men, taking lunches out in haversacks had become an accepted practice. Our party, working only half days and eating meals in camp, had no need of haversacks, but no attention was paid when first one, then another of us bobbed up for work with one dangling over a shoulder. Bars of chocolate and boxes of cheese, easily smuggled out in pockets which were never investigated, could be stored in haversacks which, concealed in the forest with small risk of discovery, were never again to enter the camp.

Strolls from the work-site, originally born of boredom, acquired a more practical purpose. We all took to indulging in the practice, both to condition the overseer to its harmlessness and to enable Cotter to hoard the smuggled food. Deliberate care had to be taken that, while we stretched the bounds of freedom to the very limit, any apprehensions aroused in the boss's breast were calculatingly soothed away. At the same time, our conduct could not be so exemplary that he would wonder 'what are those damned Engländer up to now?' The persistent morning raids came to our assistance; we had every excuse to disperse when the sirens began to wail and to re-emerge only with the all-clear, when we would set to work as if nothing were further from our thoughts than to abuse the 'privilege' of dispersal.

Not all air-raids were allies to our cause. One, the only one by the R.A.F., strengthened conviction that the camp was not the healthiest place in which to last out the war, while a casualty from another came near to exposing and thwarting our plans. Since the Americans had failed to take out the factory, the British had a go as well, with even less result. It was the one and only night raid. The bomber buzzed over us for half an hour or more, but, although its flares lit up the whole factory and camp as brilliantly as daylight, the only visible, lasting effect of the raid was to leave a new, round clearing in the vicinity of the Ukrainian village.

It was a Flying Fortress which inadvertently put our scheme momentarily at risk. Towards the end of a glorious morning the lone bomber came into view from the north. It was so obviously labouring that no one thought of shelter or dispersal although factory and camp lay right in its path. The plane was too low and too slow, and the beat of its engines was irregular and unhealthy. Only too conscious that we were about to witness a disaster, we wasted energy in frenzied waves and gesticulations to the plane to veer off, and breath in shouting encouragement and instruction. The 88s stayed silent, holding their fire till their victim became the sitting duck it had to be. It was like waiting for an execution.

The doomed Fortress flew into a hail of shells, but kept steadily on course as if determined to allow nothing to deflect its agonising, limping progress. A torch of red, searing flame swept back from the outer port engine. Still the plane kept going. The engine came away, heading for earth like a flaming meteor, while the severed wing floated gently above it. The dismembered craft started a slow, spiralling plunge, and then exploded. The whole sky seemed full of floating fragments and hurtling engines. Everyone fell silent: the guns stopped. All thoughts were on the crew.

'God Almighty! They've bought it!'

Then came the first cry: 'A parachute! Look!'

'There's another!'

'And another!'

We came to life again. The excitement was intense, the suspense unbearable.

Most of the crew must have baled out in the split second before the fragmentation of the fuselage. Long after the tumbling sheets of metal had sunk into the trees, we were still watching airmen floating away beyond the factory roofs. Ubiquitous Cotter, at work in the forest, was the first to reach one of the flyers. The American, badly shocked and suffering a broken leg among other injuries, seemed not to absorb Cotter's assertions that he was an Australian, and wouldn't trust his assurances that, if there were papers or valuables to be kept out of German hands, they would be safe in those of Cotter.

The greater part of one wing, shining aluminium with a large

176

white star, lay only two hundred yards from our work-site, while smaller debris, among other things a bright yellow cylinder, littered the surrounding area. For days, the search for odd remnants attracted far more attention from military bigwigs as well as from their underlings than was healthy for our plot, especially for our secret food store. It lay no farther from the site than did the severed wing, but, fortunately, it was concealed in the opposite direction and the wing acted as a magnet to attract the majority of searchers and curious strollers. When the Kommandant returned to camp with the yellow cylinder proudly tucked under his arm, we decided it was time to shift our hoard to a safer distance. That operation completed, we breathed more easily.

The escape party had grown to ten men with the inclusion of Sergeants Jennings and Adams, who, not being of our working gang, could not be automatically and legitimately positioned with us on the site. They would have to find their own way of joining us: if they failed, we would move without them. Thanks to the German reliance on successive barriers and checks, we had no doubt of our ability to get the two Australians out of the camp and factory, for the very complexity of the inner defences had a gaping flaw which would work to our advantage. Scorning safe simplicity, the Germans, instead of being content to count off each party at the morning Appell and then hand it over to the escorts in the security of the compound, had evolved a lengthy procedure of consecutive checks and counts, starting with the main count of the entire complement in the compound and ending with an individual count of each separate party by its own escort outside the factory perimeter. In practice, instead of quadrupled security they had achieved doubled insecurity. After the main count, the working prisoners, always almost the entire strength of the camp, were herded rather than checked past the sentries into the assembly enclosure; there was no difficulty in adding an additional man or two. The surplus men had only to hover around between two loosely grouped parties to be overlooked by overseers who were only concerned that they had the number of men signed for; all others they disregarded as being the responsibility of someone else. As for the works police, they were so busy checking civilians at the outer gate that they were only too ready to take it on trust that when an overseer's chit said eight men that was the number of prisoners milling among the civilians. Jennings's and Adams's difficulties would begin outside the factory: there they would have to rely on our having sufficiently brainwashed the overseer.

The time came to announce that a serious, big breakout was on: we couldn't be foiled by another, unwitting prisoner bringing the jackboot down on the camp by making a bid for freedom a day or so before we were ready. Neither could we risk anyone else exploiting the flaw discovered in the morning check-out. When we announced our intentions, we received a big shock. We were not the only ones going.

Another escape party, also of ten men, and also lured on by the prospect of an airlift, was being organised under the leadership of an Englishman, Sid Paling. Employed as one of a big working party who went to work by train and, at some remote stretch of the track, helped to maintain the line, he had intentions very like our own. Unless both attempts were synchronised, one or other would never get off the ground and, with autumn just around the corner there would be insufficient time for the predictable uproar and tightened security to die away to allow the thwarted party another chance before spring. The parties faced widely different problems in making the initial getaway: Paling's men had to break away from armed guards, while we had merely to outwit an unarmed civilian. On the other hand, Paling would find no great barrier between himself and the hills, whereas we would be in a tight trap, hemmed in on one side by a wide, exposed river, and on the other by a series of obstacles, a main road, easily patrolled, a strip of forest containing factory and Ukrainian village, an exposed railway line bristling with flak batteries and searchlights, and a wide glider field offering no cover at all.

Assuming equal initial success for both parties, we would still be bogged down in the forest when Paling was ensconcing himself in the hills and, at the same time, drawing patrols across our path. Our ideas to move behind the search rather than in front of it had arisen from experience of enemy counter-moves, and by recognition that, however long it might take the Germans to react and organise a containing ring, we could not hope to reach and cross the open ground bordering the railway on both sides before that part of the trap was closed. The added knowledge that Paling's party would be escaping from a point farther along that same railway line a good half-hour before we could hope to reach it, demolished all doubts as to the rightness of our original thinking. It also robbed us of the flexibility we had depended on for fixing the zero-hour and lengthened the odds against our ability to move at all.

Employment in the forest had not been wholly continuous and there was no method by which we could guarantee we would be conveniently stationed on site on any chosen day. At one period we had been diverted for more than a week to mending the factory fence; another time a lorry had carted us for miles to a brickworks where the morning had been spent watching bare-footed women working in mud and conditions no self-respecting British prisoner would have been expected to tolerate. No warning was given for such departures from routine. Those surprise deviations were not the only hazards we had to contemplate: the Kommandant sometimes did the rounds of the sites; occasionally, too, the big bosses from Heigl un Schwab favoured us with an inspection, in order, amongst other things, to knock out of me any conceit about my proficiency in German — for the biggest boss, physically and in status, rarely failed to correct my interpreting. He may, in his stiff, formal way, have been genuinely trying to improve me, but he always did so while leaving the impression he was 'taking the mickey'.

It was essential that the break be made in the vicinity of our food store and intended shelter. The sporadic switches from the regular site, and the unexpected intrusions of unwelcome visitors might put us in the wrong place or in unfavourable circumstances on the selected day. That mattered little while we still retained the freedom to postpone the attempt on a daily basis. That freedom had been assumed, even for the not-impossible event of the regular, conditioned gaffer being replaced temporarily by someone more alert and suspicious. Synchronising the 'off' with another party which could not be contacted once we had left the assembly area on 'the day' substantially increased the risk of being left high and dry at the last, vital moment. There would be only one chance once the day were set; it would be a matter of ill-luck if we were thwarted rather than detected or caught. One resolve we did make: if the only, or main, obstacle were to be a too-keen overseer, we would tie him up, without hurting him.

Paling and Cotter had not yet agreed on a date and time for the unprecedented mass-escape, when an opportunity was

179

thrust on us for testing some of our theories and, at the same time, for snatching a comrade from the clutches of the German law. I had finished my midday meal prior to an afternoon shift when Cotter paid one of his rare visits to my room. The very fact that he had come was in itself a sign that he had something both important and urgent to communicate, for in less than half an hour we would both have been on our way to work together with plenty of opportunity to talk. He came to the point without preamble: he proposed smuggling a ninth, an additional prisoner out in the working party.

As was usual at lunchtime, the pervs had taken their fill of the female talent parading alongside the wires. Works police had moved in purposefully on the girls, extracted one from their midst, and escorted her away. Those of the pervs normally employed inside the factory area had recognised the detainee as a young girl between whom an Englishman, Winstanley, scribbled billets-doux had been surreptitiously passing for some time. There were any number of misdemeanours or breaches of discipline of which the girl might have been suspected, and her arrest could have been attributable to any one of them, including consorting with an enemy prisoner. Whatever the motive behind the police swoop, Winstanley was at risk if a search of the girl's belongings turned up a note either to or from him. Cotter had decided to get Winstanley out of the camp before the enemy could pounce.

The party of eight paraded and waited in the assembly enclosure. In place of Cotter's busy, bustling figure, stood a bulkier, paler and somewhat apprehensive-looking Winstanley. The overseer noticed the strange face, and pointed, questioningly. Impatiently, Poidevin cut his query short, more through gestures than the effect of his limited German:

'Eins, zwei, drei, vier, fünf, sechs, sieben, acht. Stimmt? Acht Mann stimmt! Los!'

Pushing his bicycle, the still puzzled man fell in behind us as we moved out on to the factory road.

Midway through the afternoon Cotter appeared on the site. The unfortunate Winstanley was nowhere to be seen: Cotter had holed him up in an overgrown hollow, barely three hundred yards away, together with the only blanket and groundsheet we had managed to sneak out of camp. There he would have to remain, dependent on us for all his food, until such time as we made our move on some future date, which was still to be determined. He was assured of not being left to starve, and a ready supply of water lay close to hand, requiring only a stealthy raid once a night to the tap-stand at the work-site. For the rest, he faced a long, nerve-racking wait of indeterminate length, during which he could do little but count the days and the stars. It was either that, with the remote prospect of us eventually leading him to freedom, or the dead certainty of a prolonged stretch in an enemy prison, into which the long, comforting arm of the Red Cross wouldn't penetrate.

One out, completely unforeseen, and twenty still to go!

The switching of Cotter – who had broken away from a party within the factory perimeter to gain the forest – for the fugitive Winstanley, although unnoticed for some time, increased the fears and confusion of the hapless overseer, who hadn't a clue what it was all about. There remained plenty of time between his first awareness of the substitution and the return to camp for him to assemble enough thought to realise that his best interests lay in being content to take the same number back through the wires as he had signed for. He was in a vice, and he knew that we knew it. As a Slav in an easy, if somewhat trying and precarious, paddock, he was, for his German masters, a convenient, expendable scapegoat. At the one extreme lay the danger of just one square of English choco-late or one stub of an English cigarette being found on his person or in his home; at the other his job could be endangered. None of us enjoyed placing the likeable fellow in such a pre-dicament, but we could only deal with the material the Germans supplied. With all their efficiency they had still been extremely foolish or trusting in not switching guards and bosses before remote indifference to their charges gave way to familiarity and vulnerability.

At the evening Appell the formal routine was enacted as usual, with the noticeable difference that the Kommandant was accompanied by more guards than was normal and that the routing out of dilatory prisoners from bunks and wash-hut was more thorough. The results of the count, correct or other-wise, roused no significant response from the Kommandant. Instead, the Senior N.C.O., a Kiwi, called out:

'Will Winstanley please step forward.'

There wasn't a prisoner on parade, including the speaker, who didn't know that Winstanley was in no position to oblige. But the request was confirmation that he was in trouble, and that our pre-emptive move had not been a needless jumping of the gun. Had it all been a scare over nothing we would have restored the fugitive to the Kommandant's care in a day or so, as easily as we had smuggled him out.

'Winstanley! Come forward, please!'

The parade resigned itself to what had, inevitably, to follow. The Germans, using every soldier who could be mustered, blocked every doorway and painstakingly worked their way through every inch of every room. Once assured that all prisoners were indeed in the compound they had only one device left, to check every disc against their lists. It was no good them studying faces: they wouldn't have recognised their man had he been right marker. Even after the disc check had confirmed that the bird had flown, the total of the Germans' knowledge was only that Winstanley was the name of the missing man. How and when he had gone or how much search time had been lost could only be guessed at, and by the time the deficiency was reported to higher authority and pursuit was organised it would be dark.

Midway through the following morning Winstanley was still in his hideout, confirming that, in spite of the stir of the previous, restless night, the instinctive reaction of our jailors was not to beat the bushes but to surround them and wait for the fugitive to move. Every passing day with the truant at large would strengthen our conviction that our thinking had been right but, in the event of his recapture, would imperil our own chances of making a break. It was too much to hope that, should the Germans pick him up on their doorstep after perhaps a week or more adrift, it would not occur to them that lightning might indeed strike in the same place twice and that they should scour the glades, just in case, as soon as our own absences were reported. There was a remote chance that they would, on the other hand, relate Winstanley's lengthy stay on the threshold of his cage to our subsequent disappearance by concluding, 'ach so! so that was what he was waiting for!', and abide by their normal, successful formula of encircling the area by patrols.

Much as we hoped that the latter line of thought would prevail should our mate be unearthed, his presence and his welfare, to which we were irrevocably committed – for, unlike ours, his escape could not be called off whatever happened – gave new urgency to our preparations, and in particular

182

concentrated our minds on a course of action with which we had been toying for some time. We decided to try to secure the assistance of the partisans from the very first step. Perhaps we could get them to come to us, guide us out of the valley trap and pass us along their lines of communication.

At first the suggestion had seemed outrageous: the more it was pondered over the less fantastic it became. We, ourselves, when driven to it, had snatched a man out of reach of the enemy on the most slender chance that the manoeuvre might succeed, regardless of the fact that the man had not been of our party and might have acted like a clot. After three-and-a-half years of repression, the Yugoslavs would certainly react in the same way, at least towards their countrymen, and would have long since established secret, underground lines for that purpose. Whether they would risk their necks for a bunch of British prisoners was another matter for, if such men existed around us, they would certainly know that the consequences for them of being caught aiding prisoners to escape would be immeasurably more severe than for the prisoners they were aiding. Two things inspired us to hope that such help might be forthcoming: the partisans relied heavily on the R.A.F. for supplies; and most days some one of the numerous Slavs in or around Marburg must be fearing the midnight knock, and making preparations accordingly. There just had to be a local movement of the type we visualised. Invaders like the Germans must have created it by their very presence: kid-gloved occupation invites resistance; ruthless rule compels it.

Approaches to the civilians on the site were ruled out. The Yugoslavs among them inspired little confidence. That all Yugoslavs were united against Hitler's hordes, as one could so easily conclude from the continued and intensified efforts of the partisans, was belied by the sight of German uniforms bearing the chequered shield of Croatia on the sleeves. It was unsafe to assume that all provinces of all occupied lands were united in opposition to the swastika: Russia's Ukrainians were hardly unanimous in their support of Stalin; France was blighted by its Vichy; and even we British had seen our Irish comrades wooed by the enemy and had heard of a Free British Brigade being recruited from the Stalags.

Two other avenues of indirect contact gave more reason for optimism: the French prisoners, and a young Yugoslav girl I had never seen. The French prisoners, veterans of captivity before any of us had met our fates, worked in the daytime without guards, compulsorily paroled by the bitter knowledge that their homes were as securely under enemy yoke as they themselves. With Paris liberated and the Allies rampaging through Northern France, and an invasion of Southern France just reported, there was a chance that many of them, now that their burden as hostages for their families (and that of their families for them) was being lifted, would be glad to stir themselves and apply the knowledge gained during the impotent years.

The other possibility not to be ignored was the assistance of any friendly Yugoslav girl. Unlike their menfolk, the women not only had no cause to associate with us, they were expressly forbidden to do so under pain of the severest penalties. The very existence of such an edict made it easier to recognise a sympathetic female than a perhaps equally sympathetic male: just a smile from the former meant an unmistakable declaration of her position, and that one fraught with terrible danger. The inimitable Cotter revealed that he had a more than nodding acquaintance with just such a girl – young, but with an understanding of which way the world was rolling. I had been unaware of her existence, but if she satisfied Cotter's stringent tests I would readily take her on trust for the job in hand, even without Poidevin's spontaneous endorsement.

The contacts with a Frenchman seemed to come good. He was willing, and full of assurances that he could fish up the end of a partisan link. The negotiations were well under way by the time Winstanley became entangled in our schemes to give them new impetus. Content with the reported progress of the talks with our unknown collaborators, we made the French contact a focal point of our further plans, while the girl, who had been sounded and found to be willing, was kept, by common consent, as reserve in the background. Her risks, compared with the Frenchman's and our own, were too disproportionately high for her to be drawn needlessly into an adventure from which she alone had nothing to gain.

Winstanley had been out well over a week when he declared that it was time he had a hot bath. The totally unexpected request should have shaken us rigid. The date and time of the two mass escapes having at last been fixed for eleven o'clock on the morning of Thursday, 14th September, he had not yet reached the halfway mark of his lonely sojourn in the forest, and we could well appreciate his dread of a Salonika-sized scruffiness shortly overtaking him. Yet, at the same time, we couldn't but wonder if he fully understood the peril he was in or the efforts already made on his behalf. The stuff of escape was wet and cold, soiled underwear and swollen, sweaty feet, certainly not glamour and comfort. I stood aside and waited for an Aussie outburst: 'Isn't that just like a Pom! They come out to Aussie to start a new life, and as soon as they discover the pub hasn't a dartboard and closes at six they're packing their sacks and heading back to the dole.' Nothing of that nature came. Instead, we calmly discussed how to cheer and freshen the hermit up, and how to provide the desired hot bath.

Since the camp possessed no tin bath, and even if it had we couldn't have smuggled it out, let alone supplied the hot water to fill it, the next, much better thing was to take the body to the shower. We had taken it out undetected, so why not a second time? The prefabricated sections of huts stacked flat about the site were mostly of uniform size and thickness, the width of a door-frame and the height of a one-storey hut. Most were solid, to be assembled into walls, a lesser number were solid for only half their depth, to allow for windows, and the smallest collection of all consisted of sections which were virtually door-frames with shallow steps and deep lintels. At a glance from any side it was impossible to distinguish one type of section from another when stacked. By taking the top five or six sections off a stack of 'solids' and replacing all but one of them with 'door-frames' before topping the stack off with one of the displaced 'solids', a hideout was constructed, the size of a doorway and deep enough for a couple of men to lie, and turn, in comparative comfort, hidden from view and shielded from the weather. Such concealment was useless in a case such as Winstanley's, since he would have been unable to leave it for any purpose during the long working days, but it did have possibilities in the event of a prisoner desiring to stay out all night. The time had come to try it.

Winstanley, somewhat crumpled, made one of the party checked into the factory by the works police that evening, and into the Lager by the unrecognising Kommandant in person. Cotter spent the night in the cavity of door-frames. The fugitive got more than his hot bath and a change into fresh underclothes; he was able to stuff himself on whatever food was available to spare from his mates' parcels. Next morning he was marched out again to effect the change-back with an immaculate-looking Cotter.

Not everyone in camp looked forward to the fateful 14th September with equal pleasure. The size and scope of the venture, beyond all experience of guards and inmates, was sufficient to ensure that the scale of the German reaction would result in an extremely uncomfortable time for everyone left within the wires. Since the sort of unprecedented upheaval which would result could only be guessed at, men quite prepared to assist escape plans were entitled to misgivings as to the outcome for themselves when left to carry the can for our dubious scheme. Moods had already been depressed by a severe reduction of Red Cross parcels since the invasion of Southern France had cut the established supply route from Portugal. Both legitimate and illegal food had been slashed, for the parcels had provided the main items for barter as well as their own balanced rations. It was understandable that members of both escape parties should feel that they owed it as much to their fellow-prisoners as to themselves to do their best to leave behind a feeling that, success or failure, the undertaking had indeed been worthwhile. Many of the owners of the astonished faces gazing on the resurrected Winstanley began to concede that we were perhaps not completely barbed-wire happy, and that there might be more to our going than merely a desire to satisfy our own egos.

The Frenchman placed a seal of reliability on his participation by agreeing to escape with us, taking a friend along as company. His decision meant that Cotter would have to ignore or forget his often-avowed resolution never again to attempt escape in a party of thirteen men. Jennings and Adams had brought the numbers up to ten; the Frenchmen increased the party to twelve; and, hidden in the bushes, awaiting our pleasure, lay Winstanley, the fatal thirteenth man. As a salve to Cotter's doubts, we all stuck to ignoring the participation of the luckless lover, and to regarding the party as being of twelve men who were prepared to have Winstanley tag along with them, since he was going the same way.

With the date of the escape only a week away, affairs had to be tidied up. The knock-out table-tennis tournament had reached the semi-final stage, and the draw had guaranteed that at least two of the semi-finalists would either be at large or languishing in the bunker from Thursday, 14th September onwards, Sergeant Honeywell and myself having come out of the hat to contest the one leg. On a sweltering evening I was dragged from my bunk, where I had been racing to finish and return an interesting book on the forms and history of cannibalism. Honeywell and I slogged it out, he in shorts and sandals, I in only shorts, until the sweat dripped off us in spite of the wide-open windows and door. His cunning defence gained him a narrow victory over my aggression after a match which was voted by far the best of the tournament. I believe my conqueror went on to win the final, with only a day or two to spare before the big day itself.

On the evening of Wednesday the 13th, I turned out my kit, and sorted out two good, warm sets of underwear, both to be worn next day under my battledress and under the brown, polo-necked sweater knitted by my girl more than two years before. The pile of carefully preserved letters went into the lighted stove. A small bundle of photographs, souvenirs from which I felt reluctant to part, were slipped into my breast pocket. Apart from the memories the pictures would evoke in later years, they would assist in identification should things go wildly wrong. I laid aside the greatcoat, just in case there was an excuse for taking it along, and placed my identity discs, British and German, around my neck as insurance that they would not be overlooked. Lastly, my accumulated surplus of Lagergeld, apart from a couple of notes of larger denomination, were laid on the table to be picked up by whoever wished.*

With a feeling of having cleared the decks for action, I took myself off for the luxury of the last, leisurely shower likely to come my way for some time. I could then resort to my bunk confident of being able to get through the last words on cannibalism before lights-out. Most of my room-mates had left to seek diversion elsewhere, leaving only Bluey Roberts sprawled on the corresponding bunk on the other side of the room. He, too, had his nose buried in a book. It was considerably later, when both of us had laid aside our reading in favour of a smoke, that conversation started. Then 'Little Pud', a cheery Australian not to be confused with 'Big Pud', Poidevin, made an entry. One of Paling's party, he was doing his farewell round.

---

* I made a mistake. Back home I was surprised to learn that the government were prepared to exchange earned Lagergeld for sterling at a fixed rate of exchange.

We wished each other luck for the morrow and exchanged promises that whoever of us was recaptured first would reserve a corner in the bunker for the other; and just in case, since we were setting out on separate missions, we should never see each other again, 'thanks for knowing you'.

Towards midnight, when most men were already asleep, Cotter crept quietly in through the shaft of light thrown from the corridor. He looked up at my bunk.

'O.K., Taff?'

'O.K., George.'

By the time I had dropped to the floor, pulled my overcoat over my pyjamas and wiggled my feet into slippers, Cotter was away. I turned left along the full length of the corridor and stepped out into the brightly lit compound. A sentry stared at me through the wires. I headed for the latrine, spent several minutes there, and returned back across the short stretch of open space, this time not into my own hut but into the corridor of its neighbour. Down at the far end a cluster of men were grouped in a doorway. At both ends of the corridor, look-outs, like everyone else in pyjamas and greatcoats, were doing their utmost to look as if they had just paid or were about to pay a visit to the toilets. The German lock of the Red Cross store had been picked. Inside, the Senior N.C.O. and others were busy rifling Canadian food parcels. Each man in the doorway received a packet of biscuits, a bar of chocolate and a box of cheese. Then, the goods concealed in his coat, he made his way back to his room at the signal of the look-outs.

Back in my room, I pulled a copy of the *Beobachter* off my shelf, and a length of vest sleeve from under my pillow. The newspaper was spread out on the table, at a page reporting the trial of the Burgermeister of Leipzig, one of the principal conspirators in the July attempt against Hitler. With the aid of an improvised, but effective flat-iron, I began crushing the biscuits and sliding the powder into the open end of the sleeve, the other end of which had been sewn up to make a bag. When the bag was judged full enough it was tested for fit in the patch pocket on the left thigh of my trousers. Each one of us would have such a bag of crumbs to supplement the cheese, corned-beef and chocolate which, together with any roots and fruit we might find unharvested, would form our staple diet until such time as we might be scooped up by the partisans.

Sleep was hard to come by. For the dozenth time I tossed

about the innumerable permutations of all the things which could yet go wrong: the overseer might fall sick; Heigl und Schwab might already have plans for our working miles from the food cache; Winstanley could even yet be stumbled upon, to draw attention to the site at the worst possible time; the Kommandant might decide to pay us a visit, or the guards, suspicious of a bulky pocket or strange face, might conduct a morning search in the assembly area. Our chances had never been rated very high, and by the time I had thought of all the mischances which could reasonably come our way through sheer bad luck or incompetent blundering, it would have taken a lot to convince me that my last full day of captivity had ended. Much more certain was that I was robbing myself of my last night's sleep on that particular bunk in that particular Arbeitskommando.

Chapter 7

TIME TO GO HOME

When the guards began their heavy-booted stamping through the corridor, calling the prisoners to 'aufstehen' and face another day's Arbeit, I was still fast asleep. Only slowly did it penetrate that this was not to be just another day of hurried wash, toast and tea, parade and count, and so to work. For a while it really would contain all those irksome routines, and then what? On into the great, so far untried land of the fugitive!

The morning ablutions lasted rather longer than usual. After my wash, and a shave which ran counter to my normal practice of a leisurely, evening scrape, I dressed methodically. The air was fresh but the sun, already up, seemed to promise another warm day to match the ones which had preceded it. Overcoats would have to be left behind: a rash of them on parade would have looked odd on youngsters who would in any case be peeling jackets off in an hour or so, and would have provided a startling contrast to the shorts and pullover garb of the day before.

As I ate my breakfast toast I tried to keep my mind on the normal babble of talk and concentrated, instead, on mentally checking that all I needed was either already on my person or lined up on the bunk. Cotter dropped in to confirm that nothing had been overlooked and to test that the powder-bag on my thigh and the box of cheese nestling at the bottom of my trouser leg about my short gaiter were unlikely to attract attention.

On the parade ground the escapees dispersed themselves among the middle and rear ranks, where bulging uniforms would be less noticeable to guards mainly concerned with counting properly. I couldn't have listed every man Paling was taking with him, but the sight of one or two men convinced me I had pinpointed intended escapers. I hoped that I had picked them out only because, being in the thick of the plot, I had known the signs to look for.

190

The first real test came in the assembly enclosure. All depended on the organisation and timing of the departures of the numerous parties – some, the more distant ones, with armed guards to escort them, others, those working inside the wires or, like us, in the forest trap, with innocent civilian overseers. Strange faces seemed to shriek out to the Germans to be recognised as, literally, displaced persons, with no right to be where they were. Our party was normal and compact; but, while waiting, we edged close to a larger party so that Jennings and Adams, both of whom should have been still in the compound, would look less conspicuously out on their own and could all the more easily be passed over by the respective overseers as belonging to the other party. The two bosses didn't know it but, if all went well, they would, between them, be responsible for conducting the two Australian sergeants, first out of the enclosure, and then out through the main factory gate.

The scene looked even more chaotic than usual; in fact, the chaos had never been more organised. Almost every prisoner, including many completely ignorant of the fact, was in a pre-arranged position and set to move off in a pre-arranged order. Our own regular overseer was there, thus removing one of our earliest points of concern. It was also noted with immense satisfaction that his bicycle was propped against the end of the guards' hut, alongside the Kommandant's window. In addition to conveniently increasing congestion at the factory gate, his bike would come in handy at the crucial hour of eleven o'clock.

Looking around at the all-too-familiar scene, it was impossible to desist from the reflection that for everybody in the small paddock, as well as for guards and prisoners out of sight in their quarters, life could hardly be quite the same after the approaching zero-hour, whatever the outcome of the bids for freedom. The prisoners knew that twenty of their number would be either on the run or in the bunker by evening, and that the remainder would be paraded and counted again and again as a prelude to a wholesale tightening of control. Kommandant, guards and civilian bosses, on the other hand, were completely oblivious of the fact that their freedom, their jobs and possibly their lives were to be rudely shattered in a matter of hours. However much of a botch and bungle Paling's and Cotter's men made of their attempts, theirs were the only fates roughly predictable, involving bunker and Straflager. For the rest, all was pure conjecture. New ground would be broken by our unprecedented mass escape.

Paling's party, with a train to catch, moved off; Honeywell and Rose were with them. Another train, the factory workers' special, came into sight, slowing to a halt behind the prison compound. It was time for us to move. Judging the moment when the bulk of the passengers would be streaming past our exit, we filed out of the enclosure. We joined and mingled with the civilians off the train. Jennings and Adams assumed stations at our heels, closely followed by the loosely grouped advance guard of the larger party we had closed up against during the party checks. Only a few yards farther on both groups were surrounded by hurrying civilian workers, while both overseers, jostling in the throng like the rest of us, ignored the two spare Australians inconspicuously sandwiched between the two parties of prisoners.

The front men of our party quickened their pace, while those at the rear slowed down to maintain only a small separation from the larger party behind. Our boss, wheeling his bicycle at the side of the road, looked to be in charge of something less than eight men, even including the two spares walking almost at his shoulder. Most of the civilians as well as the following party of prisoners peeled off from the road but were almost immediately replaced by workers coming off night shift crowding us in. Our party of ten, scattered among the crowd, were now the only prisoners making for the main gate but our overseer still pushed his bike along, more concerned about his steering than the number of men he was escorting. The works police had no chance at all of checking the correctness of the numbers shown on the Kommandant's chit: we were too widely dispersed among the pushing impatient crowd, and the police, accustomed to our regular exit, placed too much reliance on the Wehrmacht having done their job thoroughly at the check parade.

Twenty or more yards outside the gate our party stopped and casually waited for the last straggler to join us. The civilian re-counted us as we moved off again. The numbers tallied: he had his eight men. Then he halted, made a questioning sound and pointed. We looked back, eyes following his outstretched fingers: the two sergeants, having got through the gate and broken away from the throng, were cutting away across the open ground, following a rough path which we had used daily when the Ukrainian village had been the scene of our labours. Waving hands in a scissors movement of dismissal, to emphasise that the two men purposefully hurrying away were nothing to do with him or with us, we reassured the overseer:

'Andere Partei! Hier acht Mann. Los.'

It looked like the end of a ten man attempt, for he looked far from convinced. For seconds neither he nor his bicycle moved an inch, although the men he was really responsible for ambled on. Then he made his decision. At what was perhaps the most crucial moment of his poor life of obedience he made, for him, the wrong choice: he fell into position behind us. None of us looked back.

So far things had gone reasonably well. Much as we would have regretted the interception of the two additional Australians, it had been well understood by everyone involved that they would have to take their chance without prejudicing the rest of us. It was now up to us to restore the still puzzled guard to a condition of trustfulness conducive to making our own break as neat and decisive as planned. We were making for our own site, within reach of food-store and thicket as well as of the long-since-browned-off Winstanley.

Our outward appearance, once the biscuit powder bags, boxes of cheese and bars of chocolate had been surreptitiously collected and smuggled away to the cache, gave no hints of anything abnormal: not a single overcoat or haversack or anything else associated with escape littered the clearing. Acting as if the morning were no whit different from any other, we pitched into the allotted work, determined to dispose of it, as always during the past weeks, by eleven o'clock. At the same time it didn't do to exaggerate the diligence. I indulged in my morning stroll, as did Cotter, and the overseer displayed no sign of additional nerves. Cotter's strolls were to some purpose: he reported Winstanley still in his hideout, and Adams and Jennings safely bedded down in our own.

The big blow fell around ten o'clock. The two Frenchmen, passing through the clearing, called Cotter aside. Their news vitally concerned our plans and every man involved in them, but we could hardly attract attention by gathering around in a huddle. The information was bandied around while backs remained bent over picks and shovels. The Frenchmen had cried off! Their fellow-prisoners had become alarmed over the possible reprisals to which they might be subjected should two of their number fail to report back off parole at the end of a day when twenty British prisoners had made a break. Our two conspirators had bowed to the storm and withdrawn from active participation in the escape attempt.

Wholly plausible as the stated reasons were, most of us received the tidings with feelings composed as much of mistrust and suspicion as of genuine sympathy and understanding. There could be no doubt that the Germans would give the French camp a rough time. But it was hard not to wonder why the Frenchmen had had to leave it so late before informing us. There was no time or means left for organising another partisan link and the thought niggled that, although the reasons given might be true, they might just as well be covering the fact that the link hadn't materialised as we had been led to believe: fantasy might have taken precedence over fact in the reports doled out to us. If the Frenchmen had been convinced and confident of their own dealings, would they have given up so easily at the first pressure?

There was nothing we could do to prevent Paling's party making their bid in less than an hour's time. The moment they took off we would be left with no alternative but to do the same thing that same morning or abandon all hope until the spring. Crawling back to camp with tails between our legs was never considered. The original plans had been based on no local partisan contact; that was a line which had arisen and been developed later. Without a dissenting voice, we decided to carry on.

At about a quarter to eleven one of the Australians went for a walk, unnoticed by the boss or by the workmen busy feeding a cement-mixer alongside the road bisecting the clearing. Shortly afterwards, the remaining seven of us began picking up jackets and cleaning boots on the tufty grass. We hung about, talking in a group, a clear indication that, contract disposed of, we were more than ready to turn our backs on the site for that day. The overseer took the broad hint. As he moved away to collect his bike, we began a saunter out of the clearing, towards camp. By the time he joined us we were at a spot on the road where a slow bend hid us from view of the civilians on the site, only a hundred yards away. It was almost on the hour.

We stopped and sat on the grass verge, explaining to the boss that there were only seven prisoners in the group. Letting him discover the fact for himself would have put him on his guard and revived memories of the suspicious happenings outside the factory gate. It was also essential that he leave us for several minutes, something he was unlikely to do unless completely without suspicions. The unfortunate civilian, baffled as to what he should do but also certain that it was no good expecting his prisoners to round up the truant, listened to impatient explanations that his man was down by the cement-mixer and, just as we hoped he would, mounted his bicycle and pedalled back into the clearing.

The moment he was out of sight, the prisoners were on their feet pounding through the trees, not in the direction of the thicket, but in the opposite direction, heading for the long ridge and the river. Any tracks we might leave would take the Germans well away from their goal and, should there have been any prying eyes among the trees, their owners would have a false idea of our destination. A ducking run brought us to the top of the ridge. Down we plunged, checking our slides by clutching at the saplings. Turning right, our course then lay along the foot of the ridge. The cover was thin, although the high rise eliminated any worry about being seen from the right. To avoid being spotted across the level fields running down to the river about three hundred yards away, it was necessary to keep inside the narrow belt of bushes nestling against the foot of the slope. In a long file, moving from cover to cover in erratic bursts, we covered a distance which we estimated would take us past both the work-site and the clearing between it and the village.

Again striking right, we pulled ourselves back up the ridge, surveyed the woods in front of us and, judging them to be clear, broke into a run again to pursue the third side of our rectangular course. The forest track from which we had made our bolt reappeared across our bows. Nothing moved on the road, nor in the trees beyond it.

'Right! One of you over. Keep your hand up as long as it looks clear. The rest of us will cross in one bunch. It's no good crossing in ones. Anyone showing on this track could take ages to get out of sight, and we haven't got the time.'

The prisoner on the other side of the road knelt under the trees, head turning from side to side. His arm rose.

'Everybody ready? Let's go. Now!'

In one mad scramble we were over. Bearing steadily right we described an arc, until, at the top of a tangled clearing, those of us who had made a prior study of the area recognised where we were. Skirting the top of the clearing we arrived at our hide-out, a rectangular plantation of young firs, unthinned and seemingly impenetrable to anyone, even a small child, walking upright. In the course of my strolls I had often viewed it end-on, but never from the side. The breathless party hurried down a narrow path with the thicket on their left, while on their right mature deciduous trees cast a shade through which only dapples of sunlight penetrated. Halfway along the side of the thicket Cotter halted his men.

'We go in here. Flat, on our stomachs. Go careful, and don't snap anything. Before we go in, take a look at this.'

Where we stood the thick crown of a huge tree fell almost to our heads. Odd branches were low enough to jump up and grasp; that Cotter had already done. Twigs and foliage of one branch hung down in front of our faces, held only by pale sinews of young wood and a strip of bark where Cotter had snapped it.

'You might have to get back here after dark. Wait till this brushes your face; then crawl in.'

Carefully, one after another, weaving in between the young, irregular trunks and ducking our backs where the needles met in a solid barrier, we crawled into the centre of the thicket. Inside, where the trees sprouted less densely than along the surrounds, three grinning faces watched our arrival – those of Sergeants Jennings, Adams and Poidevin, the last-named being the missing prisoner the overseer had pedalled away to round up.

Everyone spread himself out as best he could among the young saplings and settled down to await the uncertain developments. There was no smoking, and talk, conducted in breathless whispers heard only by immediate neighbours, was restricted to the minimum needed to convey essential orders and warnings.

The party which was sprawled silently in the heart of the thicket, hardly half a mile from the site where it had toiled for months at the behest of the enemy, consisted of seven Australians, one New Zealander, one Englishman, and myself. Australians had a not undeserved reputation for being averse to discipline, in the sense in which that much-overworked word is used in the British army. Had a British private, trussed up in webbing and equipment like a Christmas tree, dared to yell down to his captain, 'Don't stand there scratching your arse; grab this rifle,' he would have been on a 252 before he'd stopped speaking; but that was exactly what I had heard one pitch-black night at El Daba when a battalion of Diggers had been disembarking from a train in darkness made deeper by a dust-storm. The officer addressed had indeed grabbed the rifle, while his piquant retort had had little of wounded pride in it. Australian troops exercised and responded to a discipline peculiarly their own, one equally as effective in times which mattered as the regimentation firmly drilled into their Pommie counterparts on the basis of tradition and 'bull'. Their concept of discipline was amply illustrated in our party: Cotter, the gunner, was undisputed leader, and in every last resort his word, no matter how hotly disputed, even by the three sergeants, carried the day.

Besides the sergeants and Cotter, the other Australian members were the small, dark-haired Jockey, a Digger of medium but solid stature, and a taller, blond man; all were seemingly close friends. The Englishman, George Cable, hailed from Dagenham and was one of the odd men out in Stalag XVIIIA; he was a sailor, not a soldier. A sick-berth attendant, he had been captured after his ship, H.M.S. *Gloucester*, had been bombed and sunk during the evacuation of Crete. The ninth escapee was the New Zealander, Viv Harper, a friend of Cable's, and a strict vegetarian. I made the tenth man. One thing we all lacked: no one had an anxious wife liable to get upset by an interruption in mail. 'Wot! No wives?'

We would have counted ourselves well content had wives been our only lack. Apart from a theory about the Germans ringing us in rather than winkling us out, a faint but diminishing trust that the Frenchman, in spite of his backing down, had indeed established some sort of partisan link, and a strong determination to remain free as long as possible, the party had little other than a hoard of food which might by severe rationing spin out for a fortnight or perhaps slightly longer. With a vague objective of aiming for Dalmatia, we had launched an escape attempt without map, compass, forged papers or usable money. Lagergeld was so much waste paper, of no value outside a camp perimeter and a sure betrayer of our identities should we try to pass any. As regards personal comfort, we were reconciled to having nothing between our bodies and the elements but the underclothes and battledress donned before leaving the

Lager. We possessed one groundsheet and one blanket, both of which were serving to keep Winstanley dry and warm a quarter of a mile away.

After much thought it had been decided to continue to hide Winstanley in isolation until we ourselves were ready to move on. For more than three weeks his hideout had proved its worth. Far from being recaptured he had hardly had a scare. Compared with our thicket his shelter lay almost in the open, so obviously unsuitable for sheltering eight refugees – that was the number the Germans would assume to have fled the site – that, assuming our basic theory didn't work, it would still not be a primary objective for any search party on our trail. Should we be the ones to be recaptured, Winstanley's prospects for further, prolonged concealment would be slim. Yet it was felt that, since his likely punishment was far more unpredictable than our own, his recapture should not be risked by admitting him too soon to the more vulnerable party of escapees, and that, in the event of our being picked up, he should have the option of either taking off on his own or of breaking back into camp, where, as surplus to strength, he might be successfully concealed and fed for further weeks, if not months.

We lay motionless, counting the minutes ticking by, and warmed by the patches of sunlight filtering through the saplings. Minds worked busily on assessing the possible timing of German reactions. We could feel fairly confident about the overall form of such reactions; but formulation of a time-scale for the inevitable counter-measures was a task hampered by the existence of too many unknown factors and was made particularly difficult by our inability to even guess at the fate of Paling's men. If their move had been made at the same time as ours, as planned, and if, in addition, it was inadvertently discovered that Jennings and Adams were also missing, the Germans might panic and assume that the morning's concerted events were even more widespread and involved even greater numbers than was actually the case. The case itself, once the sums were done, would still prove far more disastrous than any local Kommandant or garrison commander had ever experienced.

What was certain, assuming that Paling's luck had equalled our own, was that the Kommandant would receive two messages, one within a short time of the other, and that both would have the same import, mass escape. On disbelieving receipt of the first he would have to take time to think and organise forces depleted by the escape's having been deliberately timed for a part of the day when the maximum number of sentries were out with working parties, and in many cases beyond reach by phone. Before his hurried plans could be put into operation, they would be nullified by the impact of the second message; and a nightmarish suspicion and fear that there might be a third or even a fourth call from an outlying party would perhaps put back the search rather than hasten it. We hoped that, once confronted with the known magnitude of the operation and fearful of attempting to handle on his own a situation which might well prove to be far worse than he imagined, the Kommandant would suffer a period of near-paralysis before thrusting the matter into the hands of his superiors at Wolfsberg and alerting the garrison in Marburg. If such were to be the rough sequence of events, it would aid the working-out of our theory; the longer it took for the available forces to be mustered for search, the less likely that further time would be lost in seeking the fugitives at the sources of the breakaways. On the contrary, it would be all the more imperative to contain them in a circle sufficiently wide to ensure that none of them could already have sneaked out of it.

So our thoughts flitted about from work-site to camp to the unknown, distant scene of Paling's activities, as we tried to visualise the events taking place in all those areas, and attempted to relate them to each other in an effort to gauge what we had to fear, and when. If all had gone well with the others, who, in spite of having had to get away from armed guards, had the distinct advantage of a starting point on the outer perimeter of the concentric defences, they would have been gaining the foothills at about the same time as we were entering the thicket. We wondered how long it had taken our overseer, first to absorb the truth that his entire band of charges had decamped, and then to pluck up courage and resolution enough to confront the Kommandant. His position was unenviable. Unlike the guards of Paling's party he would have had no one with whom to consult, no one to share and confirm his worst fears, no one to share both blame and wrath. If he reported too soon, before it was certain we had taken off, he would face blame and be berated for a stupid Slav fool: if he left it too late, he would be accused of adding tardiness and indecision to his original crimes of excess of trust and lack of vigilance. The consequences of such a combination of failings were incalculable. The longer the images were tossed about, the greater became the confusion whirling in our brains.

An hour or two passed with no sign of life outside the refuge. From time to time the muffled sound of heavy vehicles on the Marburg–Celje road reached us; otherwise, nothing seemed to be stirring. The period of immediate danger was slowly passing to bolster confidence in the rightness of our thinking. Fervently we prayed that the other escapees would remain at large, compelling the Germans to think the two separate attempts were of one common plan and giving them no excuse for tightening the circle. With each hour that passed we became more sure that all encircling moves had been taken, that road, river and railway hemming us in were being patrolled in strength, and that we could breathe more easily.

It was time for a meal. Slivers of corned-beef and cheese went down well, although no one had an appetite. Carefully measured spoonfuls of biscuit powder proved harder to swallow with mouths and throats dry from tension, and we made inroads into the water supply in order to wash the stuff down.

In the middle of the long afternoon the sun began to lose its strength as the sky dulled over. Hours before dark the first fine dewdrops of light moisture settled, glistening on blouses and trousers, and sparkling on conifer needles. By the time premature darkness, for which we had been longing as confirmation that we had won the first round of the uneven contest, encased us, light rain had turned to a thick drizzle, so we collected the haversacks which had previously remained within reach of individual owners in case of the need for flight, and piled them as protection for the vulnerable bags of biscuit powder. At best the night was going to be wet, cold and unpleasant, although welcomingly protective.

In cancelling his participation the Frenchman had assured Cotter that the partisan connection still held good, an assurance which was a matter for doubt. In our hearts we were convinced that, even if it were valid, no local partisan courier would venture forth that night amid all the increased enemy activity, but it was best to be prepared for that eventuality, as well as for the sudden appearance of the Germans.

It was decided that water must be collected shortly after dark so that the party would not be dispersed should friendly help arrive. Since Cotter and I were the men most familiar with the network of paths, and Cotter himself was to continue the role of supplier for Winstanley, I volunteered to fill the bottles. One of the Aussies, as glad of the chance to stretch his cramped legs and regain a little warmth as I was myself, elected to accompany me. Carefully we crawled out of cover. Soon we found ourselves on paths I had trodden many times. In spite of the rain and the need to walk through the longer, sodden grass under cover of the trees, it was exhilarating to be moving freely after years of supervision and confinement. The whole forest seemed to be ours alone. At the work-site we had to move out into the open. Somewhere away to the right would be Winstanley, couched down in his blanket and groundsheet, better protected than we were likely to be in the thicket. If awake, he might even have heard us.

The water stanchion rose up about three feet above the side of the road. The nearest trees stood almost thirty yards away, with the intervening space covered by rough shrubs, except where heaps of excavated rubble framed a sump boxed in under the tap. We surveyed the area from the shrubbery behind the rubble. Everything was still, the only noticeable sound, as we strained to catch a hint of footsteps on the road, being the dripping of the rain shed by the leaves. I stepped round the rubble while the Aussie kept a look-out from the cover of the undergrowth.

Filling the bottles was a slow and noisy process. The tap, designed to take a hose-pipe, was wide and threaded, while the tapering necks of the bottles were narrow. However one turned the tap, partially open or full on, water escaped down the outsides of the bottles to spill into the sump with a loud splashing. Rather than risk being overheard by anyone approaching while I was deafened, I had to take my time with a slow but steady stream of water slowly increasing the weight of the bottles till I felt the overflow pooling up on my hands. All the while I kept a look-out along the light ribbon marking the course of the road through the dark edges of trees. The operation seemed ludicrous, for only a hundred yards away along that same track lay the spot from which we had bolted that morning.

The rain got steadily heavier. By midnight it was a downpour which showed no sign of slackening: we had chosen the wrong day in relation to the one factor we had confidently considered the most reliable in the whole of our reckonings, the weather. Our staunchest ally had let us down; it had broken too soon. Obstinately, we lay where we were, each man a separate huddle optimistically presenting one side to the weather in the forlorn hope that, if he refrained from turning until the rain had passed, the underside of his body as well as the patch of earth underneath it would stay dry. The close-growing trees ruled out huddling together to shelter each other and share body warmth, and instead of affording limited shelter actually collected and directed the heavy drops, transforming them into rivulets impossible to avoid. We got colder and colder as our layers of underclothes, intended to keep us snug and warm, sopped up the rain. Wet, cold, numb and miserable, one after another, we had to give in and turn in order to try restoring warmth and circulation to sides continuously exposed to the penetrating moisture and the bitter cold. Soon, dry sides which had been relatively less cold suffered the same fate as the cold sponges on which we then lay. Paradise, at that stage, would have been a bug-infested, wooden bunk, a straw palliasse and a couple of rough blankets in a room still redolent with supper toast.

In the early hours, with the rain still beating down as if it had been saved up for weeks in anticipation of our brainstorm, the position became intolerable. Through uniforms and underclothes everyone was soaked to the skin and cold to the marrow: the clothes weighed a ton. Even if the rain were to stop, we would still have to stick to the clothes, with no prospect of drying them out except on our bodies. A whispered conference through chattering teeth was the prelude to squelching out of our cover in order to seek better shelter under one of the larger deciduous trees. Groping around in the dark, we found the best spot seemed to be under the trunk of the tree whose branch had been broken to provide a face-swish to guide us in our thicket. We lay down in a row, packed closely fronts to backs, knees raised into the hollows of the men in front.

'Nobody turns till we all turn.'

It was some improvement on our previous state, but everyone had become numb and saturated: all that could be hoped for was to prevent ourselves getting colder and stiffer. The two men on the ends of the row had the worst of it: I was one of them. In spite of the expressed reluctance of one or two men in the middle, the order to turn was given and, eventually, obeyed several times before the sky began to lighten behind the canopy of mist and foliage. It was time to think about slithering back into cover. The very thought was daunting, for the rain seemed not to have eased. In the midst of a discussion as to the wisdom of delaying any longer, someone hissed:

'Shshshshuuuuush!'

Barely twenty-five yards away, an old lady, dressed all in black, with matching headscarf, was moving slowly in the half light. Over her arm was a basket: she was searching for kindling. Every few paces she bent down to pick up a piece of wood. We lay there and watched. One moment her back was towards us, the next she was facing us as she spotted her next twig. It looked as if we might be lucky and remain unseen. Then she straightened up as much as her aged frame would allow and her old, perhaps weak and tired eyes fixed in our direction. We stayed motionless, wondering what her dim vision made of what she saw outlined in the dull twilight under the huge, spreading tree.

Whatever the poor lady had seen, she did not investigate. The bent figure moved off slowly on a continued search for the wherewithal to warm her worn-out frame.

'Did she see us?'

'I'm sure she did. There's nothing to fear there. Any poor bugger who has to come out on a morning like this to dig up a few twigs has nothing to thank Hitler or anyone else for. She most probably hasn't a clue what she was looking at. She'll leave us in peace.'

'The rotten bitch! Why the hell can't she call a cop!' That would have been one way out of our misery! A dry bunker, with a roof on!

Back in the thicket, away from the heavier dripping of the bigger branches, the rain seemed to have let up a little. It was mid-morning before it stopped, and shortly afterwards the sun broke through gaps in the clouds. Spirits began to revive. It would be hours before the sun could even begin to make an impression on our soggy clothes and shivering bodies, but it was heaven to feel a little direct warmth on faces and hands. More encouraging was the thought that we had survived the first twenty-four hours. If one could hold out for one day, one could hold out for two, or three, or more. The same applied to the shelter: if we could hole up in one for days, why not in another, and another? The only thing to be proved was the ability to move in the right direction.

203

The day passed as had the previous one. We lay still, scarcely daring to breathe, fully clothed and unmoving, cat-napping as the twin effects of the sun and our body heat started to dry out our clothing. From outside came no alarms.

The only real event of the day was the discovery that if one crawled a little way along the centre of the thicket for toilet needs, one came to a small, circular clearing. Slightly off centre, an iron bar rose a couple of feet out of the ground, and at its top it supported a vertical disc. The frame of the disc, like its support, was of iron but its centre was rough, like pink, sandy cement. Its purpose was made clear by the fact that towering above the trees on one side of the thicket stood a tall, wooden scaffolding surmounted by a roofed platform. We had taken refuge against a deer-snare, a place where marksmen on the tower could take pot-shots at the deer licking the salt-disc.

It seemed unbelievable that in all our reconnoitring we had never noticed the tower. The more we thought about it, after the first shock, the more confident we became. Who would expect us to lie low in a perfect 'black spot' at the base of a shooting tower commanding a magnificent view of the forest?

As soon as it was dark enough, the routine of the previous night was repeated: I went for water and Cotter set off to succour the lonely Winstanley. Then once more we lay back, this time hopefully awaiting some indication that the partisans might be about. The vigil was drier than the night before, the results, however, were just the same. The forest stayed still and deserted.

Saturday came and slowly went. It seemed as if we had been out for a lifetime, and the temptation to assume that the way ahead was now clear had grown stronger. As midnight approached we became certain that no partisan link had been made and that, when we were ready to move, we would have to do so on our own. But there was one more chance worth taking. Accordingly, at midnight, Cotter slipped out of cover, confident that he could not only reach the village but also track down his girl contact. The hours which followed were anxious ones. Every time someone heard a stirring in the darkness he would whisper:

'That you, George?'

Time after time the answer was the same: 'No. He's still not back. I hope nothing's happened.'

The long night dragged away, with everyone alert and

imagining the worst. It was not far short of dawn when the unmistakable sound of someone brushing into the shelter had us all reaching out for our haversacks.

'Don't panic. It's only me.'

'Thank God! Everything O.K.? You've been gone a hell of a time. You had us all worried.'

'It'll be O.K. I'll tell you in the morning.'

The news, when finally imparted, was encouraging. The girl had been confident she could bring the partisans to our aid. There had been little she could do in the middle of the night, but in the morning she would set about the task and in the afternoon she would bring us definite information. It sounded like the answer to our prayers and much too easy and good to be true.

It was Sunday, 17th September, and the day was developing warm and beautiful in harmony with our improved spirits. It was pleasant sprawled under the saplings, wallowing in the satisfaction of having outwitted the Germans for three whole days and having possibly already established a record for the largest party ever to have been on the loose for so long without advancing one step. The picnic lunch of the unchanging corned-beef, cheese and crushed biscuit tasted a bit more appetising than on previous days.

Cotter took up station in the fringe of the thicket in order to receive his girl-friend. The rest of us, like relatives about to assess the merits of a prospective in-law, brushed hair out of our eyes and tugged at uniforms to do justice to the distinguished visitor. When she arrived, she arrived on hands and knees, crawling in by the back door, and chaperoned by a girl-friend who entered literally on her heels. Cotter formed the rearguard.

Both girls were young, perhaps not yet twenty years of age, the one dark, the other fair. They were also pretty – and both, turned out in their Sunday best, were likely to convey the impression that their stroll through the woods was merely for the parading of their obvious charms. They had, however, taken care to display a purpose for their walk. Like the old woman who surprised us at Friday's dawn, Cotter's contact carried a basket of wood. As they squatted before our admiring gazes, there was little about their merry faces or their almost-giggling voices to indicate that they were taking their very lives in their hands. But the eager, whispered conversation soon convinced me that they were not empty-headed or blind to the possible consequences of what they were doing.

Under the wood in the basket was a cloth. When the cloth was lifted, bread, cheese and fruit came to light. Someone other than the girls must have co-operated in helping us, for food enough for a reasonable meal for ten men represented the sacrifices of more than just two spirited girls.

Their news was as heartening as their company and food. They assured us (and we were convinced by information volunteered as frankly as if nothing more important than the trimming of a bonnet was at stake), that they had been in touch with partisan sympathisers, that they would come for us when all was ready, and that, if all went well, we would be contacted on the Tuesday night. Until then we had to lie low. It was great news. And it couldn't have been conveyed by pleasanter emissaries. As for the breakouts, the girls, though with little of substance to report, had no evil tidings: there had been no talk of recaptured prisoners, and those in camp had been kept there all Friday after having been hastily recalled from their work-sites on Thursday morning.

While we'd been whispering, loud, unrestrained chatter and periodic bursts of laughter drifting from a distance had given early warning of a threat we had never considered. Never having been at work in the forest on a Sunday, we had not thought that the Russians, with free time on their hands and little welcome among the fleshpots of the town, would resort to the woods to pursue the delights of courtship. On a day so warm and inviting our thicket itself might be invaded and, from what we had seen of the Ukrainians, we felt ill-disposed to chance the fate of our venture to their discretion should they stumble upon our lair. As soon as it seemed the Russians had moved away, the conference broke up, and the girls were ushered out of the plantation.

In the early evening the forest was alive with youthful voices. The noisy horseplay of groups of youngsters continued for hours, sometimes with the parties settled in fixed spots, sometimes with the sounds gradually approaching and receding before dying away. There were intervals when all was quiet and the forest seemingly empty, and then, just as we were beginning to relax, the same voices would rise from the same direction and distance as previously. The strumming of a balalaika mingled with the shouts and screams of a large band which still disturbed the peace after everyone else had grown silent or departed, and it was dark before we heard the last of their rowdy play.

Reluctant to venture out of cover before it was certain that no couple remained hidden in the trees or promenading along the paths, we left it later than usual for filling the water-bottles. Sergeant Jennings went with me. Taking even more care than before, in case a twist in a path brought us face to face with an intruder left over from the revelries, we got to the tap without incident. Jennings took his post in the bushes.

The water flow proved as frustrating as ever. I was reduced to turning the tap off after every few seconds in order to check whether we, Jennings invisible in the undergrowth and myself horrifyingly exposed on the road, were still alone. All went smoothly until the last bottle was almost full. Turning off the tap, I heard footsteps, heavy and hurrying. Over my left shoulder, in the direction of the sound, I saw two figures hastening towards we. Marching in step, and wearing uniform, they were emerging from the trees and entering the clearing. I started a dash for the bushes. After only two or three steps the clatter of my boots on the loose rubble seemed deafening. I flung myself down on the near side of the heap, instinctively conscious that my only hope lay in lying where I was, visible from the road only three yards away, but with my khaki perhaps blending into the brown earth under me. My face was turned away from the advancing men, and I pressed my hands, still clutching the bottle, under my chest. The hurrying footsteps grew louder and louder, sounding as if they would walk right over my bunched-up legs. As they passed behind me there was no break in the timing, no hesitation. Still perfectly in step, the men went on. Not daring to breathe or move, I fixed my eyes on the retreating backs, and followed their progress till the shade of the trees once again swallowed them up, just short of the gentle bend we had raced from on Thursday morning.

As I rose to my feet my heart was pounding, and I felt the blood returning to my face. The front of my blouse was soaked by the water lost from the bottle. Stepping over the rubble, I joined Jennings in the bushes.

'Didn't you hear me whistle?'

'No. Did you whistle? You heard them coming?'

'I whistled and whistled. I was afraid to whistle any louder in case they heard. I thought you were a goner.'

'It's that blasted tap. It was lucky I turned it off when I did.'

The party had had a narrow escape, for had I been spotted, let alone picked up, the whole weight of renewed German efforts would instantly have been switched to the one place which had most probably been dismissed as too absurd to be seriously considered. It would have been a sad end after the increased optimism of the day. I was convinced that I had not been seen or heard by the two Germans, who had possibly been making so much clatter themselves as their jackboots pounded the stones that they had heard neither the splashing in the sump nor the rubble giving way under my feet. Yet I couldn't help but relive the moments and ponder over them through the long night. We would soon know, if the Germans descended. By the time I was due to repeat my nightly chore all misgivings on the matter had gone: no one invaded our sanctuary nor flung forces into the forest.

My doubts were soon replaced by others more concrete than the vague fear that a German soldier might fancy he had seen a heap of stones with a suspiciously human shape. We lost Winstanley. One day he was there, exactly as he had been for over three weeks; the next, and the very day when Cotter was to warn him to be ready to move at a moment's notice, he was not to be found. What was worse, there was no trace of his kit; even our blanket and groundsheet had gone.

There could be only one explanation. The idea that he might have taken off on his own was ludicrous. If he had disappeared to answer one of nature's calls, he would hardly have taken his kit. Had a scare caused him to bed down elsewhere, surely he would have waylaid Cotter, one of whose many virtues had been that he stuck to a set time-table for visiting Winstanley, in order that the latter would not be panicked by the approach of unexpected footsteps. How were we to find out what had happened? We could hardly explore for clues.

We racked our brains to discover if there were any means by which the Germans could link our present whereabouts with the presence of Winstanley under their noses after an absence of weeks. It might have given them a clue as to how he got there in the first place, and also have explained how he had managed to survive in such good condition. We could only hope that they wouldn't work out why he was still there after his apparent source of supply had also fled. We tended to hope that the enemy would attribute his well-being to assistance rendered by friends of the girl who had contributed to his downfall, or, if they attributed it to us, would repeat their previous mistake of assuming that the moment we discovered they had retaken our mate we would be panicked into a flight which would take us into the arms of renewed patrols. They might think that, now that our game had been exposed, we would have to try a new tack. So we decided to stay on course and trust to our basic theory's working a second time. We prayed it would work, at least until nightfall. It was a gamble; but so had it all been, right from the very start.

We stayed crouched in our lair, haversacks ready for rapid departure and still fully clad in uniforms and boots which hadn't left our bodies for a second the whole five long days and nights. Longing for nightfall was more intense than ever. We were inspired by hopes which had not existed five days earlier, and urged on by the fear that the Germans would surely return to search the glades once we'd avoided a second time falling into their traps.

Night eventually fell, and we were still free to greet it. I went for water early, and returned safely. Hours passed; but, as on every other night save the Sunday, the forest seemed to be ours alone. Long after doubt and dismay had crept back, the girl arrived. This time her escort was both more sinister and more welcome than the friend of the Sunday — two shadowy figures with firm handclasps who carried long-barrelled fire-arms. It was hard to believe that this dramatic scene was really being enacted less than a mile from the Lager and only hundreds of yards from our work-site.

The partisans took the lead, stealthily escorting us through the woods and then, to our surprise, out from the comforting shelter of the trees into the third big clearing bisected by the track to the village. They motioned us down into the long grass. For a short while the partisans stood starkly silhouetted against the sky, discussing some point of interest before they, too, went to ground. Presently the silence was broken by a low, distant, double hiss.

We pricked up our ears. An answer went back: 'Sssssssssss . . . Sssssssssss.'

Again came the distant hiss. Our escort stood up. Peering through the grass, we made out dark shapes advancing to meet our men. A short conference ensued among the armed shadows and then we were beckoned to our feet. As we assembled, another party, totalling perhaps a dozen, rose into view and came forward to join us. They were unarmed civilians, recruits culled from the villages and suburbs of Marburg, and destined to swell the ranks of Tito's guerrillas. The partisans marshalled everyone into single file, taking up their own positions in the van and rear. Following one man, scouting ahead, the column moved off back under the trees. Behind us, the brave girl we had just thanked vanished into the night.

Striking a course at a diagonal to the road, the partisans cautiously and quietly moved through the forest. The main road itself was safely crossed, the armed men taking up firing positions as the rest of us quickly slipped over the wide grass verges and the white tarmac. Our further progress took us well wide of the Ukrainian village until, suddenly, miles farther on, the sky lightened before us and we were out of the trees. In front, the ground was open to give a clear view of the railway embankment three hundred yards away and a suggestion of the promised land of hills rising beyond it.

The sight would have been heartening had there not been a long, glaring, tapering shaft of light picking out trees, promontories and embankment as it slowly swung towards us in a vast circle. The searchlight, hidden from view by a small copse, the only cover between forest and embankment, was located on the railway to our right. We retreated back under the trees as the brilliant light painted a wide band of green above our heads. Then the light went out.

Dismay had been clearly visible on all faces. Separated into knots of partisans, civilians and prisoners, everyone stood silent, waiting for the next move. After barely a minute's interval, the searchlight stabbed on to begin another sweep of the line and its bare approaches. When it went off again we began to count the seconds before its next probe; and when it came on we took stock of its direction of aim and its point of dousing. It soon became clear that, even by using the blind spot presented by the copse, the periods of darkness would be too short for a man to make a dash of a hundred yards, climb the embankment, and gain cover, which might be hundreds of yards away on the other side; also, that it was no good making a run for it as soon as the beam passed over our heads, for it was switched on and off indiscriminately, sometimes making only a three-quarter circle, at others passing every spot twice before plunging us back into darkness. In addition, there was no pattern to the direction it was facing each time it sprang to life. Was it also being operated in conjunction with foot patrols?

As long as the light was scanning the ground there was no getting across. There had to be a reason for the exercise, and to find that reason one might not have to look farther than where we were standing. A single fugitive might risk a slow crawl by freezing every time the light threatened to pick him out, but for a party as large as that sheltering under the trees and consisting mainly of undisciplined civilians it was a risk which could very well end in horrible disaster.

The civilians were taken aside and led back along the track we had travelled with such high hopes a short while earlier. They were being returned to their homes or friendly cover to await a more favourable night for reaching the hills. Three armed men remained with us. They led us out into some open ground strewn with maize stalks – which, had they been standing unharvested would have provided excellent, tall cover to within a hundred yards of the line. As it was, they constituted a straw-coloured mat against which our dark figures could be spotted a mile away.

About fifty yards clear of the forest, two of the partisans held us back while the third continued cautiously on and began bending over the field as if searching. He found what he was looking for and, laying down his rifle, groped and scraped among the stalks. When he straightened up it was the signal for us to advance and join him. A square of blackness yawned at his feet, marking the entrance to a hole in the ground. Bending down at his invitation to examine the cavity more closely, we discovered that it was the end of a trench thickly covered by long, sturdy stalks.

The trench was to be our hideout until the next night. The spokesman for the partisans conveyed as clearly as he could in his limited German that we would be safe there until they returned to renew the attempt to cross the railway, and that he would see to it that we were fed. The last point was emphasised by the motion of his arms vaguely pointing down the valley in the direction of what we understood to be the invisible farmhouse to which the maize paddock was attached. With mixed feelings, we watched the men depart. The seachlight was spotlighting the hills.

Shaped in the form of a letter 'T', the trench was the ideal size for our party. Wide enough to allow two men to stretch out

211

side by side, and long enough for three pairs to bed down in the longer leg and one pair in each of the shorter side arms, the shelter, with its earth floor liberally carpeted with maize leaves, was a much more comfortable sleeping billet than the thicket. Although the walls were brown, damp earth, about four feet deep, there was protection from the wind and, once we had replaced the stalks to hide the entrance, a shield against the chilly, dewy night air.

There were indeed obvious drawbacks compared with the large thicket as regards safety. The position, which might have been admirably camouflaged by the growing crop of maize, was so exposed on all sides that every excursion outside in daylight would prove a hazard. With a whole day before us and with the certainty that every man would have to make at least one bid for the shelter of the trees during that period regardless of what precautions we took by creeping out before dawn, we would be more vulnerable than at any time since breakout.

Whatever grounds for concern the exposed position gave us, and in spite of a natural disappointment that a night which had started so incredibly well should end with us holed up only a few short miles from our starting point, we knew that our prospects had improved immeasurably. We had never kidded ourselves that we had anything more than the slenderest of chances; neither had we been blind to the fact that risks would have to be taken in conjunction with the breaks which fell in our path. Having proof of partisan assistance in such tangible form as to be lying in one of their hideouts awaiting their further help signalled complete success in that part of the original plans in which we had had the least confidence. The omens were good. We were even going to be fed. Exhilaration was in no way dampened by the thought that we had now involved ourselves in a situation which would ensure far stiffer penalties should we yet be caught.

Next day passed without incident. The farmer brought food and water, remaining with us while we ate. We kept fingers crossed each time someone, after a wary survey of the ground with head poked up like a rabbit's through the gap in the covering stalks, made a bolt for the bushes; but when darkness returned there was nothing adverse to report. As in the forest, we passed the long hours cat-napping; but by the time daylight faded it was the unanimous decision of us all that, although the trench was a warmer, cosier place in which to spend the night, its stuffy dampness by day couldn't compare with the fresh warmth of the thicket in sunlight.

The ensuing hours of darkness stretched endlessly as we waited in vain for the escort to return. Ready as we were to appreciate that any one of a number of small, innocent causes might upset the best-laid plans of partisans, we could not ignore the possibility of more sinister causes for the silence outside. When all hope of the partisans' reappearance had vanished, we had already gone a long way towards analysing the possible implications for ourselves. The worst fear was that the men might have been intercepted, perhaps even killed, the previous night. There had to be a reason why the searchlight had probed so insistently the night before, yet had stayed so strangely inactive twenty-four hours later. Had the Germans achieved the result they'd been seeking?

Simple explanations in plenty served to relieve our minds a little. The partisans could have been switched to another, more urgent task; they could have decided to wait an additional day in order to check whether the searchlight was to be a regular, nightly hazard; or they could be waiting for someone else in their pipe-line who was to be taken through the enemy lines, on the simple principle of not risking two journeys when one would suffice. Above all, we comforted ourselves, no matter what had happened, we were still sheltered in a partisan hideout, constructed by them for their own purposes long before they had ever heard of us. Surely they would want continued use of the trench for the job for which it was initially constructed with such care and labour, and would, therefore, return.

Thursday and Friday passed with neither a sign of the partisans nor any information from the farmer, who still continued to feed us. Doubts multiplied; and when the return of the rain not only made our abode uncomfortable but also rendered it conspicuous, we began seriously to consider moving on of our own volition. The stalks across the trench could not be waterproofed. We were not exposed to the direct rain; instead, we sat helplessly under the steady dripping which threatened to saturate our clothing. We could not, as in our former shelter, spread ourselves in the sun when it shone nor benefit from a drying breeze, so wet clothes had to be endured for as long as it took our cold bodies to dry them out. We noticed that we had begun to smell, a smell suggestive of body odour, sour air and damp soil.

In order to return to the trench after an expedition into the trees one had to take care to get one's bearings right or dangerous minutes of exposure would be spent finding the hole cunningly concealed in the uniform carpet of maize. A combination of the right or, for us, wrong conditions of temperature and humidity produced a situation where the most careless of oafs, with no sense of direction, could have homed on the target in a straight line. From a couple of hundred yards away, the site of the hideout was marked by a flat, low cloud of steam hanging over the ground as the overloaded, damp trench smoked away like some witch's cauldron. The most innocent passer-by, spotting it, wouldn't have been able to resist the temptation to investigate the curious, 'natural phenomenon'. The sight was alarming, not only spelling danger for us, but also threatening to deprive the partisans, through us, of a much-needed refuge. Saturday night found us seemingly severed for ever from contact with the partisans, and with our minds made up. We couldn't lie there doing nothing for ourselves and repaying our helpers by exposing the trench to grave risk of discovery. It was bitter to contemplate casting aside the local aid for which we had prayed, and which only a short while before had enabled us to regard successful escape as no longer impossible. The decisive factor was the recognition that we could apply to our own plans some of the lessons we had learned during our brief encounter with the guerrillas. In the light of that experience our next move would not be into the hills, as originally planned, but down the valley.

The escape attempt had taken on a new dimension with the advent of the Yugoslavs and, although we had lost them, we now knew that they existed within reach. Brief as the encounter was, it gave us some knowledge of how they operated and against what background. Like ours, their target had been the inviting hills, but they had operated in the valley with the assistance of farmers and villagers in whose hands they had placed their lives. The same friendship or fear protecting the nocturnal prowlers might shelter and feed us until the moment when those same emotions prompted our shelterers to unload us back on to the partisans. There was also the chance that, since persons other than the escort who had not returned knew what had been done with us, other men sympathetic to our cause might make discreet enquiries as to our whereabouts once it was known we had vacated the trench.

The farmer was informed when he came to feed us on the Sunday, our tenth day at large. The searchlight was out as we set off, and there was no sign of its coming to life. Spirits noticeably lifted once we were on the move, surrounded by the friendly forest. We had to be prepared for a challenge – either in German, from an enemy, or in Yugoslav, from a friend – and were only too conscious that any wrong, instinctive reaction could just as easily result in our being sprayed with friendly as with hostile bullets, that we could become victims of 'a regrettable incident'. Our progress, pleasantly exhilarating after the days of inactivity, continued with nothing more exciting than the distant barking of wakeful dogs. At times we stopped to study furtively some farm and its outbuildings only to conclude that none of them suited the chancy purpose we had in mind.

The farm ultimately selected seemed to possess most of the qualities we had been seeking. As far as we were able to make out, it was not affluent enough to have housed either a German landowner or a fortune-seeking Slav; nor did its size and condition of repair suggest that the farmer had given up an unequal struggle. It was also isolated, and there were no tell-tale wires to indicate a phone link with the outside world. Trees ran right up to the sizeable barn, offering a reasonable chance of quick evacuation should it be necessary.

While the rest of us stood out of sight alongside the barn, two men went up to the front door of the darkened house. Their mission was to part request, part demand shelter for ten men, in English or German, either of which, we hoped, would be mostly incomprehensible to the occupant, except for the one liberally-scattered word 'partisan'. This, plus the sight of outlandish uniforms, recognisable only as not being German, would utterly confuse him yet, at the same time, evoke a fearful compliance with a request seemingly backed by weight of numbers and the awful authority of one of the two forces in the land most to be placated.

The emissaries, the two biggest members of the party, loomed back out of the darkness. They returned with fair tidings: the farmer, in spite of not knowing what to make of his late callers, seemed willing to help, even though his manner implied that he would have preferred us to have knocked up someone else. That suited us fine: it would have been a very long shot if we had picked on the home of an active partisan sympathiser; all we'd hoped for was someone just wanting to be left alone, for that was the type unlikely to advertise his predicament except to someone able to remove the encumbrances without fuss. And that ruled out informing the Germans.

We took stock of the barn with the aid of an oil-lamp brought by the farmer, a middle-aged man with a worried but reassuring countenance. There was a half-attic. Loose hay, several feet deep, covered the attic floor from wall to wall, and it was in the hay that we bedded down, but not before sliding up one of the grooved roof-tiles to produce a slit through which we could command a view of the clearing and the only approach road.

Our stay at the farm confirmed that in one sense we had chosen well, for we were fed and snugly protected from the uncertain elements. But in respect of our other hope, that the farmer would bring in the partisans to solve his dilemma, we had dismayingly miscalculated. Whether he thought we were simply awaiting their inevitable arrival, or whether he assumed we would soon be departing for a pre-arranged rendezvous, it was impossible to tell, all communication being conducted through his very young daughter, a small child of eight or nine years of age.

It was the girl who twice daily climbed the ladder with the bowl of broth, and stayed with us while we spooned it down. She would watch us, as she lay on the slope of hay just above the ladder, the only visible part of her, her small, pinched, worldly-wise face, cupped in her hands. She was intelligent rather than precocious, curious rather than prying. She had begun to learn German in school, and we were impressed that she talked to us without seeming to be overawed by the strange company mysteriously tucked away in her father's barn. It would have been superfluous to have cautioned her to keep mum about what she was doing and seeing.

We were not long in discovering the virtues of hay as an aid to comfort. At first we had just lain down on it and pulled a thin layer over us, but soon came the realisation that by excavating a long grave, wide enough for a man to stretch across its width, we could arrange ourselves side by side in its depth, while one man for whom a place had been reserved in the middle of the line, heaped hay to a depth of feet above us and

216

trampled it firmly down. Once we got used to the tickling of the stalks it was comfort indeed, and perfect concealment.

The farmer, whom we felt might have dropped a hint of our presence in any company suspected of partisan sympathies, stayed obstinately indoors. He might have been living alone with his daughter, for we saw no one else about the household, but the regular supply of plain, wholesome food suggested that there might have been a farmer's wife, kept discreetly uninvolved. Ideal as the barn was as a hideout, it was hardly furthering our plans unless the partisans showed. Each day we spent cooped up in the loft tempted us to declare it the last; but, after debate, we would decide to give the partisans another day.

We had arrived on a Sunday and intended to leave the next Sunday. In the event our stay was cut short by one day. On the Saturday morning the farmer so far departed from custom as to visit us, accompanied by his daughter. They lay facing us as the girl recited a prepared speech on which they had no doubt collaborated all morning. The father hardly took his fond eyes off the girl, except to scan our faces to judge the reception of her words. The gist of the speech was that her father was very worried at our continued presence, for the neighbourhood was dangerous and there were many Germans about. I doubt if I have ever seen such obvious pride in a man's eyes as that in those of the farmer as he saw that the words of the child of his advancing years were being understood and well received by the ten unshaven, unkempt foreigners perched in his hay. There was only one answer we could have given, even had we not already made the decision for ourselves. The pride gleamed even more brilliantly in the farmer's eyes as his girl translated our reply: tell him not to worry; we'll be off tonight. We all felt sorry we had no chocolate left to slip over the hay.

It was well before midnight when we slunk away through the woods. The night was dry, but a weak, watery moon cast deceptive shadows over the track running, narrow and straight, under the dark trees. Glad to be under way again, we took it in turns to scout ahead. Hour after hour we maintained a steady pace, pausing only to listen hard before crossing the few junctions when other tracks crossed our path. The strategy had been worked out at the farm: we would make as much ground as possible; then, just an hour or so before dawn, we would find another farm, survey it thoroughly, and make for shelter in the woods. There we would sleep the day away before revisiting the farm, where we would obtain food by threat or persuasion and then get as far away as possible before morning, when the process would begin again. If the weather turned bad, the farms would have to shelter us. Having twice endured the miseries of being soaked to the skin and having also savoured the comforts of a bed of hay, we saw little sense in adding the risks of dying of pneumonia to the others in front of us while there was a hayloft to be occupied, with or without the knowledge or consent of the owner.

By about four in the morning we were feeling justifiably elated by our progress. Soon it would be time to start scouting for our farmhouse. Then we ran into the first of our troubles. Steadily the moon had receded behind high clouds and the night had darkened. When we saw the light we stopped dead in our tracks. It was the first we had seen for hours, and it appeared to be right ahead of us, on the road itself. Creeping as close as we safely could, we studied it hard but could make nothing of it. Perhaps it was a vehicle facing us on the right-hand verge. We moved into the cover of the bushes to the left of the road and advanced, trying to pick out the companion light which should have been there if indeed it was a lorry or car. Still we saw only one light, and the darkness as well as the background of trees made it impossible to discern any outline of cab or bodywork, especially with the light shining directly towards us.

We swung farther into the bushes, creeping along in a wide arc. The light ducked out of sight. Suddenly the stillness was broken by the most horrible clattering in the bushes ahead. I stopped, frozen to the spot. A second outburst of loud clattering joined the first, and suppressed Aussie oaths floated up from somewhere below me. I took one step forward and then I, too, was away, skidding uncontrollably downwards. Loose shale rattled under and around me as, with arms flailing, I tried to steady myself and remain upright. I landed at the bottom on my back. On both sides of me men were cursing as they picked themselves up, while the continued rush of bodies and noisy stones indicated where others were still on their precipitate ways down to join us. The alarm had been sufficient to wake the dead – to say nothing of a driver akip in his cab. The absurd situation, after weeks of confining our every conversation to whispers, was so ludicrous and had burst upon us so suddenly that tension broke and we stood bunched at the bottom of the shale pit, limp with laughter which brought tears to the eyes.

The laughter died away as abruptly as it had started. We sobered up with the realisation that the darkness was as still as it had been before the sudden outburst of noise. We might not have been heard; the sooner we started acting as if we hadn't, the better. Slowly, and even more warily than before, we made our way over the crumbling floor of the quarry. We found a way up the wall of the pit, where older workings had been abandoned long enough before for stunted bushes to provide handgrips and for the shale to have stabilised. At the top, back in the welcome cover of the undergrowth, there was a pause while we listened intently for sounds which might betray whether anyone was moving nearby. There was nothing but our own suppressed breathing.

Poking cautiously out of the bushes, we saw across our bows, not the road we had expected, but the railway line. The tracks were double, and the signal wires, like toy telegraph lines on short poles, convinced us we were looking at the main line, not at some branch track laid down to serve the shale pits. The sight offered an explanation for the light. Craning our necks to the right, we picked out the side of the light and its long reflection running towards us along the shining top of the nearest rail. It had been the warning light of a level crossing. Under our gaze lay the obstacle which had turned back the partisans and caused us to cower in a trench for five days. It still commanded Cotter's respect.

'Everyone take his boots off!'

We stared as if none of us had heard right.

'Take off our boots? After all that bloody clatter?'

'Yes. We cross this in bare feet. The din below was bad enough, but it wouldn't have carried half as far as the sound will travel along these rails if one of us kicks it.'

'We'll never get them back on.'

'Never mind getting them back on! I'll never get mine off. They must be welded on after all this time!'

None of the heated, hissed protests moved Cotter. Sitting on the wet grass back in the bushes, muttering under our breath or shaking with silent mirth, we removed boots which had encased our feet without break for sixteen days and nights. The wet

219

coldness of the dew was refreshing through the stiff socks. As, side by side, we hobbled gingerly over the signal wires, I heard someone mutter:

'All I want now is for one of you dingos to drop a bastard boot on a rail.'

It took a lot of hard tugging to get the boots back on to swollen, no longer hot feet, over saturated socks.

With further, uneventful miles behind us, our concern became that it would shortly start to grow light and that there had been no sign of a farmhouse since crossing the line. Not even a dog had barked to give a clue of habitation. The sky began to show traces of light. To the left the cover began to thin out and we could make out the outlines of wooden huts scattered well back from the road. Soundlessly, we crept past and were grateful for the return of the bushes. Self-congratulation didn't last long.

The right of the road had been bordered by a ditch with uninterrupted woods stretching away behind it. Suddenly, although both ditch and woods were still there, we found that a high, netting-wire fence, topped with barbed-wire, had crept out from the forest and was running alongside us between ditch and trees. The fence was identical to that surrounding the factory at Thesen – tall, concrete posts with angled crowns carrying sturdy mesh designed to do more than keep out stray animals. We hastened, as best we could while maintaining caution, to reach the end of the enclosed stretch, but were brought up with a jerk when we saw that the bushes to the left were petering out again to reveal more than a smattering of huts like those we had just passed. Still at least fifty yards from the road, they stood much closer together and appeared to cover the ground ahead as far as we could see in the dim light. There were lights in several of the buildings, including one some considerable way ahead. To make matters worse a dog began to bark from one of the nearer huts directly opposite, a door opened to send a shaft of bright light in our direction and the form of a man showed black in the doorway. We felt trapped.

We held a conference in the ditch. To retrace our steps was out of the question, for that would have meant repassing the other huts. The outline of the hilltops was already beginning to show faintly over the huts opposite. The way to the left was blocked by the colony coming to life before our eyes. The only hope lay either to the right, under the fence, or straight on into the unknown. The fence intrigued us. Behind it nothing showed through the trees, and the base of each pole, while not surrounded by freshly turned earth, was uncluttered by tufty grass as had been the case at Thesen. Considering the comparative newness of the fence in relation to the density of the huts across the road there was a strong likelihood that we had blundered inside an enclosure, through an open side not yet fenced in.

Selecting a spot where the ground sank midway between two posts, we prised the wire up. Two men had already struggled under, towing their haversacks behind them, when someone whispered:

'Hold it! We're getting inside.'

The operation stopped.

'Remember the factory. The wires were on the inside. If this one's the same, we're getting in.'

'Are you sure?'

'Yes. Remember? When we repaired the fence? We put the wires on the inside.'

'Right! Back out. Quick.'

The two men were hauled back to our side. Nothing remained but to go on. Keeping low, we crept along the ditch. The bellowing dog had been joined by another, equally deep-throated, and lights seemed to have been switched on in every other hut. Those few moments nearly put me off dogs for life. And the occupants of the estate seemed never to have heard of black-out. Our position was no longer tricky, it was desperate. Fortunately, bushes reappeared on the other side of the road to blot out all view from the threatening huts. Hardly had we straightened up and surged forward when we saw that we were in even worse trouble. As we turned a shallow corner, a glaring object only fifty yards ahead gave us the biggest shock of the eventful night: we were staring at the red, black and white chevrons on the side of a German sentry box!

This time there was nothing to debate; only one recourse was left to us. One tip-toeing rush took us over the road into the bushes. We began a detour to the right to curve around the sentry box. Much too soon by our reckonings the road again confronted us. It ran uphill from left to right and, as we looked up the slope, we found ourselves staring at the box, and with relief. It was empty. Hardly trusting our eyes, or our luck, we wasted no time in re-crossing the road. It was almost daylight, with the hills clearly visible in all their features. It had been a close shave. I will never know whether the box was actually unoccupied, or whether the sentry had obliged us by leaving his box at the right moment, perhaps to investigate a noise we ourselves had made.

All plans about a suitable farmhouse had to be abandoned. We were thankful just to have extricated ourselves from the tangled web in which we had so nearly become enmeshed. One thought only was uppermost in our minds, to work ourselves well away from the danger zone before hiding up for an uncomfortable, chilly and, most probably, wet day. The dawn showed that the sky we had watched hazing over for hours had become overcast and threatening. Ominous as it looked, that too might have helped towards our salvation by delaying the daylight for vital minutes. The cover remained dense enough for us to continue moving diagonally away from the road and, after a mile or two, we considered ourselves as safe as we could be from anyone except an aimless stroller stumbling on us.

Curling up in the bushes we tried to get what sleep we could. The rain moved in gently at first and, while not as heavy as the downpour of the night in the thicket, it grew steadily heavier, while we became wetter and colder. By dusk we were more than ready to seek shelter under a roof.

The first likely building we found looked like a farm which had been steadily going downhill for years. The barn in the centre of the muddy yard was attached end-on to the house. We tried the door. Creakingly the one leaf yielded. Apart from odd bits of antiquated machinery the place was empty and neglected-looking. By the light of spluttering matches we came across a ladder and discovered that the end of the barn nearest to the house boasted a hay-loft similar to, though very much smaller than the one we had left the night before. An important difference was that this one showed no welcoming hay. The man who climbed to investigate reported that there was indeed hay, very thinly spread. It would certainly not bury us, nor dry us out but, scraped together, it could be packed around our bodies to help retain our own heat. The hay was dry, too, and the roof sound. We decided to weather out the storm up on the uncomfortable platform.

The long miserable night had turned into a day which, in the dim light of the barn, looked particularly uninviting (an impression confirmed by the continued beating of the rain just over our heads), when the creaking door opened. Slowly everyone prised himself into a sitting position to gain a glimpse of the visitor. We were too far back from the edge of the platform to see anything except the gap of light through the partly open door. Below us someone was shuffling around. The top of the ladder moved slightly as if the bottom was taking a weight. We waited, listening to the heavy breathing of whoever was climbing the ladder. A head came into view, bent down, ensuring the safety of the owner. It lifted to reveal the wrinkled face of an old woman. The eyes slowly took in the scene confronting them, and the mouth fell open. Out of it came one, long-drawn-out word:

'Jesus!'

The steps retreated back down the ladder much more quickly than they had come up. A long silence followed. Then the shuffling of feet started up again and was followed by the creaking of the door as the woman left her barn.

We felt perfectly safe. In the half-light of the morning the woman would have had no idea of what she had actually seen, other than that her barn was full of men. Nothing was more certain than that an old woman confronted by such a frightening sight in that troubled land would nurse her shock and pretend she had seen nothing. Thankful that we had not caused her to fall off the ladder, we decided that it suited our purpose to play along with her pretence and to leave her alone in what peace she could obtain as long as she suspected her loft was sheltering unknown intruders.

The farm was almost part of a village strung out along a road. All day, through a slit in the tiles we kept watch on the movements in the village street, the fields and the road. Twice we saw the village policeman cycle past and were reassured by the sight, for his journeys smacked of irksome routine with no hint of interest in prisoners or partisans.

The day continued wet and the damp air allowed our clothes to dry only slowly on our bodies. Eager as we were to get going again and to emulate the progress of two nights before (hopefully without its upsets), we had to stay where we were. We now realised that getting out of captivity was something akin to going into it, a matter of endurance rather than heroics, and knew the wisdom of avoiding the needless discomforts inflicted by our enemy's most powerful allies, the rain and the cold. But some calculated risks still had to be taken. Late in the night, two Australians undertook a sortie into the village to view the terrain and, if possible, raise a sympathetic contact.

Seemingly endless hours passed without us hearing the creak of the door which would announce the return of the two scouts. All hope had been given up, together with the two men, when finally we heard, not the warning creaking, but the low murmuring of Australian voices interspersed with what sounded suspiciously like laughter. The door squealed open and squealed shut again, one of the arrivals warned his companion to be quiet, footsteps stumbled towards the ladder and then the wanderers were among us, filling the air with boozy breath.

'Where the hell have you been?'

They had been entertained in one of the village houses by a local who had plied them with potent drink and, in an intoxicated, blurred fashion had promised help and more booze next day. The man struck us as sounding not too capable of producing the goods and unlikely to advance our cause substantially, an opinion not too hotly contested by the two contented, sleepy men who had been his guests.

Next morning the rain had stopped and the sun came out at intervals. Nothing was seen in or around the village to alarm us. The old lady reappeared to snoop around her barn, inside and out; but whether it was to round up stray chickens or to investigate surreptitiously whether or not she was still entertaining uninvited guests was difficult to tell, for apart from a glimpse of her head, the only clue to her presence was the shuffling of her aged, ill-shod feet.

An hour or two after dark we set off. Not a chink of light showed in the village as we plodded boldly up the main street; the good citizens had shut themselves up for the night. Clear of the houses we struck off across the fields, heading for hills sharply lit by the moon shining through the high, scattered clouds. We had had our fill of the valley. The path began to run downhill through an orchard where the trees were heavy with fruit hanging conveniently low. We restocked our almost empty haversacks.

Two or three of us were still busy plucking the fruit by the time the rest of the party had moved down the muddy slope into the full moonlight. We were hastening to catch them up, planting our feet on the grassy verge at the side of the treacherous, slimy track, when the shout came and we saw the men in front suddenly halt. There seemed no explanation for the cry. Before we could arrest our headlong slide, the group ahead surged forward again, in a wild, arm-waving run. Then I saw the cause of the excitement. Coming slowly up the hill to meet them was a solitary figure, clutching a tommy-gun. A partisan! The men were shouting:

'Inglese! Inglese! English! English! Freund! Engländer!'

Everyone converged into a tight mass, hugging the large, shaggy figure.

The shout I had heard had come from one of our party. I had not heard a previous shout, a challenge from the partisan who had been lying concealed in a ditch and had held his fire until sure we were not Germans. There was a lot to be said for moonlight!

The armed man, young, with a face as round and rosy as any of the apples we had plucked, seemed as delighted to see us as we to see him. His whole appearance was large and hairy. A rough fur cape and cap fitted in well with his monstrous bristling moustache, and made him a truly formidable-looking figure. The Germans must have had him in mind when they used the word 'banditen'. Suddenly, in the midst of the unrestrained jubilation, the young man turned away, as if he had forgotten something, and gave a low, long whistle. Out of the ditch, twenty yards below us, two other figures rose up, one from either side of the path. Both were armed, like their companion and leader, and both were small and slender: they were girls. Greetings began afresh. The delighted giant explained part of the reason for his delight; it wasn't on every twenty-first birthday that one got ten escaping English prisoners.

'Where have you come from?'

'From Maribor. Marburg.'

'That's a long way. You've done well. When?'

'Nearly three weeks. Fourteenth of September.'

'That's a long time. Now you will be safe.'

This time we felt that we would be.

'I will take you into the hills, but only a little way. You will be safe until I come for you tomorrow. Then I will take you right into the hills. The people in the hills haven't got much. What they have they will share.'

Once securely in the foothills, the partisan drew us up outside a small farm and disappeared inside. When he came out again, a short while later, he had obtained billets for five men, including myself. The other half of the party followed him back into the night.

The building into which my reduced party was conducted hardly warranted the title of farm. That the homestead was poor was hardly surprising, for the rounded hills we had observed on our way up had been wooded for the most part, except where small, sloping clearings had been won back from the woods to provide precarious islands of cultivation. In the tiny house itself we found comfort and welcome. The farmer, his wife and two small children presented a domestic setting such as none of us had shared for years. The living-room was warm, especially to men who had scarcely recovered from drying out saturated clothes on shivering bodies, and the woman of the house had our mouths watering as she heated a stew-pot over the crackling log fire.

The farmer opened a small door high up in the gable-end of his living-room-cum-kitchen and revealed a tiny loft almost half full of hay. The heat of the fire rising up from the room made burrowing needless; we lay on top of the hay and relaxed. Any dampness remaining in our clothing would evaporate in no time. Had it only been possible, at last, to remove our clothing and boots it would have been heavenly, but the partisan had warned us to be ready to make a bolt – of that need there would be warning, though only a short one – and, in case we were forced to step outside in daylight, always to keep the house between us and any glasses scanning the hills from the valley below.

The farmer and his wife looked after us well. Meals, drinks, and a large basket of freshly-picked, blooming peaches were passed up to us next day. In the early hours of the following morning the farmer roused us. The rest of the party were already waiting in the darkness together with a number of armed men, including our hirsute friend of the night before, and a larger party made up of civilians who, for good or ill, from patriotism or fear, had taken the plunge into the life of partisan resisters. By the time the sky had begun to lighten we were high in the mountains, having passed crest after crest with the heartening assurance that there were even more ahead. Even though, up to that moment, all movements had been confined to the dark, and we know only too well that the whole range was encircled by valleys securely under German control, there was already a feeling of passing out of enemy overlordship. Our company had fought for years, had never stopped fighting, yet had not known the inside of an enemy cage.

As if to mark the auspicious occasion, the dawn was the most colourful I'd ever seen. The whole eastern sky, stretching beyond fold after fold of seemingly endless hills, was a huge frieze of ever-changing light, a magic display of greys, greens, purples and reds. Never have I had a better chance or vantage point from which to observe it, or been in a more receptive mood to appreciate it. And, as the light strengthened, tongues loosened to allow us to speak in natural voices for the first time since our break-out. It was symbolic of our new, lightened, hopeful mood.

Late in the morning, the jolly young partisan who had begun it all by his challenge in the orchard said his farewells and departed, taking with him a couple of armed companions and our most grateful thanks for his timely intervention. Everyone else continued on through the hills, across grassy slopes, along sparkling mountain streams, past hedgerows heavy with berries, and over moors colourful with ferns and heathers.

The afternoon was well advanced when we reached our destination, a simple barn on a gentle slope between meadow and woods; what distinguished it from any other barn was that it was already occupied by forty or fifty armed men and that its approaches were well guarded. Judged purely by outward appearance, the men dossed down in the hay or strolling about outside the barn justified the German dismissal of them as 'banditen'. No bunch of warriors could have looked less like an army detachment or have seemed less capable of taking on a disciplined unit. Amidst the variety of military jackets and the multiplicity of insignia, the only things uniform in their dress were its soiled, threadbare, civilian foundation, and a small red star displayed on the front of their caps. Mauser rifles and Luger revolvers, Italian carbines, German stick-bombs and British Mills bombs were in the minority; most weapons must have had their heydays in Balkan wars long since legendary. Yet the contribution these 'banditen' made to the overthrow of Prussian might and Nazi fanaticism is nothing short of epic, and it would be presumptuous of someone like myself to attempt to explain or describe it.

The partisans immediately solved our main problem, that of feeding ourselves. As an added treat the food was both hot and plentiful – mostly stew, served up twice a day, and liberally stiffened with meat, meal and vegetables. Even the vegetarian Kiwi was able to satisfy his appetite for, after transferring visible traces of flesh from his bowl to that of his friend Cable, he still had left a meal of real substance which was vastly superior to any served up to their prisoners by the Germans.

It was important, for the survival and continued existence of an effective partisan harassing force, that each unit rarely stay more than two nights in the same rough, remote bivouac; and for two very sound reasons. They could not allow the enemy time to pinpoint their whereabouts and organise a striking force; neither could they impose too continuous and heavy a burden of 'taxation' on the sparse, impoverished mountain population on which they depended for their food supplies. Wherever they settled for the night they exacted a compulsory levy on the neighbouring farms – a cow, a couple of bags of meal and potatoes and whatever else was available to sustain them – until, two nights later, they moved on to pastures new. The area in which they operated had to be large enough for their nomadic existence not to denude the farms of the means of providing for their needs.

The band of partisans which had received us was steadily reinforced throughout all of the next day, until its strength was that of a skeleton brigade, totalling several hundred men and one solitary, sturdily-built woman, who looked more than capable of holding her own among the tough company into which fate had plunged her. There was no mistaking the brigade commander: he was almost alone in wearing a complete, though much-faded and worn, light greenish-blue uniform; but his predominant colour, which made him stand out in the midst of his sombre-toned followers, was white. His youthful, athletic figure was crowned by a mane of pale-blond hair, he rode a white charger, and both hands were heavily swathed in white bandages.

The steady build-up in numbers was accompanied by an increasing crop of rumours that the night's move to new quarters was to be something far more risky and adventurous than the usual quiet slipping away to forage fresh grounds in greater safety. Dark hints were dropped to the effect that the range of mountains was likely to become untenable as the Germans, in preparation for a future defence against the still distant Russians, set about constructing a line of strong-points.

The brigade was in danger of being sealed off in an area too small for viable resistance. Our arrival had been well-timed.

In the gathering dusk, the huge stew cauldrons were scoured for transporting on the backs of pack-horses, and the units were marshalled into line of march. The meadows emptied as company after company slipped away into the darkness. The chosen way down the mountain lay along a narrow gulley, shaded throughout its entire length, and the darkness was so intense under the close canopy of trees that it was impossible to distinguish the outline of the man in front. Loose stones rolled and slid from under one's feet, one found oneself brought up suddenly in a heap as the line suddenly stopped, or, equally suddenly, jerked or pushed forward as the movement was resumed. To help maintain contact haversacks were slung around shoulders to be gripped by the men behind and, eventually, shoulders grew sore from the jerking pulls; knees, too, took a drubbing from slithering blindly over loose stones. The downhill path continued for hours with no break in the wall of blackness, though muttered oaths gradually gave way to more useful warnings as we began to adapt to the erratic, uneven progress.

The lower the column descended, the more frequent became the enforced halts, some of them lengthy; we could only speculate as to the causes. When finally we burst out from the trees it was to be dazzled by the glaring whiteness of a large church rearing up alongside us. The sudden, unexpected contrast of light and space was breathtaking. Before us lay a flat valley, with the opposite hills too far away to be detected even in the moonlight, and straight away the recent stops and starts made sense. To get hundreds of outlawed rebels across that exposed plain, dominated by the Germans, required meticulous planning and strict discipline, and to prevent a massacre in case of surprise by superior forces the partisans had to undertake the venture in small, well-protected, self-contained groups. We found ourselves hustled into the open at a brisk run for several hundreds of yards, then ordered down into the long grass. While we were catching our breath, partisans who had protected our run jog-trotted past to cover the next stretch.

The leap-frogging progress of protectors and protected continued right across the valley, past houses and through villages where shadowy figures could be seen posted at doors and on balconies to prevent curious inmates from prying into the extraordinary happenings outdoors. Day was breaking before the ground began perceptibly to rise; and by the time the railway line, whose polished metals indicated that it was still actively functioning as a German supply link, had been left behind us we could look back and survey the distinct, irregular peaks of the range we had quitted stretching in an unbroken chain along the far side of the valley. As we struggled up to the safety of the new range, muffled explosions in the plain below us announced that the railway line had been put out of action.

That day was the beginning of a confusing, nomadic wandering. Even more than before we became creatures of the night, taking our rest by day and moving only when the embracing cover of darkness concealed our wanderings. For a week or so the general direction of the brigade's migration served our objective of reaching the Dalmatian coast. At the same time, while we tried to pick up what information we could as to the existence and whereabouts of British missions, a new, easily understood yet mystifying word fell on our ears more and more often, to conjure up pictures of a luxury we knew couldn't possibly exist: the word was 'transport'.

From every context in which the attractive-sounding word was used, it was obvious that 'transport' concerned us rather than the speakers and that it referred to the method by which we would be leaving their company. The first 'transport' was an escort of half a dozen partisans detailed to walk us and several of their own people through the night away from the brigade and deliver us safely into the keeping of other units operating farther south. Night after night, sometimes under clear frosty stars, sometimes drenched by cold driving rain, we were passed through gullies and passes and over mountain peaks and bare, exposed moorlands.

The escorts of the 'transports' were, for the most part, unfamiliar with their surroundings and entirely dependent on a chain of guides provided by the local hill farms. It became a fascinating game to speculate on who the next guide would be as, halted after hours of plodding, we crouched down to shelter from the wind or lay flat on our backs on the muddy track to await the arrival of a fresh guide (the previous one having travelled to the limit of his territory). The figure which then emerged from the darkness was usually a young or middle-aged man, although the partisan service seemingly never discriminated against anyone on account of age or sex. Once it was a small boy who preceded us for half a night before turning back to find his black, lonely way back to the humble shelter he had left long miles behind us. Another time it was an old woman, bent and walking with a stick. I can still hear her tapping her way home down a stony, echoing hillside.

We learned the true value of hay as bedding on mornings when we arrived at our hide-outs soaked and chilled to the marrow from the dead weight of saturated uniforms and underclothes. Deep hay ensured not only sound sleep, but also warmth and comfort and, by some miracle, dry clothes on our bodies when we finally crawled forth. We lost count of the number and variety of barns we slept in; the only ones which stood out in memory were those where the hay was sparse when we were in need of the deep burrow.

The 'community bowl', as we somewhat disparagingly termed it, first came to our aid in a small village high in the mountains. The one street was accessible only to mules and pedestrians and the villagers appeared to be descendants of the Turkish Empire. The rough table would be laid with nothing but a ring of spoons, one for each 'guest'; the food, usually stew or mashed potatoes, was placed in the centre of the table in one big bowl; and everyone sitting or sometimes standing around the table would pitch in with his spoon. There was an unwritten law restricting spoon-dipping to the imaginary segment directly facing one; any straying spoon would be sharply rapped back into its legitimate sphere of activity. The table would soon resemble a rectangular wheel, with spokes of droppings radiating out from the central bowl. Had we ever been forced to flee in the middle of a meal, the Germans would have had no trouble checking the number of men they had surprised – one for each spoke.

With each night's march, each change of billet and each new, strange escort, guide, or travelling companion it became more difficult to retrace our wanderings in our minds; harder still to verify our whereabouts in a strange country where all travel took place in the dead of night with a deliberate skirting of those few places or landmarks which might have struck a faint chord. There were times when we seemed to be retracing the steps of the night before, and there were others when the direction was difficult to reconcile with that which we ourselves would have taken had we been finding our own ways, assisted only by the stars and the immediate lie of the land.

The discovery that lice had caught up with us, while not exactly lifting our spirits, had nothing of the earth-shattering impact of the infection at Salonika, even though we realised we would have to live with the brutes until either success or recapture put us out of our misery. Indeed, once the initial shock had registered, a peculiar process of perverse logic inspired us to regard the return of the parasites as a not entirely unwelcome portent for the future: we had gone into captivity through a barrier of lice, so what could be more natural than that we should have to penetrate it once again on the way out?

Far more joyous was participation in the impromptu celebrations to mark the liberation of Belgrade, hundreds of miles to the south. By a lucky chance of timing we entered a town, the first we had come across in partisan hands, early in the morning of the very day when the glad tidings arrived. We rejoiced with the townsfolk and, in the evening, joined them in dancing around a huge bonfire and in hugging and being hugged by a populace delirious at the prospect of an end to their years of repression.

There were also moments of fear and plentiful signs of the precariousness of the partisan hold. Twice an all-night slog through the mountains found us back at the point from which we had started, the way ahead having been effectively blocked. On another occasion we had been bedded down for only a couple of hours after a long weary night when, long before the hay had had time to dry us out, the villagers suddenly roused us. On a wooded slope where the bushes dripped ceaselessly we crouched the morning through, gazing at a straggling column of Germans plodding along the opposite crest. And there were nights when every single building which loomed up out of the darkness in the course of our stealthy trek was nothing but the burnt-out shell of what had once housed a patient farmer and his family; a blackened symbol of revenge to suggest that children hadn't played and laughed but had escorted armed men through the night.

It was a startling contrast when we found ourselves wandering around a partisan-held town, and in daylight, a day or two after the celebrations over the liberation of Belgrade. The lady in whose house we were billeted thrilled us by mentioning, rather casually, that there was a British mission not many miles away. The partisans had given no indication that there was a mission located in the area. Sensing our disbelief, our hostess lost no time in producing visible evidence that British officers in the Yugoslavian mountains were no figment of her imagination: she produced a photograph.

The group photograph, of about forty or fifty men and women sitting and standing in several rows, was a good, clear and convincing vindication of the lady's unexpected statement. Everyone had dressed to honour and impress and, conspicuous among them, in a gown which did justice to her bearing and beauty, sat our hostess, whose finger, as she analysed the group for our benefit, rested on the Sam Browne of a British officer. The photo showed two British officers and, equally unmistakable, a couple of American and Russian uniforms. Venturing along a road outside the town later in the day, we came across the lines of a field telephone snaking under the hedgerows. Those tell-tale lines could possibly lead us to the mysterious British mission, and we resolved to test the idea in the afternoon.

It was not to be. We returned to town only to be confronted by the populace streaming out to meet us laden with whatever stocks of food they could hump on their backs or trundle on handcarts into the protecting hills. The Germans were conducting a probe in strength into the valley and their leading columns were already approaching the town. Throughout the afternoon, partisan units hastily concentrated to assist the brigade which, on a rougher, hidden, parallel course, had stalked the enemy for days; thus assembled and deployed they were waiting for the moment to close the trap, annihilate the extended columns, and so preserve the stores and granaries so vital for the survival of the small community. The confrontation never reached battle stage: the Germans withdrew before night and the encircling guerrillas severed the German lines of communication and destroyed their ability to fall back on their base at Laibach. The citizens could return.

The old routine of nocturnal wanderings, shadowy guides and distant, wakeful barking was resumed and everyone was heartened and impressed by the amount of solid progress made. Then everything came to a shuddering halt: the way was blocked by the swollen river Sava. The night before our arrival on its northern bank its waters had become impassable: the rains which had soaked and chilled us now barred entry to the

Croatia which our escorting partisans had assured us would provide a haven more hospitable and secure than the areas through which we had passed to date.

After a week of delay, perilously endured on a hillside where surprise attack would have found us in an indefensible position with our backs to an impassable barrier, the partisans themselves began to be anxious for the safety of the parties they were escorting, while we grew concerned at the signs of approaching winter. Day after day, on a vantage point from which we could see the river deep down in the gorge, we stood and endeavoured to gauge any lessening in the volume of water. We studied the smashed pillars of a blasted railway bridge which had once carried the line from Laibach to Zagreb over the Sava and deluded ourselves that the patches of dancing white which marked the spots where the river threw itself against the ruined columns were perceptibly smaller and less agitated than when we had last looked. Food was scarce, and our days were spent scouring the few harvested fields, rooting out overlooked potatoes, carrots and parsnips for roasting in a wood fire. Viv Harper proved a capable forager. That the Germans were in strength not too far away was demonstrated when a British bomber, passing low over our heads, crossed over the hill behind us only to run into a barrage of flak. The stiff breeze carried the white powder puffs in clusters into the sky above us.

'Over the Sava' became the symbol of our future hopes and sufficient cause for nightmares. One of the Aussies declared that if ever he got out to fulfil his ambition of owning a racehorse it could be given only one name: 'Over the Sava'. As the hold-up lengthened to almost a fortnight, we seriously discussed the feasibility of going it alone and trying to swim the river, a topic accompanied by visions of corpses being fished out from under the bridges of Zagreb. Almost as if the partisans had overheard and understood, things began to show signs of moving. There was a false start; one half of us were taken down to the river at dead of night, only to be escorted back, cold, wet and shivering some hours later.

The following night all went well: the crossing was successfully made, and without splitting the party. The night could hardly have been darker nor the setting more sinister for the secretive purpose. It was impossible to distinguish where land ended and water began; the man in front was a sound rather than a shape, and the boat, returning from a prior trip, thrust into the reeds before its outline could be picked up from the rushing blackness of the Sava. We had to feel our way into the small craft, assisted by groping hands which ensured that we were stowed in such fashion as not to endanger the balance of the boat. The two boatmen stood, one in the prow and one in the stern, tall silhouettes clutching long poles. A final check that the human cargo was stable and we were off, swirling down the current, the boatmen's poles rhythmically pushing us farther and farther from the bank, the only sounds in our ears the wild rushing of water. We had to stay motionless, crouched down on imaginary seats with hands firmly grasping both sides of the boat. How far downstream we were carried it was impossible to tell, for the only landmarks were not of this earth, just a couple of stars fitfully peeping through the racing clouds.

A grinding shudder and we were no longer plunging through the night. Then we were standing on shingle which scraped under our boots and against its light background it was possible to trace the dark edge of noisy water. The landing had been made on a long, exposed spit which was severed from the farther bank by another band of black, but more peaceful water. A second boat got us across with a few powerful shoves.

Lost time had to be made up. That and subsequent nights taxed feet and general fitness to the limit as the long, dark, often eerie miles fell behind us; but there was a new magnet to draw us forward, a new name never mentioned on the other side of the Sava – Novo Mesto. That was the place where we would find a British mission and, better still, one of those landing fields which had beckoned us from afar to attempt our crazy expedition. The partisans seemed to fall in with our mood and aspirations. For them, too, Novo Mesto was a goal to be reached, a haven where lay comparative safety and release from responsibility for their charges, who were, after all, mostly their own countrymen.

Our travel companions had often changed. Some had remained constantly with us, the most conspicuous among them two young, barefooted Yugoslav brothers roped together at the wrists, and a German soldier. The two boys, scarcely in their teens, were in close custody to await partisan justice: their crime had been that they had passed on information to the Germans. They must have suffered badly from the weather with their bare, filthy legs permanently blue with cold, but their escorts treated them kindly and showed no signs of malice or ill-will.

The German, who claimed to have surrendered himself as a refugee from the vengeance due to fall on his regiment for participating in the 20th July attempt at overthrowing Hitler, clung to us like a limpet, perhaps because he felt his chances of protection and fair treatment would be enhanced in our company. After all the years of German domination and captivity, it seemed strange and incongruous to be travelling towards freedom side by side with an enemy equally hell-bent on quitting it.

With Novo Mesto still tantalisingly at a distance which varied considerably according to which particular partisan supplied the measurement (which was always given in days, never in miles or kilometres), there came the first foretaste of the winter we were hastening to avoid. On a night of cold rain, the thin, stretched-out column was ascending the zig-zag of a mountain pass. As we lifted our eyes to scan the way ahead we saw the snowline clearly marked where it cut across the road. In a matter of a dozen paces the chilling rain turned to soft, clinging snow and the ground showed a black, irregular, mushy furrow, ploughed by scuffling feet. Our dismay as we watched each other being transformed into snowmen had less to do with our present discomfort and lack of suitable clothing than with the implications for future progress. Towards morning, the descent to lower ground dispelled the worst of our forebodings, for the snow gradually softened again and finally turned back into the rain into which we had set out.

Some nights later our wanderings took us into a medium-sized town as dawn was breaking. Partisans milled around the drab streets of shuttered and apparently abandoned shops and offices and the buildings commandeered to house the rough-and-ready administration. Our guides, escorts and travel companions dispersed on their various, mysterious missions and left us hanging around the forecourt and vestibule of a headquarter office, where everyone seemed at a loss as to what to do with us. Of food and shelter there was no mention, and less hope. To all enquiries, whatever their nature, every answer was the same: hang around and an unspecified someone else will see to you, some time.

Eventually someone did. In spite of tiredness and empty stomachs we stepped out with renewed vigour. In front walked one lone, armed man, combined guide and escort; and, ringing in our ears, joyfully, was his assurance that the day's march would end at Novo Mesto, in a British mission. Even without the knowledge that our goal was nearer than anticipated, the fact that the journey was being made in daylight under the flimsiest of protection, would have lifted the cold depression of early morning; but, to heighten spirits further, the autumn sun shone brilliantly in our faces. A mile or two out of town a gang of workmen came into view repairing a long section of road with the most basic of tools – shovels and picks. A familiar figure in field-grey uniform and with corn-coloured hair stopped work, half bent over his shovel, and watched us stride by: it was our German. I hadn't missed him. When, where and by what means he had been separated from us in town I don't know. As I looked at him, I felt I was looking at a ghost of myself three years earlier, and that I was helping to condemn him to the life I was forsaking. Somehow, I felt sorry for the man, and for his dashed hopes, and I called out to him: 'Alles Gute!'

For all our revived zeal and rekindled energy, harsh reality took its toll as the morning wore on. Freed from the previous irksome restraints of keeping together in one tight bunch we stepped out briskly; but gradually men began to fall back as stiffened muscles, sore feet and aching limbs made themselves felt. In a scattered village my companion for the moment and I stopped to warm ourselves at a workmen's brazier, and waited for the laggards to catch up. Judging by the time it took for the last hobbling couple to limp into sight, our sparse column must have been spread over two or three miles of road. Once reunited, we slowed the pace down.

The contraption which came speeding towards us might have passed without stopping, for the vehicle's occupants must long since have become used to seeing partisans in British battle-dress. Its like had not existed in our pre-capture days, and it took some time for tired minds to absorb what heavy eyes were regarding. It was when our attention switched from the flimsy skeleton to its two-man crew that our brains sprang to life, and voices found the word to describe the wonder we had heard of but never seen: 'A jeep!' The shout, loud and violent from half a dozen throats, arrested the contraption's rattling career. It slewed to a halt as the driver, after a momentary hesitation, caught the Australian accents and a glimpse of flashes decorating long-weathered uniforms. We jog-trotted back down the road towards the men strolling to meet us. It was an historic meeting: they were New Zealand officers, spruce in battledress which made us look like the tramps we were.

We had made it! Incredibly, we had actually done it; we had rejoined our own forces. The confidence of the last hours made the impact hardly less stunning. The fact that those forces, represented by just two officers, were only a small contingent operating deep inside German-occupied Europe was neither here nor there. Nothing, not even recapture within the hour, would ever be able to alter the record: against all odds we had actually made it.

The day was Saturday, 11th November, Armistice Day, the fifty-eighth day at large, the anniversary not only of the end of the Great War but also of the day when I had left Stalag one year earlier full of vague ideas about escaping to Northern Italy to await our advancing forces.

In response to our eager questions, the New Zealanders assured us they were attached to a mission, that Novo Mesto lay not many more miles along the road, and that there was indeed an airstrip. All doubts assuaged, we came down to earth and back to immediate practicalities.

'Got any smokes?'

The scene was reminiscent of the morning of my capture, when the Germans had pulled out Craven A and Woodbines, but this time everything, the mood, the setting, and future prospects were more conducive to enjoyment. As we lit up the State Express 333s the one officer passed round and puffed clouds of delicious, tingling blue smoke into the fresh morning air, the other Kiwi strolled to the jeep to return with several more packets of the same brand.

Like all else in a land where almost everyone existed in a permanent state of readiness for instant departure, the British mission proved to be a scattered, nebulous affair. Its arms received us but we neither saw nor felt its body. An hour or two after leaving Novo Mesto we approached a small farm cottage in the hills. There to receive us was a British captain, a British sergeant, and a bare, unfurnished ground floor room pleasantly warmed by a projecting Kachelofen. It was an austere paradise refound. Greetings over, the inevitable questions were not long in coming.

'How long will we have to wait for a plane?'

'I'm afraid there'll be no more planes till after winter. The snow's arrived. The last one took off last week.'

It was the one setback we had never expected. It might have been easier to take had there been no landing-strip. To reach the goal, find it actually existed and then to be told it was out of action for the winter was not merely to mock our distress but also to dash all hopes of finding another field. The deeper into winter, the deeper the snow. We ought to have sat down and cried, but tricks of fate were something we had long since become accustomed to. Not all turns of fortune had been against us, or we wouldn't have been where we were. Then someone, turning the unpropitious answer over in his mind, burst out with the one further question which, instantly, dragged us up from the depths, and redirected our thoughts to what we had achieved.

'Last week? Were there other prisoners on it?'

Jerked back to life by an affirmative answer, we sprayed the captain with a barrage of names.

'Can you remember a Paling? Honeywell? Rose?'

The officer tried to fasten on to certain names, whilst others were still being fired at him.

'Yes, I believe I remember a Paling. Sounds as if they were your men.'

The others had done it, too! And in time to get a lift out! Although it would be idle to suggest that we felt no trace of envy on hearing the news, the predominant feeling was one of elation. We had not been competing in a race, and it had been granted all along that, given equal success, Paling's party should have had at least a week's lead, even without our long delay at the Sava. A conviction that they must have met the same fate as the unfortunate Winstanley had grown with each day that passed without word of them at the innumerable staging posts to Novo Mesto.

Having undertaken our venture more in the hope of establishing a record or two than of reaching the elusive freedom, the knowledge that we had indeed performed the fantastic feat of bringing all ten of our party out of lengthy captivity was a matter for pride, almost of disbelief which, amongst ourselves, couldn't be disguised. The discovery that our fellow-conspirators, given up for lost, had also had luck which had held doubled the sense of accomplishment. Between us we must

239

have completed a record difficult to beat, and gained freedom as well: one-hundred-per-cent success, all twenty out of the bag. If there was one thing we wished at that moment, other than the plane we knew wouldn't arrive, it was that the mission start buzzing the news to Italy so that the facts be recorded in case of future mishap.

The captain outlined the immediate plans: 'they' would rest us up for a week before passing us along to Major Randolph Churchill's mission, some days further south. We celebrated our freedom that same night by washing ourselves free of the accumulated grime and sweat of the previous two months alongside a wood fire blazing twenty yards from the house. We washed in pairs, each man with one leg apiece in a petrol can of hot water heated on the fire. The night wind was bitter on our naked bodies. One side roasted against the blaze while the other rose in goose-pimples like rough sandpaper. Feeling more wholesome in body and more peaceful in mind than for weeks, we ended the momentous day sprawled on the bare, hard floor of the warm room.

The only slightly discordant note came when, next morning, the lady of the house reproached us for having bathed naked under the bedroom window of her two small daughters. We weren't enlightened as to whether she herself had watched the performance or whether she was simply reporting second-hand.

The stay at the house was not to be uneventful. Next afternoon found the area swarming with partisan units, rushed to the defence of the town which, as had happened to the previous town boasting a mission in its vicinity, lay under threat of enemy attack. However, as on the former occasion, the heavy concentration of guerrillas persuaded the Germans that discretion was the better part of valour. By Monday night the isolated farm had been left once again to the woman of the house, her two young children and her ten guests.

The file of men which trooped into the room a night or so later showed signs of weariness and strain. Even had there not been a sprinkling of R.A.F. blue among the familiar khaki, most of us in the room would have been able to distinguish the crashed airmen from the escaped prisoners. A large group of ten men showed, both in the state of their uniforms and the exhaustion of their bodies, more obvious traces of wear and tear; but the fitter-looking men in blue appeared more bewildered and out of place. The ex-prisoners resembled our own tired but triumphant selves of a few days earlier; the airmen, our dejected selves of 1941. There was a striking contrast between the tired faces lit up by confidence, hope and achievement, and the fresh ones, cast down by uncertainty, doubt and recent shock; between men succeeding in a long familiar element and men still bemused at finding themselves out of their depth; between prisoners with the scent of freedom, home and reunion strong in their nostrils, and airmen with fear of capture, exile and separation clouding every thought.

As if to emphasise to the airmen that their new surroundings might not be so strange and hopeless as they seemed, an excited reunion took place there and then. Among the new arrivals I detected a face I was certain I had seen before, though I couldn't recollect where. With another face there was no need to tax my memory: I could effortlessly recall the exact date when I had last seen it – Armistice Day, 1943, the day I had been slung out of Stalag in favour of Marburg. He was the Digger who had almost burst getting out the 'S' of Sydney. One or two of my Aussie companions also knew him by name, possibly as a long unseen unit comrade. The ten men had also escaped from a working camp of Stalag XVIIIA. Our score had jumped to thirty!

The sudden influx and subsequent overcrowding doubtless hastened our departure from the mission. The intended week's stay had not quite elapsed before we were under way again; but this time we were better shielded against the elements, for each man had been issued with an American lightweight raincoat, with shoulders doubly protected by a flap. The additional waterproofing was all the more welcome since it was raining as we left, and also because the restful stay in the warm mission had, somehow, given men who had endured weeks of soakings and exposure without apparent ill-effect, snuffling colds.

The Australians, with a revival of the same enthusiasm which had caused them to volunteer for a British war years before, were heartened by the prospect of meeting Major Churchill. Few things then within their immediate grasp could have provided better compensation for the disappointment of not being able to convert a technical success into the reality of homecoming than for that setback to bring them face to face, behind enemy lines, with the son of the greatest and proudest leader of the British war effort which they had travelled so far to support. Had one day's further walk brought us to an airfield with a plane ready to take off for Italy, they would have boarded with one regret – that they had narrowly missed shaking hands with the bearer of the proud name.

George Cotter, while as keen as any of his countrymen to meet Major Churchill, had other schemes in his fertile mind. His once far-fetched schemes were coming to fruition, but one would remain unfulfilled if we just kept walking blithely forward. High on the list of his declared aims had been his ambition to celebrate victory in London; and he was the last man to allow that one, additional goal to be lost by default or to be snatched from his grasp for lack of prior planning. So it was that, at Novo Mesto, he revived a plan of which I was intended to be the lynch-pin. We would swop identities.

Exchanging identities, while not the most common of practices, was still a manoeuvre far from unknown among prisoners. All the escapers in our party had gone into captivity from the Middle East Command and it was natural to assume that, since we were heading home in the direction of that same command, the moment military organisations took us back in charge we would be separated – the Anzacs to be shipped home direct to the Antipodes, and Cable and I via the Straits to Britain. In order to forestall that disaster, Cotter's eyes turned towards me: unlike Cable, I had no sweetheart to rush home to. I was nothing averse to the project, a further plot, ready-made for minds long since habituated to scheming. Although Cotter's accent would never pass for Welsh, and there was a good chance that I would find myself plunged right away into an Australian camp, there were compensating factors likely to assist us: Cotter would not have to stand a test among real Welshmen in a real Welsh unit until some time after reaching Britain; and I, having lived so long in the midst of Australians, could easily submerge my voice into a passable imitation of a first-generation Digger, plus which I would have a supporting cast of six dinkum Aussies to bail me out should I put a foot wrong. The compact was made: if and when we reached Italy, we would study the situation on the ground and then, at the right moment, the boat-burning move would be made.

There was still a lot of hard walking in front of us. One of the party began to suffer the peculiar affliction of having to be propped up when walking downhill, though he was still as sprightly as the rest of us at getting up slopes. A tall, warrior-like Serb who was making his way laboriously to his home in

Belgrade – a long, dangerous journey through territory still mainly in German hands – became our constant companion. He thought his best chance might lie in sticking to us until Italy and then hitching a flight back to his native land. Wherever we went, whenever we moved, he and his imposing, bristling moustache were with us, not at our heels, but quietly in our midst, unobtrusive, helpful and completely accepted.

At Metlika or Karlovac, a Captain Bird who was attached to Major Churchill's mission took us in charge. Of the great man himself there was no sight, and the information which filtered down from him gave little promise of our being quickly snatched out of the country. The most we could hope for was that Italy would be radioed for warm clothes to see us through until spring. Debating among ourselves and eyeing our Serb, we began to evolve the outline of other plans: if need be we would break away on our own and try our luck at getting some sort of boat on the Dalmatian coast. It might be risky, and obstacles might be placed in our path, but we felt that it was too easy to sit back and let others finish the job we had started; and there was no reason to assume that the missions, however useful they might be as stepping stones, ought to take all responsibility for furthering our legitimate, patriotic ends.

We had been in Karlovac some days when Captain Bird announced that a film show had been arranged in the town, and that we were invited. Major Churchill would be leaving his H.Q. in the vicinity of Glina to attend. The following night we made ourselves as presentable as possible and were escorted through the blacked-out streets, the Serb, as ever, in our midst. The cinema was closed, its front as dark and uninviting as those of its neighbours. Groups of men stood about on the pavement, like ourselves puzzled as to what was happening. Captain Bird, who had buzzed around seeking information, finally announced that the show was off, the films hadn't arrived, or something of that nature.

A car drove up and stopped at the kerb alongside us. Two men got out, followed by two ladies. Against the dim head-lights the men could pick them out as being British officers. Suddenly one of them was bawling into the night: 'Bird! Bird!' Captain Bird came up, and explained what he had learned. The ladies got back into the car, followed by their escorts, and the car drove off. On the emptying pavement around me, my Australian friends loomed large, motionless, and unusually silent. They had had their meeting with Major Randolph Churchill. I was thankful for the darkness as, on the way back to our improvised billets, I made the few, sorry excuses I could muster, a task I found particularly difficult since I believed none of them myself.

The fiasco of that evening strengthened the determination to make our own way to the coast; but a morning or two later Captain Bird, who, like his counterpart at the previous mission, had earned our respect, had us waiting in the sleet for a 'transport'. When it arrived it really was a conveyance, in the form of an ancient lorry and, when it drove off with our party crouched on the open back to get what shelter we could from the cab, we had a new companion, a South African fighter-pilot, whose plane had failed to make it back to Italy.

The South African officer proved not to be the last crashed flyer we were to stumble on. Accommodation was almost impossible to come by in the overcrowded town of Slunj. The only available space where we could bed down was on the floor of the sole bedroom in a small house, around the bedstead occupied at night by the aged couple of the house. There was never any discussion whether thirteen to a bedroom, two in bed and eleven on the floor, was an omen of impending misfortune but, after the first night, much of our time was spent probing into all seemingly empty buildings which might have served our needs. That was how we stumbled on the Yanks, the crew of a Flying Fortress. As with their British counterparts back at Novo Mesto, shock and bewilderment seemed to have rendered them temporarily incapable of appreciating their good fortune or of realising how favourable were their chances of evading capture. Having been through it all before, we could well understand their feelings; what they made of us, rummaging through the town, was more difficult to tell.

Much of our energy was directed at trying to get a lift by lorry. For the first time we had reached a town where four-wheeled transport consisted of more than pre-war vehicles cannibalised back into service. There was a sprinkling of almost-new Dodge trucks which could hardly have been landed or dropped from the air. The logical conclusion that Slunj probably had an occasional outlet to the coast, opened up a new dimension. It would have been foolish to imagine that our pleadings, cajolings and arguments would persuade partisans to divert one of their few, precious lorries, ancient or modern, from its essential task of provisioning the hard-pressed enclave, but the unceasing pressure we exerted would, we hoped, keep our need constantly in their minds. There is no way of telling whether our efforts in any way influenced the subsequent course of events but, in any case, several days later, we, together with the Yanks and the South African, left Slunj crammed among as many Yugoslavs on the back of another lorry which had seen its heyday.

The blizzard hit us before dark, after a couple of hours' driving, when we were committed to the lower slopes of the pass. The higher we climbed, the more blinding became the snow, and the more frozen we felt under our raincoats. Miraculously, the aged vehicle continued to chug along until headlights stabbing the swirling flakes on a parallel, rising course suggested that the top of the pass would have been in sight had it not been for the darkness and the blinding curtain of white. Then the lorry slewed into the side of the road, its gallant attempt over.

There was nothing for it but to shake off the snow which blanketed our clothes and plod on through the night. The only heartening sight was the small convoy coming to meet us; there were a dozen brand-new Dodge lorries, a sure sign that the road to the coast was still open. Fortunately, the vintage lorry had broken the back of the journey and the remainder of the way continued downhill until, in the light of the dawn, we tramped into a small town in the valley.

A British Major bobbed up from somewhere and took us in charge. Things began to move quickly. The Major produced a lorry. Next morning found us on the Dalmatian coast, well clear of, and below the snow-line. In a larger coastal town the efficient Major immediately set to work battling with partisan officialdom and returned to re-load us on to our lorry. Within hours, in the port of Zadar, we were walking to the quayside, hardly daring to conjecture what might happen next. From the front of the shambling file a voice called back:

'A White Ensign! The Navy's here!'

'Where? You're seeing things.'

Through a gap in the buildings to our right, the duster lazily dangling against the tallest mast certainly looked white, and there was a suggestion of red and blue in the top corner. Stubbornly, the breeze refused to lift. The next few minutes were agonising, until we turned a corner and started down the quayside. It had been no mirage. There was no mistaking the flag fluttering only two hundred yards ahead, and the ship on which it was flying bristled with guns. In all our plottings we had never reckoned on getting out on a British warship. A voice muttered huskily, and joyfully:

'They're only three-and-a-half years late, but it's the loveliest sight I've ever seen.'

The day was Saturday, 2nd December, the eightieth day of our once-seemingly-hopeless escape attempt. The ship was H.M.S. *Colombo*, an anti-aircraft cruiser. Accompanied by two Infantry Landing Craft, she had entered the port of Zadar only two days earlier, reputedly the first British warship to do so since war began, a claim which was most probably true for, because of a three-cornered wrangle involving the communist partisans, the Yugoslav government in exile and the British government, the *Colombo*'s sailors were still not permitted to set foot ashore. Our arrival had been perfectly timed!

The first man to board was the South African pilot. The Americans followed, leaving us to bring up the rear. The one step down from the gang-plank on to the firm deck, under the calm gaze of officers and orderlies drawn up to receive us, was the most emotion-stirring I have ever taken. In a brief second the impact that it was all really true struck with full force. It took a mental effort to refrain from planting lips on the hard unyielding metal. A voice quietly said, 'Welcome on board', and an orderly fell out smartly to precede me to a mess-deck.

The matelots treated us handsomely. A Petty Officer arrived from another mess, attracted by the rumour of a Welch shoulder badge.

'What part of Wales are you from, Taff?'

'Monmouthshire. From a little place about twelve miles from Newport.'

'Monmouthshire! I'm from Newbridge.'

'Newbridge! I'm from Blackwood.'

'That's just over the tump.'

Later on a marine appeared.

'I hear you're from Blackwood, Taff.'

'Yes. Do you know it?'

'I'm from Tiryberth.'

'We're almost Townies.'

I believe it was the marine who used the phrase 'it's a small

246

world'. How small it was struck home forcibly when, in the early evening, after a wash and shave with borrowed kit, I stepped out on deck for the first time. A group stood at the rails only yards in front of me: the Australians, several American airmen, and a Petty Officer from the ship. Poidevin popped the question even before I could cover the intervening few yards.

'Ever come across a prisoner called Barlow, Taff?'

'Yes. Two. Why?'

'The Petty Officer here is writing to him.'

'The one was a Scotsman. He came to the camp I was at before Thesen, just to escape. He stayed only one day.'

'That's not him.'

'The other was from Manchester, a boy called Earnie Barlow.'

'That's the one. You really know him?'

'Very well indeed. He's at a place called Weissenbach, or he was a year ago, at Arbeitskommando 785/GW.'

'That's the address. I'd almost finished a letter to him before I came up for some air. Want to send a message?'

'I'd be delighted. And Barlow and the boys will be even more bucked. This is unbelievable.'

'What shall I say?'

'That's easy. Tell him you've just been talking to an old mate of his, Taff Williams, tell him I've just come in from a long walk, and then add I've been telling you about the wonderful times I used to have with Earnie and . . .' I dictated a short list of carefully selected names of men, British and Dominion, none of whom could have ever been together with Earnie Barlow and Taff Williams except in one place, the Paper Mill in Weissenbach a.d. Enns. That unexpected longshot rounded off my day.

Next night one of the L.C.I.s ferried us across the Adriatic to Bari. In the rest camp, north of the town, we were separated according to nationalities and dispersed throughout the camp, with orders to report in mid-morning to the Intelligence Hut for interrogation and vetting. We agreed to meet before the appointed time to compare notes on what we might have discovered about our future movements. As soon as we re-met it was obvious the Australians had something exciting to impart.

'We're being repatriated through England, all except Viv.'

'Through England! Sounds crazy.'

'It's true. We're all going to Britain. Viv goes via Suez.'

Although delighted that Cotter was to get that much nearer to fulfilling his one outstanding ambition, I felt a twinge of regret. It would have compensated for a lot to have finished up my war by having a free, unauthorised look at Diggerland, especially under the guidance of my friends. Scheming gets into the blood.

'Is there anyone you wish to mention as being pro-German, anyone who collaborated?'

As the interrogator put the question, Salonika Tanky sprang immediately to mind. At that moment, he and his ultimate fate were matters of complete indifference to me, the passage of time having made his conduct less and less significant. I wouldn't have put it past him to have done a Vicar-of-Bray act, to finish up by winning as much credit as a tormentor of his captors as he had earned hatred as a tormentor of his fellow-captives, but there had been less destructive thoughts to occupy one's mind in captivity than planning revenge on a man who had been revealed day by day as a mean, stupid, little creature who had prematurely backed the wrong horse.

I wouldn't have walked a yard to report Tanky, but there was a vast difference between filing a complaint and condoning, or conniving at his conduct by lying or evading a direct question. Besides which, any subsequent repatriated prisoner with more cause than I to bring the man to account would be badly served if everyone else were to forgo a deliberate invitation to supply corroboration. The more I thought about it, the more repulsive became the vision of a reformed Tanky lording it over future generations of unsuspecting 'rookies' at Aldershot with the same authority he had abused in Salonika. I related what I knew.

Interrogation over, we decided to go our own ways until evening, to re-establish long-severed links with home and catch up on sleep, before meeting in the wet canteen for a celebratory drink to our joint success. I was the last to arrive at the bar. The Australians were already seated at a nearby table. I had hardly greeted them and leaned on the bar to attract service when Cotter, of all people, made the startling, seemingly absurd remark:

'There's a couple of chaps in here who know you, Taff.'

Considering that all of us had been adrift for over three

years, that none of us had been in Italy before, except as prisoners (among whose number I couldn't be included), and that none of my companions knew my first name, nothing seemed less likely than that anyone could seriously imagine he knew Taff Williams of the Welch. Taff Joneses, Taff Evanses and Taff Williamses in a Welsh unit were as common as ducks going barefoot, and had to be distinguished by numbers, although sometimes rank, trade or personal characteristics provided a more convenient way of pin-pointing a man, as with Dai Pioneer, Evans the Meat, or Cough-drop Jones. Devoid of rank or trade, and minus a wart on my nose, I had been plain 22 Williams, not to be confused with 32 ('Doc') Williams or 52 Williams. Behind me another voice continued:

'They've been hiding out in Greece.'

It just couldn't be! The whole thing was crazy. The names hadn't been on the list; they hadn't been missing.

'Here they are now.'

I glanced across the dimly-lit Naafi hut and, in spite of fore-warning, nearly spilt the beer I had just lifted off the bar. Sauntering towards us, carefully balancing and sipping their drinks, were two ghosts from the past, two men in fresh, un-decorated battledress, whom I'd last seen in filthy, tropical drill in July 1941, on the hot, dusty, brown compound at Salonika. There was no doubt of it! Ash and Ashford! It was unbeliev-ably wonderful to see them. And a marvellous excuse for a double celebration. My fellow-Welshmen had escaped through the drain and had lived in Salonika, under the noses of the Germans, from July 1941, until liberated in September or October 1944! The incredible, marathon feat made our piffling eighty days appear like a Sunday-afternoon saunter. And my loner days were over.

We boarded the troopship *Worcestershire* at Naples, in which city we had celebrated our first Christmas as free men again. Having settled into my berth, I set off on the obligatory tour to find Cotter, Poidevin and company. My narrow passage was blocked by kit belonging to a couple of soldiers who, stand-ing on lower bunks, were busy stowing their belongings on berths above. As I waited for the gangway to clear, one of the men glanced down. Our eyes met.

'Rowlands!'

'Williams, isn't it?'

We had been in the same call-up squad, had trained together, been posted overseas in the same ship and had served together until our involuntary separation on Crete. At last I had done something right: I had caught the same ship which would have carried me home had I not been captured. Dispersed among its holds were the remnants of my draft, now being repatriated after completing their tour of four-and-a-half years overseas.

The ship swung round the buoy in the bay at Gibraltar while the convoy assembled; then, with the New Year only a day or two old, it steamed through the Straits and out into the Atlantic. As the coast of Spain dropped behind us, we stood at the rails, old unit comrades, Ash and Ashford, the Australians and Cable, gazing at the ships spread widely over the sea ahead. A frigate raced back to curve past us. Over the loudhailer came the order:

'Whip her up, *Worcestershire*. Your place is astern of the *Capetown Castle*.'

It was indeed. Very much astern. Early promenaders next morning reported nothing to be seen but an empty ocean, with not a wisp of smoke smudging the grey horizon. Our old tub was too slow to keep station. But who really cared? We were on the Home Straight.

EPILOGUE

Apart from a letter from Sergeant Poidevin from Bourne-mouth early in 1945, I have had no further contact with any of the men who so intimately shared the many, different stages of my captivity. Whether George Cotter ever danced around Trafalgar Square or whether a horse called 'Over the Sava' ever limped home last of the field are just two of many questions I cannot answer.

I am, however, indebted to the Naafi canteen on Shrewsbury station for providing the venue for three separate, unarranged meetings with three different soldiers, none of whom I could recall ever having seen previously. On all three occasions I had slipped into the canteen for a cup of tea while waiting for a connection to Newport on my way home on leave.

At the first meeting a man of the Welch enquired if I had been with the 1st Welch on Crete. On finding that I had been, he produced an evening paper: the soldier charged with the murder of P.S.M. Simms on Crete in 1941 had been re-arrested in London on his return after four years as a P.O.W. He was subsequently tried and convicted at the Old Bailey.

A couple of months later, my tea-sipping was interrupted by a soldier who asked, somewhat uncertainly:

'Weren't you a prisoner at Marburg?'

He had also been there at the time of the escapes, but was unaware he was talking to one of the escapees, about whose fate he knew nothing. I imparted the news that we had not upset the boys' lives for nothing. In return he was able to tell me that there had been such consternation and upheaval in the camp that the Germans had closed it down in a hurry and transported the prisoners to safer areas.

'Do you know what happened to Winstanley?' I asked.

And he replied: 'He was recaptured.'

It was at the third encounter that I received the one item of news I most wanted to hear. The soldier who thought he recognised me opened the conversation by asking:

'Is your name Williams?'

'Yes. How do you know? Should I know you?'

'I was at Weissenbach. I was there when you left for Stalag. Didn't you escape?'

"Yes, I did. How do you know?"

'One of the boys had a letter.'

The Petty Officer from the *Colombo* had done the trick. His letter had got through, message received and understood.

RUTH ALIAV & PEGGY MANN

THE LAST ESCAPE

THE LAST ESCAPE is the true story of how just ten
people managed to save the lives of many thousands of
Jews who would otherwise have been doomed to die in
Hitler's concentration camps. Told in the first person,
the book describes the desperate and exciting ad-
ventures of Ruth Kluger herself. A beautiful and determined young woman, her part in this secret operation
has made her into an almost legendary figure.

With incredibly meagre resources, Ruth Kluger over-
came unbelievable obstacles – finding shipowners
willing to lease ancient vessels at a premium; cajoling
sailors into working the leaky boats; calming passengers
confined to a few feet of a darkened, airless hold, sometimes for weeks on end; bribing border officials, station-
masters, harbourmasters and embassies; and at all
times raising money. And in the midst of all the turmoil
and danger, she even found time for a beautiful but tragic
love affair.

CORONET BOOKS

SIM KESSEL

HANGED AT AUSCHWITZ

Time after time he was condemned to die. But each time, miraculously, he escaped, becoming one of the longest-surviving inmates of the dreaded death camp.

The author was arrested by the Gestapo in 1942 and sent to Auschwitz because of his Jewish origin and his work with the French Resistance. But his pre-war days as a boxer had given him both physical stamina and the will to win. Reprieve after reprieve showed that he was lucky. And, somehow, he lived to tell the tale.

In this personal account of concentration camp life, Sim Kessel has provided a moving testimony to the fate of the other prisoners, the many millions who did not survive. This is a true story and a terrible one; one man's account of the horror that engulfed him and almost wiped him from the face of the earth.

CORONET BOOKS

HENRI FRENAY

THE NIGHT WILL END

Thirty years have passed since the victory of the Allies in World War II. Now, for the first time, Henri Frenay, the man who was the inspiration behind the French Resistance, tells the story of those bitter war years in occupied France – when his country lay crushed beneath the ruthless foot of German domination. Though France's position seemed hopeless, Frenay was determined that the spirit of patriotism should not die. For him and for his countrymen the night *would* end . . .

Frenay's memoirs cover the secret growth of organised resistance to Nazi persecution: the early development of 'Combat'; the creation of *Vérités*, an underground newspaper to counteract Nazi propaganda; the formation of a Secret Army. He describes the astonishing courage of all those who took part in the Resistance, whether infiltrating government departments as spies, printing illegal pamphlets – or simply spreading hope through the darkness.

This is the inside story of a historic and vital underground movement told by its creator. It is also one of the most extraordinary autobiographies of our time.

CORONET BOOKS

ALSO AVAILABLE IN CORONET BOOKS

All these books are available at your local bookshop or newsagent, or can be ordered direct from the publisher. Just tick the titles you want and fill in the form below.

Prices and availability subject to change without notice.

CORONET BOOKS, P.O. Box 11, Falmouth, Cornwall.

Please send cheque or postal order, and allow the following for postage and packing:

U.K. – One book 22p plus 10p per copy for each additional book ordered, up to a maximum of 82p.

B.F.P.O. and EIRE – 22p for the first book plus 10p per copy for the next 6 books, thereafter 4p per book.

OTHER OVERSEAS CUSTOMERS – 30p for the first book and 10p per copy for each additional book.

Name ....

Address ....

....